Magic Chef®

The Magic of Microwave

Cookbook

GOLDEN PRESS • NEW YORK
Western Publishing Company, Inc.
Racine, Wisconsin

We're glad you've chosen Magic Chef for your first microwave oven. We think you'll be glad, too, when you see the new ideas that Magic Chef has put into their new ovens. Ideas like "heat control" and "quick defrosting", that give microwave cooking more flexibility than a conventional range. (A quick glance at the pictures in this book will give you a hint of what you can do with your Magic Chef Microwave Oven.)

Heat control opens up a complete range of microwave cooking, from appetizers to desserts.

This cookbook places special emphasis on meats. With heat control, roasts cook with a minimum of time and attention. You can simmer pot roasts and stews to fork tenderness.

For those who have never used a microwave oven before, you will find a mini-course illustrating the basic techniques of microwave cookery. Read the introductory pages, then enjoy your new oven.

All the foods shown in the photographs were prepared from the recipes in this book and photographed just as they came out of the microwave oven, without any special treatment.

We wish to thank the University of Wisconsin-Stout, where the recipes and techniques were tested under the direction of Dr. Helen Van Zante. The recipes have also been tested by homemakers just like you.

Magic Chef is proud of its long standing reputation as the oven of "cooking experts". We want you to become as "expert" as possible in microwave cookery. Your new oven, along with this cookbook will get you off to a great start. If you have any questions, or need additional advice, please write me.

Joanne Crocker

Joanne Crocker
Magic Chef, Microwave Division
P.O. Box 2369
Anniston, Alabama 36202

Library of Congress Catalog Card Number: 76-9419

Golden® and Golden Press® are trademarks of Western Publishing Company, Inc.

Contents

The Magic of Microwave.........................4

Precautions to Avoid Possible Exposure
    to Excessive Microwave Energy 5

How to Use This Cookbook 6

Utensils...10

Let's Get Started....................................12

Microwave Cooking Techniques 18

Defrosting & Defrosting Charts................20

Microwave Menus..................................25

Appetizers 35

Sandwiches 44

Soups & Beverages...............................53

Fish & Seafood 60

Beef 71

Ground Beef 80

Veal 84

Pork..86

Lamb...92

Bacon, Sausage & Specialty Meats 96

Poultry...99

Casserole Cookery 108

Eggs & Cheese 125

Vegetables..133

Rice, Pasta & Cereals...........................152

Sauces & Toppings 156

Baking..160

Desserts..167

Candy & Cookies 181

Jams, Preserves & Relishes 186

Convenience Foods..............................190

Drying Flowers 198

Recipe Index.......................................200

The Magic of Microwave

Almost everyone knows that microwave cooking is fast. Saving time is generally the first reason for buying a microwave oven. But microwave does a lot more than save cooking time. Foods cooked by microwave retain their natural flavor. You use less seasoning in microwave cooking because seasonings don't cook away.

Microwave cooking saves nutrients; foods with a high natural moisture content need little or no water, others use far less than conventional cooking. Foods cook in their own natural juices, which enhances flavor.

A microwave oven saves energy; not only because it cooks faster, but because it doesn't consume energy heating up, or waste it cooling down.

Microwave cooking lets you keep your cool. The kitchen doesn't heat up; even the oven doesn't heat up. As for the cook . . . you'll be unhurried, unworried, with more time for your family, your friends and yourself.

Microwave makes your freezer more convenient. No more worry if you forgot to defrost the meat. You can defrost and cook in about the same time or less than you are used to cooking in. If you grow your own vegetables, or freeze vegetables in season, microwave can help prepare small portions for the freezer, then defrost and cook them in the same container.

Every cook knows that preparing a meal is only half the battle. Microwave cooking saves clean-up time, too. Many of your favorite serving dishes can be used to mix and cook as well as serve. You can even cook on disposable plates for an absolutely no-clean-up meal. Spatters and spills don't bake on with a microwave oven, so it's easy to keep the oven clean.

What is Microwave Energy

Electrical energy is transformed into electro-magnetic energy or microwave energy by a tube called a magnetron. This tube is like a broadcasting station sending out waves of high frequency energy in the cavity of the microwave oven where they are reflected off the metallic side walls, floor and ceiling of the oven and are eventually absorbed by the food. This electro-magnetic energy causes the molecules of the food to agitate. This agitation produces friction which in turn causes it to cook. Because all the heat is produced in the food itself no heat is wasted in preheating the oven or heating the utensils. Microwaves are high frequency radio waves, they cannot cause a chemical change or a breakdown in your foods.

How Microwave Cooks

Microwaves react differently with different substances.

1. They are *reflected* by metal or foil, just as light is reflected by a mirror. The cooking cavity is made of metal in order to bounce energy back to the food. Any metal in the oven will reflect or bounce energy. The cooking shelf is positioned in the oven to take best advantage of the reflected energy.

2. Microwaves pass *through* certain substances, such as paper, plastic, glass and ceramic, as light passes through a window. These materials may warm up eventually, as heat transfers from the food to them.

3. Microwaves are absorbed by food and liquids, causing the molecules of the food to agitate, produce friction and in turn heat. Microwaves penetrate about ½ to 1½-inches, depending on the density of the food and after that heating occurs through transference or conduction.

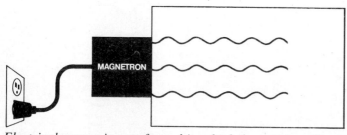

Electrical energy is transformed into high frequency radio waves.

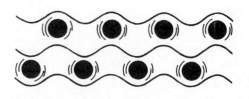

The radio waves agitate the food molecules causing heat by friction.

How Heat Control Works

Your conventional oven gives you a variety of temperatures on which to cook. After you select the temperature setting, your oven preheats to the desired temperature, then goes on and off to maintain that temperature level. If you wish to choose a lower level, or turn it off, it will retain heat as it "coasts" to cool. Heat control microwave ovens are never preheated and respond to changes instantly.

The earliest microwave ovens had one setting, ON. Energy was constant, and cooking was regulated only by time. Rest periods were needed for food to "equalize" or transfer heat to the interior, especially in defrosting, where the outside might cook before the inside was defrosted. This technique was also necessary for many foods which require a slower, more gentle cooking.

Microwave ovens with defrost heat control provide equalizing by cycling energy on and off at a fixed rate. It has two settings HIGH and DEFROST. The defrost setting permits preparation of large cuts of meat or dense casseroles which require frequent equalizing times, as well as defrosting.

Many foods require different proportions of on to off time to give a high quality product. Microwave ovens with variable heat control offer a range of useable settings, in a limited area, such as those with numbers of 1 through 5 and High. These settings vary the percentage of on to off time, thereby changing the rate at which foods cook.

The faster these cycles and the more settings available on a microwave oven, the more control you have. Solid state heat control provides an infinite number of settings from 1 to 10 with shorter and more frequent pulses of energy to give more precise cooking performance.

Precautions to Avoid Possible Exposure to Excessive Microwave Energy

(a) Do not attempt to operate this oven with the door open since open-door operation can result in harmful exposure to microwave energy. It is important not to defeat or tamper with the safety interlocks.

(b) Do not place any object between the oven front face and the door or allow soil or cleaner residue to accumulate on sealing surfaces.

(c) Do not operate the oven if it is damaged. It is particularly important that the oven door close properly and that there is no damage to the: (1) Door (bent), (2) Hinges and latches (broken or loosened), (3) Door seals and sealing surfaces.

(d) The oven should not be adjusted or repaired by anyone except properly qualified service personnel.

The above is printed in compliance with the Food and Drug Administration, Department of Health, Education, and Welfare, Performance Standards for Microwave and Radio Frequency Emitting Products, 21 CFR 1030.10.

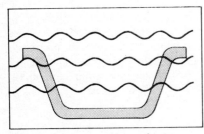

Microwaves pass through some materials like glass and paper.

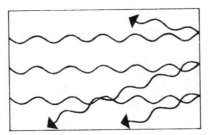

Microwaves are reflected by metal.

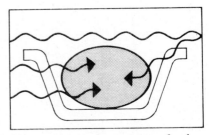

Microwaves only penetrate food and cause heat by agitation.

How To Use This Cookbook

American life styles are changing rapidly. People don't have time to spend long hours cooking. Serving meals means clean-up, too. A sink full of dirty pots and pans can double the time spent in the kitchen.

Microwave helps solve all these problems. This cookbook is designed to help you make the best use of your microwave oven, and easily find the recipes which suit your life style.

Learning to Cook with Microwave. If you're a new owner of a microwave oven, you'll want to read the chapters on cooking utensils and techniques. A special chapter, Let's Get Started, is a mini-course in microwave cooking. By following the pictures and step-by-step directions, you'll learn to cook with microwave through experience.

HOW TO READ THE RECIPES

All recipes in this cookbook are set up according to the following example:

NAME OF RECIPE

Number of servings
Microwave cooking
utensils needed

*Ingredients
listed in order
of use*

Procedures include covering, stirring, times, heat control settings, changes in settings and tests for doneness. An explanation of each of these key components follows:

Number of Servings. Most of the recipes are for 4 to 6 servings. If you wish to make fewer servings, cut the recipe ingredients and cooking time in half. Check for doneness and add more time if necessary.

Microwave Cooking Utensils. The size and type of cooking utensils which will be used in the microwave oven are listed at the upper right of each recipe. Read the section on cooking utensils to make sure that your casseroles or dishes are suitable for microwave use. If you do not have the size casserole called for, you may substitute a larger one, although cooking times may be affected. A casserole smaller than the one listed is not recommended, because foods which boil need room to expand.

Covering. When a recipe directs you to cover, you may use a casserole lid or plastic wrap. If a cover is not mentioned, the food is to be cooked uncovered. Some dishes are cooked covered at one time and uncovered at another.

Stirring. Microwave cooking requires less stirring than conventional cooking. When a recipe directs you to stir once, do so about halfway through the cooking period. Two or more stirrings should be done at approximately even intervals, but it is not necessary to be precise.

Foods which cannot be stirred are turned over, rearranged or repositioned by turning the dish. Since the oven shuts off when the door is opened, stirring does not affect cooking time.

Heat Control Setting. The recipes in this cookbook have been developed around ovens with heat control. Many include a change of setting during cooking.

Testing for Doneness. Line voltage is higher in some parts of the country. Your house power may fluctuate during the day, or vary from summer to winter. To reduce the possibility of overcooking, the recipes give minimum times, with directions for checking doneness and further cooking if needed. It's easy to add more time, but nothing can be done for foods that are overcooked.

Throughout the cookbook, easy-to-find symbols identify recipes which are especially suited to particular life styles. Some recipes carry more than one symbol.

HOW TO USE THE LIFE STYLE SYMBOLS

Microwave Show-offs

In each of the general recipe sections you'll find special dishes, some of them simple to prepare, which are spectacular when cooked by microwave. The magic of microwave will be evident in anything you cook with it, but these recipes show off microwave's difference dramatically. When entertaining, include a Microwave Show-off as part of the meal.

Try serving appetizers which cook at the same heat and time. Guests assemble their own plates and operate the oven.

For an informal lunch or supper, try Magic Meltwiches. Let each guest create and heat his own sandwich.

The Microwave/Freezer Team

The home freezer is a basic appliance, but not all families make the same use of it. If you "live from the freezer", you probably bought a microwave oven as a "flash defroster". It can be much more than that. Many of these recipes freeze beautifully. Make two at a time. Serve one now, change the other with one of the simple variations, and freeze it. Make your own TV dinners, using plastic or paper plates or shallow foil trays. Use boil-in-bags to freeze leftovers in single portions for faster freezing and reheating.

When freezing vegetables, prepare them as you plan to use them; whole, halved, sliced or diced. Under cook them slightly and add to your favorite dishes as needed.

No Time to Cook

Increasing numbers of American women are active outside the home. They want to serve nourishing and interesting meals, but they can't follow time-consuming traditional methods. Whether she works in the home or away from it, every woman has days when she hasn't time to cook.

If you have little time to cook, you already make good use of ready-prepared and convenience foods, but you may want more variety. The recipes in this category are all quick to prepare, with minimum clean-up, and use ingredients you can keep on hand in the freezer, the refrigerator, or on your pantry shelf.

Leftovers

With microwave cooking, leftovers don't taste leftover. Extra portions can be heated next day for "just cooked" flavor, or made into frozen entrees or dinners. Since microwave reheats foods without flavor or quality loss, larger quantities make fresh-tasting new dishes. The cookbook includes recipes which start with cooked meats, and others which can be varied for a second meal.

Make-ahead Meals

There are times when you like to prepare dinner in advance. If the family plans a Sunday outing, make Sunday dinner on Saturday afternoon. When dinner time comes, the meal is hot on the table before anyone says, ''when's dinner?''

Heating Meals

Foods can be reheated in a microwave to serving temperature without further cooking. Rare meat can stay rare. Vegetables don't get mushy. In all these cases, heat, don't over heat. Remember that foods continue to heat, so you can remove one, heat another and still serve everything hot.

Heat dense items, such as baked beans or mashed potatoes first, since they retain heat longer than other foods. Cover the dish and stir occasionally to speed heating. Heating times will increase in proportion to the number of servings, and refrigerated foods will take longer than those at room temperature.

If a roast has cooled to room temperature, heat it whole before carving. Turn it during heating, just as you do when cooking.

Whether cooked conventionally or by microwave, roasts need to stand after they are removed from the oven in order to retain their juices. During this time they continue to heat. After standing time, carve the meat in ½-inch slices. Arrange, slightly over-lapping, on a microwave-safe platter. If the meat has cooled during carving, cover loosely with waxed paper and heat by microwave. To keep rare meat rare, use '5' as a setting.

Split Shift Dinners

Busy families often eat in split shifts. With a microwave oven you cook when it's convenient, arrange the food on individual plates, and everyone can have a good hot meal when he wants it. A microwave oven is so simple, a child can reheat his own dinner.

Arranging Plates for Split Shift Dinners

A sauce keeps meat from drying out while it stands. For fastest heating, arrange food in a thin, even layer. Slow to heat items, like meat and mashed potatoes are arranged around the outside of the plate. Make a depression in the center of mashed potatoes. Quick-heating foods, like peas go in the center of the plate. Irregular pieces, like chicken legs or pork chops should be arranged with the thickest parts to the outside. Spoon sauce over meat. Cover with waxed paper and cool to room temperature. For a long wait, refrigerate.

When reheating, start with a short time and add more if needed. Test heat by feeling the bottom of the plate. When the plate feels warm, foods have heated enough to transfer warmth to the plate, and are ready to serve.

Company's Coming

There are times when you want to serve something special; for parties or holidays. Happy occasions should be fun for the cook, too. With a microwave oven, your dinner can be as simple or elaborate as you wish.

Everything will come out right on time, looking and tasting its best. With microwave, ''last minute'' dishes aren't last minute any more. You can plan an entire menu to be reheated by microwave, or you can team up your microwave and conventional range. Use your conventional oven for things it can do; use the microwave oven for things microwave does best. (Please, this includes vegetables and sea food.)

See Microwave Show-offs for new ideas in entertaining and Heating Meals for tips on making everything come out on time.

How to Convert Your Favorite Recipes To Microwave Recipes

Many of your favorite dishes can be cooked in the microwave oven with few, if any, changes. Use a similar recipe from this cookbook, or the cooking charts as a guide to method, time and heat control setting.

Fish, Meats, Poultry, Casseroles, Soups. Any recipes which call for steaming, covering or cooking in liquid will work well in the microwave oven. Pot roasts, stews, and other foods which call for long cooking can be prepared in one-third to one-half the time, using a lower heat control setting.

Your microwave oven cooks so quickly that seasonings aren't cooked away, so reduce the amount of seasonings. Add salt *after* you cook meats. Presoak dried ingredients such as dry beans. Otherwise, quick cooking won't allow them time to soften.

Cut up meat for stews into pieces of uniform size and shape. If your recipe calls for flouring and browning the meat, coat it — the flour is still needed to thicken the gravy — but skip the browning.

When you prepare foods for the freezer, don't use corn starch, because it breaks down when frozen.

For maximum microwave efficiency, choose recipes which serve four to six. Because cooking time depends on volume, very large quantities take almost as long to cook by microwave as they do conventionally.

Baking. In the Baking, Desserts, and Candy and Cookies chapters, you'll find sections on ''Basics,'' which tell you what recipes are best for converting to microwave baking, how to use mixes, and more. Keep in mind that baked goods rise more in a microwave oven, so reduce leavening by one-fourth and fill pans only half full. And for best results, choose cakes made with whole eggs.

Our Microwave Recipes for Your Microwave Oven

These recipes were developed for Magic Chef heat control microwave ovens with 600-650 watts of power. But every one of them can be adapted to any microwave oven. There's only one thing to remember: ''High'' setting in this book means the full power of 600-650 watts. A setting of 9 means 90% of 600-650 watts, and 5 means 50% of 600-650 watts.

If Your Heat Control Oven Is Not A Magic Chef

This test will tell you how to match your oven's settings with the settings in this book: Fill a 2-cup measure with cold water. Take the temperature of the water. Microwave 1 minute on High. Take the temperature again. Write down the difference. When the measuring cup cools, use fresh water and make the test again, using another setting. Now, divide the temperature difference on the second setting by the temperature difference on the High setting.

Example:

	Test on High	2nd Test
Temperature after heating	95°	77.5°
Starting water temperature	−60°	−60.0°
Difference	35°	17.5°
Second difference divided by first difference		$35\overline{)17.5}^{\,.5}$

The answer in this example is 5. When the setting you are testing gives an answer of 5, use it — no matter what it is — whenever a recipe in this book calls for a setting of 5. Test all your settings and make a list of the corresponding Magic Chef settings.

If Your Oven Has Settings for High and Defrost

When a recipe calls for a heat level other than 5 (your defrost cycle's level) or High, we've printed an adaptation at the end of the recipe. Do use the test above to make sure your defrost cycle measures 5. If it should measure 4, just cook a little longer.

If Your Oven Has An On (High) Setting Only

You don't have to be able to adjust the power level; adjust the cooking time instead. When you choose a recipe with a setting of 5, instead of cutting the heat to 50%, cut the time to 50%. When the directions say to cook at 6, use 60% of the recommended time. For times longer than 2 minutes, do watch your foods carefully and turn, stir, rearrange, or rest as you think appropriate.

If Your Oven Has Lower Power

If your oven's power is 400 to 500 watts, its power level on High is just right for recipes in this book that call for settings of 7 or 8. When a recipe calls for High, cook it a bit longer than the recommended time. If it calls for a setting lower than 7, don't cook as long. All the recipes include doneness tests, so you'll be able to judge timing.

Read your own Care and Use manual carefully. Follow your manufacturer's instructions regarding the use of metal in your oven, and pay attention to all the safety precautions. And follow the pattern of turning, stirring, or rotating recommended by your manufacturer.

Cooking Utensils

Microwave allows you to use a variety of cooking utensils never possible before. You can heat and serve with paper plates and napkins, or china and glass. You won't be using metal pots and pans, but you don't need a whole new set of cookware. Many things you already own will go into the microwave and on to the table, saving both serving and clean-up time.

Metal. Some metals can be used in the microwave oven, but an understanding of do's and don'ts is necessary. Do not use metal pots, pans and baking sheets, dishes trimmed with gold or silver, glass or ceramic glass utensils with metal screws, bands or handles. When cooking or defrosting in plastic bags, remove metal ties. Since metal reflects microwave energy, there would be no heat at the metal surface. This would create uneven heating patterns. Metal containers may create conditions which can cause a static discharge within the oven. It won't hurt you, but it may deface the oven.

Usable Metal. There are a few exceptions to the rule against metal. If your oven is not a Magic Chef, consult your use and care manual. *None of these metal pieces should be allowed to touch the oven walls.* Small pieces or strips of aluminum foil may be used to shield the thin ends of roasts, tips of chicken wings and legs, or any parts which might over-cook before the thicker parts are done. See recipes for when to remove the foil for even cooking. Metal clamps on the legs of frozen turkeys need not be removed. If the turkey is to be cooked by microwave, remove the clamp after defrosting. When there is a large amount of food in proportion to metal, you may use metal skewers for shish kabob or a metal rack for roasting. TV dinners in shallow (¾'') foil trays may be heated by microwave; replace the foil cover with wax paper or plastic wrap. Even where metal is permitted, it will slow cooking and you may prefer wooden hibachi skewers or an inverted saucer. TV dinners will heat much faster if you pop the food out and arrange it on an ordinary (non-metalic) dinner plate.

Glass, China and Pottery. As long as they have no metallic trim china and glass are not affected by microwave. You can warm dessert in a glass dish, heat coffee right in the cup. Foods can be heated to serving temperature right in your serving dishes, platters or plates. Since serving dishes will absorb heat from hot foods, you may not want to cook in them. Before cooking in china dishes, use the test for pottery. Naturally, dishes designed to withstand conventional oven heat, such as stoneware, porcelain souffle dishes or pottery casseroles, work well in microwave, unless they have metal in their glaze or composition. Examples of suitable ovenware are the ''French Chef'' line by Marsh Industries and Temper-ware by Lenox®.

To make sure that a dish is suitable, use this test. Place empty dish in oven. Microwave 30 seconds on High. If the dish becomes warm, do not use in the microwave oven. If the dish becomes lukewarm it is suitable for heating but not cooking. If dish remains cool it can be used for cooking. Many suitable serving dishes or casseroles may not have covers. Where the recipe calls for covering, an inverted plate or one of the recommended plastic wraps can be used.

Oven Glass/Glass Ceramic. These materials are excellent for microwave, unless they have metal trim or metal parts, such as clamps, screws or handles. Manufacturers are adding new items all the time. Check for labels such as "Good for Microwave", "Freezer-to-Oven", or "Oven-Proof". Fire King ® cookware by Anchor Hocking, Pyrex® and Creative Glass® by Corning are examples of oven glass. Teflon-coated oven glass can be used in the microwave oven, and does not affect cooking time.

Corning Ware® cookware, without metal trim, is an example of suitable glass ceramic. Corning Corelle® Livingware may be used in the microwave oven, except for the closed-handle cups.

Browning Dish. The microwave browning dish was developed for use in microwave ovens with foods which cook too quickly to develop a browned surface. This glass ceramic dish has a special coating on the bottom which becomes hot enough to brown foods. If you use a microwave browning dish, follow manufacturer's instructions carefully.

Paper. For reheating and low-heat or short-term cooking, paper plates, hot beverage cups, paper towels and napkins, even cardboard, becoming cooking utensils. Paper plates do differ, use "hot cups" for coffee, as you normally would. Uncoated paper plates are fine for a warm sandwich, but get soggy under spaghetti. Wax-coated dishes may melt. Some manufacturers of plastic coated plates are now labeling their products for microwave. You can defrost in paper cartons or freezer wrap. Check frozen fruit packages for metal ends and remove. *Watch out for foil-lined paper bags.* Use paper towels when cooking bacon to absorb grease and to absorb moisture when heating rolls or baking potatoes. Paper towels or waxed paper can be used to cover dishes or casseroles when reheating. They prevent splatters without further steaming of food.

Plastic. Plastic foam cups and dishes, or dishwasher-safe plastic containers can be used for low-heat microwave cooking and reheating. Even safe containers may develop burned spots or distortion with foods high in fat or sugar content. Melamine plastics are not microwave-oven-safe; Melmac plastics are, but may discolor. To test plastic dishes and glasses; place ¼ cup water in container and bring to a boil in microwave oven. Then check for distortion where the hot water came in contact with the plastic. Notice any discernable odors.

Non-Stretch Plastic Wrap. This may be used to cover utensils, such as casseroles which do not have suitable covers. Foods may be cooked directly in oven-wrap or boil-in-bags without foil strips or metal ties. Substitute string when sealing. Boil-in-bags should be pierced or slit. Be careful of escaping steam when plastic wrap is removed.

Straw and Wood. These materials can be used for quick warm-ups, such as heating rolls or baked Alaska. Large wooden items may dry out and crack with prolonged heat.

11

Let's Get Started *a mini-course in microwave cooking*

If you've never cooked with a microwave oven before, this chapter shows you some quick and easy things you can do right away. It illustrates the basic cooking methods and terms explained in the sections on microwave utensils and cooking techniques.

As you prepare these foods, you'll be learning how to use your microwave oven, and seeing some of the magic of microwave in action. So, if you've just brought home a new microwave oven, microwave yourself a quick cup of coffee. Relax, and read this chapter.

Instant Coffee, Tea or Cocoa. Microwave heats small amounts of liquid in about half the time of the average range burner. Three servings of coffee heat faster in individual cups than they do in a single large container.

Fill a hot beverage or foam cup, or a regular coffee cup (no metal trim) with hot tap water. MICROWAVE 1 to 2 MINUTES on HIGH, or until water is steaming hot. Add instant coffee, tea or cocoa to taste. Stir. Notice, while water is steaming hot or boiling, the handle of the cup remains cool, unless decorated with shiny metallic glaze.

Cold perked coffee can be reheated as needed, for a fresh just-perked taste.

Demonstrates: speed, heating in a cup, reheating and warning against metal, see utensil chapter.

Warm Rolls. Rolls warm quickly in the microwave oven. If rolls are over heated they become hard or tough. Be careful when heating sweet rolls; sugar or fruit filling becomes very hot. You may burn your tongue.

Place roll on a paper napkin to double as a plate and absorb moisture. If roll is placed directly on a plate, trapped steam will make the bottom of the roll soggy. MICROWAVE 10 to 15 SECONDS on HIGH. When surface is barely warm, interior will be hot. A pat of butter placed on the warm roll will begin to melt. When heating more than one roll add ⅔ of original time for each additional roll.

Demonstrates: warming, heating properties of sugar and use of paper with breads to absorb moisture.

Bacon. In the microwave oven, bacon turns crisp and brown without curling.

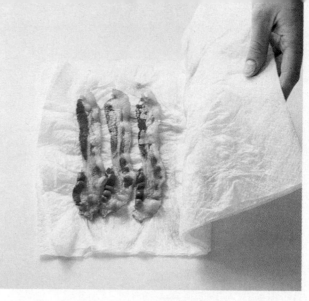

Arrange 3 slices of bacon on three layers of paper towels. Cover with paper towel and press down to prevent spattering and reduce shrinkage. MICROWAVE 2 to 3 MINUTES on HIGH, depending on thickness of bacon and desired doneness. Slight discoloration of paper towel is normal.

Foods with high fat content become very hot. Allow bacon to cool slightly or remove with tongs. If there is grease on the oven floor after bacon is cooked, wipe it up easily with dry paper towels. Bacon can also be cooked on roasting rack, see meat chapter.

Demonstrates: cooking on paper, covering to prevent spatters, heating properties of fats and easy clean-up.

Scrambled Eggs. Eggs scrambled in a microwave oven give greater volume per egg, and you don't have a crusty frying pan to clean. If you are on a low cholesterol diet, egg substitutes work well in the microwave oven.

Place 1 to 2 teaspoons butter in a 2-cup measure. MICROWAVE on HIGH until butter is melted. Break 2 eggs into cup. Add 2 tablespoons milk. Mix with fork to scramble eggs. MICROWAVE 40 SECONDS on HIGH.

The eggs will have begun to set around the outside of the cup, demonstrating the microwave cooking pattern clearly. With a fork, break up cooked portions and stir them to the center. In microwave cooking, stirring is always done from outside to center.

MICROWAVE 30 to 40 SECONDS on HIGH. Stir. The eggs will not be completely set. Let stand 1 to 3 minutes to complete cooking. Do not over cook, eggs will toughen.

Demonstrates: stirring and stand time to complete cooking.

Frozen Fruit. For a fresh, cool flavor, remove frozen fruit from oven while there are still a few ice crystals present. Pouches of frozen fruit may be placed directly on oven floor.

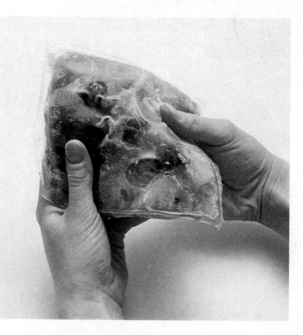

It is not necessary to prick the pouch, as there will be no steam. MICROWAVE 30 SECONDS on HIGH. Flex pouch briefly, to separate fruit and help distribute heat. MICROWAVE 30 SECONDS on '5'. Flex. Let stand 3 to 5 minutes before serving.

If you use fruit frozen in cartons with metal ends, pry off ends and place carton in serving dish. MICROWAVE 30 SECONDS on HIGH, until fruit can be loosened from carton. Break up with fork. MICROWAVE 30 SECONDS on '5'. Stir. Let stand 3 to 5 minutes before serving.

Demonstrates: use of plastic pouch, flexing to distribute heat and removal of metal.

13

No Clean-up Instant Lunch. Mix canned soup in glass or plastic storage container. Any left-over soup can be refrigerated for a fresh-tasting cup next day. Place one serving of soup in foam cup or coffee mug. MICROWAVE 1 to 2 MINUTES on HIGH, or until hot.

Place split bun on paper napkin. Place hot dog on open bun. MICROWAVE 30 SECONDS on HIGH.

Demonstrates: convenience and no clean up.

Muffins From a Mix. Three paper cupcake liners nested together are sturdy enough to hold batter without pans, or use glass baking cups with paper liners. Prepare batter according to directions on box. Fill cups one-half full. Sprinkle with cinnamon and sugar. Place 3 to 4 at a time in oven. MICROWAVE 20 to 30 SECONDS on HIGH per muffin.

Moist spots may appear on surface of muffins. Disregard these unless they penetrate to interior, thrusting toothpick into a dry spot near center. If it comes out clean, muffin is done.

Demonstrates: testing baked goods for doneness.

S'mores. The microwave oven softens or melts butter, cheese or chocolate in seconds. This favorite treat is even more popular when cooked in the microwave oven. Because of its high sugar content, the marshmallow heats first. During standing time, heat from the marshmallow melts the chocolate. If you heat a S'more long enough to melt the chocolate, the marshmallow will have scorched spots on the inside.

Place 4 squares of milk chocolate candy bar on a graham cracker. Top with marshmallow. Place on paper napkin. MICROWAVE 15 to 20 SECONDS on HIGH, or until marshmallow puffs. Top with another graham cracker for ease in eating. Let stand 1 minute.

To heat several at a time, add 15 seconds for each additional S'more.

Demonstrates: softening, standing to complete heating, simple cooking children can do.

A Microwave Show-off. Children can watch the marshmallow puff.

14

Hot and Creamy Shrimp Dip. With a microwave oven you can mix and cook right in the serving dish. This dip is ready to serve in 3 to 4 minutes.

2½ cups
1-quart bowl

1 *package (8-ounces) cream cheese*
1 *can (10¾-ounces) cream of shrimp soup, undiluted*
4 *green onions, including green tops, finely sliced*

Place cream cheese in bowl. MICROWAVE 30 SEC-ONDS to 1 MINUTE on '8', or until cheese is softened.

Stir in soup and onions. MICROWAVE 2 MINUTES on '6', or until dip is hot. Stir once halfway through cooking time.

For ovens without solid state heat control, follow above directions, using a setting of '5'. Add 30 seconds to final cooking time.

Demonstrates: softening, mixing, cooking and serving in one dish.

Microwave Stack-ups. Microwave heating enhances the flavors of foods. In this delicious appetizer, each food retains its own taste and texture. Heating reduces the onion's sharpness without transferring flavor to meat and cheese.

16 pieces
Plate

4 *slices bacon cooked and cut in ¾-inch pieces*
16 *¾-inch cubes of thuringer or cervelat*
16 *onion squares*
16 *¾-inch squares cheddar cheese, ⅛ to ¼-inch thick*

To make onion squares, halve a small onion from root to stem, separate a few layers and cut into ½-inch squares.

To assemble: place bacon pieces on thuringer cubes. Top with onion squares and cheddar cheese. Secure with toothpicks. Place on paper plate or serving dish. MICRO-WAVE 40 to 50 SECONDS on HIGH, or until cheese softens.

Demonstrates: Flavor enhancement and cooking on serving dish.

Speedy Baked Potato. Foods continue to cook after they are removed from the oven. If you cook the baked potato until it feels soft, it will be over-cooked by serving time.

Place a paper towel on oven floor. Place one medium baking potato in center of oven. MICROWAVE 4 to 5 MINUTES on HIGH, or until potato yields slightly when pressed. Wrap in aluminum foil and let stand 5 to 10 minutes. When microwaving dinner, do potatoes first, then remainder of the meal. Potatoes, wrapped in foil, hold their heat 20 to 30 minutes.

Demonstrates: standing time and covering to complete cooking.

Browning Dish Hamburgers. The browning dish has a special coating on the bottom which absorbs microwave energy. When the empty dish is pre-heated, the bottom becomes hot enough to brown foods. Be careful not to touch the bottom of the dish when removing it from the oven.

Form 1 pound ground beef into 4 patties, ½-inch thick. Place empty browning dish in oven. MICROWAVE 5 MINUTES on HIGH. Without removing dish from oven, place hamburgers in browner. MICROWAVE ½ to 1 MINUTE on HIGH. Turn hamburgers over. MICRO-WAVE ½ to 1 MINUTE on HIGH, depending on doneness preferred.

Demonstrates: use of browning dish.

Pork Chop Bake. Proper arrangement of foods assures even cooking and eliminates turning. The Pork Chop Bake was photographed before cooking, to illustrate placement. Soup will be spooned over chops, and will turn golden brown during cooking.

4 servings
12 x 8-inch utility dish

1 *can (16-ounces) sauerkraut, drained*
1 *small onion, chopped*
2 *tablespoons brown sugar*
4 *pork chops*
Salt and pepper
1 *can (10¾-ounces) condensed cream of chicken soup, undiluted*

Combine sauerkraut, onion and brown sugar in (12 x 8-inch) utility dish. Toss lightly with fork. Sprinkle chops with salt and pepper. Arrange over sauerkraut with meaty portions toward outside of dish. Top with soup. MICRO-WAVE 18 MINUTES on '8', or until pork chops are fork tender.

For ovens without solid state heat control, MICROWAVE 8 MINUTES on HIGH. Turn dish and MICROWAVE 8 MINUTES more. Let stand 5 minutes before serving.

Demonstrates: arranging foods, heat control.

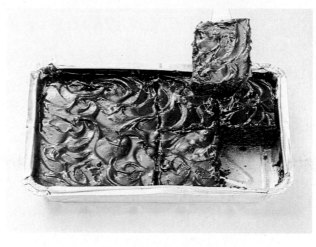

Frozen Peas and Onions Cooked in Serving Dish. Place vegetables in serving dish. Add 1 tablespoon butter, if desired. Cover tightly with plastic wrap. MICROWAVE 3 to 4 MINUTES on HIGH, or until vegetables are tender-crisp, shaking dish after 2 minutes. Remove cover with care because of steam.

Demonstrates: cooking in serving dish and shaking to stir.

Microwave Menu. A hearty family meal made with the recipes and techniques you've used in this chapter. Notice the order in which foods are prepared.

> ### After-The-Game Family Supper
>
> *Microwave Stack-ups, page 15*
>
> *Pork Chop Bake, page 16*
>
> *Baked Potatoes, page 15*
>
> *Peas and Onions, see above*
>
> *Sliced Tomatoes and Onion Rings, Marinated in Italian Dressing*
>
> *Brownies, see above*
>
> *Early in the day:*
> Slice tomatoes, scatter onion rings on top. Pour on dressing. Cover. Refrigerate.
> Assemble stack-ups.
>
> *25 to 30 minutes before serving time:*
> Bake potatoes. Let stand wrapped in foil.
> Assemble pork chop bake.
> Heat stack-ups. Start pork chops. Serve and enjoy stack-ups with the family.
> Cook peas and onions when chops are done.
> Heat brownies while clearing the table.

Demonstrates: menu planning and order of preparation.

Frozen Brownies. Frozen brownies can be defrosted right in the foil pan. Frosting will not melt. Timing is for brownies stored in a 0° freezer.

Remove lid from pan. Place brownies in center of oven, so that foil pan does not touch oven walls. MICROWAVE 1½ to 2 MINUTES on '5'.

Demonstrates: use of metal in microwave oven.

Advantages of Heat Control. Heat control gives the microwave oven the flexibility of your conventional range.

Use high to bring liquids to a boil quickly, then reduce the setting for gentle simmering.

Select the defrost setting which is best for the type and volume of food you are defrosting.

Use the lower settings to:

Simmer soups and stews to blend flavors and tenderize meat.

Cook sauces without scorching or excessive stirring.

Prepare many foods normally cooked in a double boiler.

Cook or reheat small portions.

Reheat rare or medium beef without further cooking.

Melt or soften butter, cheese and chocolate gently.

Defrost frozen whipped topping and puddings.

Warm baby bottle and foods.

Use very low settings to:

Defrost and proof frozen bread dough.

Proof homemade bread dough

Keep foods warm for up to one half hour without further cooking, on setting '1' (low). If foods must wait longer, refrigerate and reheat.

Look for other suggestions throughout the cookbook.

Microwave Cooking Techniques

You don't have to learn to cook all over again with micro-wave, but like any appliance, a microwave oven has special features that make it different. Things cook much faster; you can use utensils you never used before. You still test meat for doneness the same way you always have, by sight and touch. Grandmother's broom straw still tells you when a cake is cooked in the center. Cooking times are approximate because food preferences and portion sizes differ. A vegetable which is "just right" for one person may taste undercooked to another. The materials or shapes of cooking dishes can make a difference, too. A large, shallow casserole heats faster than a deep one of the same capacity. Some microwave cooking "tips" are just as good in conventional cooking; you notice the difference faster with microwave because microwave cooks faster.

Food Shapes. If you are cooking a stew on a conventional range, you know that large chunks of meat, carrots or potatoes take longer to cook. If you want peas, you add them at the end. Oriental cooks, who are experts at instant cooking, cut everything up into small pieces, which cook quickly and uniformly. Microwave cooking is just the same; large pieces take longer to defrost or cook than small ones. When several foods are cooked together, they should be similar in size and shape, so that everything is done at the same time.

Quantities. In conventional cooking, a chicken takes longer than a game hen. Even three TV dinners take longer than two. Microwave is just the same, except you

notice the difference faster because microwave heats the food, not the oven. In microwave cooking it is sometimes faster to cook two three-portion servings than one six-portion serving. In doubling a recipe add approximately two-thirds of the original cooking time.

Starting Temperature. In both conventional and micro-wave cooking, the starting temperature of food affects cooking time. Frozen dishes take longer than refrigerated. Refrigerated food takes longer than food at room tempera-ture. Warm foods need only a few seconds by microwave to make them piping hot.

Stirring. When cooking on a conventional range top, you stir things up from the bottom to redistribute the heated parts. In microwave cooking, you stir from the outside in, for the same reason. Sauces and puddings which call for "constant stirring" in conventional recipes need only occasional stirring in microwave.

Some foods cannot be stirred. In microwave cooking two techniques are used to achieve the same result.

1. *Rearranging.* Roasts and whole birds are turned over during cooking. Smaller items, such as chicken parts or ribs can be turned over and repositioned in the dish.

2. *Turning Dish.* With cakes, quiches and souffles, which can neither be stirred nor rearranged, the cooking dish is rotated for even heating. Turn the side of the dish which is near the oven door until it is near the back of the oven. This technique is also used when foods which cook best at a lower setting must be cooked on High.

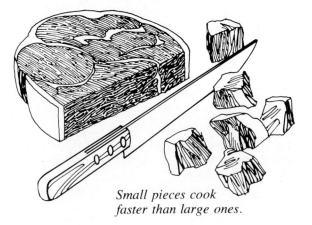

Small pieces cook faster than large ones.

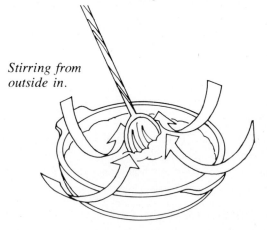

Stirring from outside in.

Standing Time. No matter how you cook them, all foods continue to cook after they are removed from the heat source. With small items, such as vegetables, this may be no longer than the time it takes to serve them. For large items such as roasts, conventional cookbooks recommend a standing time to finish cooking, retain juices and facilitate carving. The same is true for microwave. If, after standing time, the food is not cooked to your liking with microwave, you can always add a few moments more. Overcooking can never be corrected, no matter how you cook.

Shielding. Here's one place where you can use foil in the microwave oven. Small pieces or strips of foil can be wrapped around delicate parts, such as the tips of chicken wings and legs, to retard cooking until the bulky parts are almost done. When foil is removed, all parts finish together. This is comparable to conventional cooking, where a turkey breast or a pie crust may be covered to prevent over-browning before the interior is cooked.

Heat Control. In conventional cooking, you control the temperature of your range burner or oven. If you are cooking a pudding, you bring it to a boil, then reduce to simmer. You select an oven temperature to suit the food you are cooking. Microwave ovens with heat control work the same way. You're completely in control, with less time and fuss than ever before. The recipes in this cookbook suggest settings, but feel free to adjust them to suit your own cooking style.

Browning. Here is one area where microwave techniques differ from conventional cooking. In conventional cooking, browning occurs because of a high outside heat source which sears the surface before the center cooks. In microwave cooking the only heat is inside the food itself. Roasts and whole chickens will brown but smaller cuts such as steak, chops or chicken parts cook so quickly they do not have time to brown. If browning is desired, it can be achieved in three ways; by pre-searing meat in a fry pan conventionally and finishing quickly with microwave; by brushing meat with bottled browning sauce (Kitchen Bouquet) or by sprinkling with dry browning powders or gravy mix; by using a microwave browning dish.

Roasting. The microwave roasting rack serves the same purpose as the metal rack in a conventional roasting pan, but is designed for use in the microwave oven. Use it under meats, to keep them from steaming in their juices, under bacon and other foods which need to drain, under breads to allow steam to escape. If you do not have a microwave roasting rack, use inverted saucers.

Covering. When you cook conventionally, you cover pans and casseroles to retain moisture and speed cooking. You do the same in microwave cooking, but the covers may be different. When our recipes direct you to cover, you may use plastic wrap which does not touch the food, an inverted plate, or a microwave-safe casserole cover. Be careful when removing these covers, as steam may burn your hand. If the recipe does not direct you to cover, the dish should be cooked uncovered.

"Cover loosely" in our recipes is comparable to "partially cover" in conventional recipes. The cover helps retain heat, but excess steam escapes. Lay a sheet of waxed paper over a casserole, or form a waxed paper "tent" over a roast.

Some recipes call for covering with paper towels or napkins. These allow steam to escape, absorb excess moisture and prevent spatters.

Three ways to brown meat.

Pre-sear in fry pan conventionally.

Brushing meat with browning sauce.

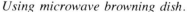
Using microwave browning dish.

Defrosting

The lower settings of heat control ovens defrost frozen foods evenly. Turkeys will need some standing time to equalize heat, but most foods only need to be turned over. To speed defrosting, foods frozen in pieces, such as fish fillets, chops or chicken parts should be separated as soon as this can be done easily.

For best results, defrost only as long as necessary. Check after the minimum time. Foods should be cool to the touch with a few icy crystals in the center. They will continue to defrost as they are prepared for cooking.

Beef

ITEM	CONTAINER	SETTING	MINUTES PER POUND	TURN OR REARRANGE	STANDING TIME
Chuck Arm Pot Roast	original package	4	3 - 5	Turn	10 min.
		4	3 - 5		
		5	2½ - 4½		
Corned Beef	original package	4	3 - 5	Turn	10 min.
		4	3 - 5		
		5	2½ - 4½		
Ground Beef	original package	4	3½ - 5½		5 min.
		4	3½ - 5½		
		5	3 - 5		
Hamburger pattie (4 oz.)	glass plate or plastic wrap	4	45 sec. - 1 min.		3 min.
		4	45 sec. - 1 min.		
		5	30 - 50 sec.		
Liver, sliced	original package	4	4 - 6	Separate and rinse in cold water	10 min.
		4	4 - 6		
		5	3½ - 7½		
Round Steak	original package	4	3½ - 5½		10 min.
		4	3½ - 5½		
		5	3 - 5		
Rump Roast (boneless)	original package	4	4 - 6	Turn once	10 min.
		4	4 - 6		
		5	3½ - 5½		
Sirloin Steak (½-inch thick)	original package	4	3½ - 5½		10 min.
		4	3½ - 5½		
		5	3 - 5		

Small items, such as fish fillets may begin to cook if defrosted too long, while meats will lose their juices.

When packaging for the freezer, use materials which can go directly into the microwave oven, such as freezer paper or plastic pouches. Aluminum foil wrappings should be removed before defrosting. If package is sealed with metal rings or twists, remove them. The metal clamp used to hold the legs of frozen turkeys may be left in place during defrosting, but should be removed if the bird is cooked in the microwave oven.

Solid State Heat Control Ovens

Variable Heat Control Ovens

Defrost Heat Control Ovens

Pork

ITEM	CONTAINER	SETTING	MINUTES PER POUND	TURN OR REARRANGE	STANDING TIME
Chops (Four ½-inch thick)	original package	4	3½ - 5½	Separate last third of time	5 min.
		4	3½ - 5½		
		5	3 - 5		
Sirloin Roast	original package	4	3½ - 5½	Turn once	10 min.
		4	3½ - 5½		
		5	3 - 4		
Spareribs	original package	4	3 - 5		10 min.
		4	3 - 5		
		5	2½ - 4½		

Veal

ITEM	CONTAINER	SETTING	MINUTES PER POUND	TURN OR REARRANGE	STANDING TIME
Roast	original package	4	5 - 7	Turn once	
		4	5 - 7		
		5	4½ - 6½		
Sliced	original package	4	4 - 6	Turn and separate	10 min.
		4	4 - 6		
		5	3½ - 5½		

Poultry

ITEM	CONTAINER	SETTING	MINUTES PER POUND	TURN OR REARRANGE	STANDING TIME
Chicken (cut up fryer)	original package	4	4½ - 6½	Turn once, rinse in cold water	10 min.
		4	4½ - 6½		
		5	4 - 6		
Duckling, Chicken (whole)	original package	4	3 - 5	Turn once, rinse in cold water	10 min.
		4	3 - 5		
		5	2½ - 4½		

Defrosting *continued*

Poultry *continued*

ITEM	CONTAINER	SETTING	MINUTES PER POUND	TURN OR REARRANGE	STANDING TIME
Rock Cornish Game Hens	original package	4	4 - 6	Turn once, rinse with water	5 - 10 min.
		4	4 - 6		
		5	3½ - 5½		
Turkey (10 - 14 pounds)	original package	4	3½ - 5½	Start breast up. Turn and rest 5 minutes halfway through defrost period. Rinse with water.	15 - 20 min.
		4	3½ - 5½		
		5	3 - 5		

Seafood

ITEM	CONTAINER	SETTING	MINUTES PER POUND	TURN OR REARRANGE	STANDING TIME
Fish Fillets	original package	4	3½ - 5	Separate last half of time.	5 min.
		4	3½ - 5		
		5	3 - 5		
Lobster Tail	original package	4	4 - 6		5 min.
		4	4 - 6		
		5	3½ - 5½		
Shrimp or Scallops	original package	2	4 - 5	Separate last half of time.	5 min.
		2	4 - 5		
		5	1½ - 2		

Breads

ITEM	CONTAINER	SETTING	MINUTES PER POUND	TURN OR REARRANGE	STANDING TIME
Loaf, sliced	original package	4	1½ - 3½		5 min.
		4	1½ - 3½		
		5	1 - 3		
Dinner Rolls (1 dozen)	original package	4	1½ - 3½		5 min.
		4	1½ - 3½		
		5	1 - 3		

ITEM	CONTAINER	SETTING	MINUTES PER POUND	TURN OR REARRANGE	STANDING TIME
Hamburger Buns (½ dozen)	original package	4	1 - 3		1 - 2 min.
		4	1 - 3		
		5	1 - 2½		

Desserts

ITEM	CONTAINER	SETTING	MINUTES PER POUND	TURN OR REARRANGE	STANDING TIME
Apple Pie, 9-inch, baked	Glass or aluminum pie plate	4	8 - 12	Cut and warm individual slices if desired.	10 min.
		4	8 - 12		
		5	6½ - 10½		
Cake	Pan	4	4 - 6		5 min.
		4	4 - 6		
		5	2½ - 5½		
Fruit	Covered casserole	High	2 - 3		5 min.
		High	2 - 3		
		High	2 - 3		

Microwave Menus

Planning a microwave menu is similar to planning a conventional menu. You need nutritional balance, contrast of color and texture, flavors that combine well. You want to cook in an orderly manner, without last-minute fussing.

Since foods reheated by microwave look and taste fresh, part of your meal may be cooked in advance. Other foods may be partially cooked and finished just before serving. Foods which require standing time to complete cooking can be set aside while you prepare the rest of the meal. "How to Cook the Dinner on the Cover", page 72, shows you the order in which foods are prepared to take advantage of partial cooking, standing and heating. The menu below illustrates a dramatic presentation for a gala dinner, made easy by microwave.

Beef Bouquetiere Dinner
(shown at left)

Italian Shrimp, page 37

Beef Bouquetiere with Lemon Garnish, pages 71 & 148

Watercress and Cherry Tomato Salad with Vinaigrette Dressing

Onion Cheese Sticks, page 163   *Corn Muffins, page 164*

Pears in Burgundy, page 177

Early in the day:

Prepare vegetables. *Under* cook them slightly. Plunge broccoli into cold water to stop cooking. Slice lemons and refrigerate.

Wash and dry watercress and tomatoes. Refrigerate. Make vinaigrette dressing.

Arrange cooled vegetables in "bouquets" around a microwave-safe platter. Leave center open. Cover with plastic wrap. Refrigerate.

Bake bread sticks. Prepare muffin batter and refrigerate until baking time.

Arrange pears in serving dish. Pour boiling syrup over. Cover with plastic wrap. Let stand on kitchen counter.

When guests arrive:

Cook shrimp. Start roast and serve shrimp. After half the cooking time, turn roast and return to guests.

While roast is standing, bake muffins. Toss salad. Let stand in refrigerator to blend.

Reheat vegetables while carving meat. Arrange slices in center of platter. If roast has cooled during carving, return platter to oven to warm briefly on '5'. Garnish with lemon.

After dinner, cook pears while clearing the table.

Family Breakfast

Orange Juice

Bacon
page 96

Scrambled Eggs
page 126

Muffins
page 165

Fresh Strawberry Jam
page 186

Day before:
Make Strawberry Jam
About 15 minutes before serving:
Cook bacon.
Mix muffins while bacon is cooking.
Bake muffins.
Scramble eggs.
Reheat bacon, if desired.

Sunday Brunch

Beautiful Baked Apples
page 178

Eggs Benedict
page 126

Asparagus Spears
page 146

Down Home Streusel Coffeecake
page 164

Early in the day:
Bake coffeecake.
Prepare apples for baking.
25 minutes before serving:
Bake apples.
Make Mock Hollandaise Sauce.
Cook asparagus spears. Toast English Muffins.
While asparagus is standing, poach eggs. Arrange ham on muffins.
Assemble Eggs Benedict. Heat.

Holiday Brunch Buffet

Holiday Fruit
Pudding
page 177

Cheese & Onion
Quiche
page 129

Link Sausage

Chilled Salmon Loaf Scandinavian
with Cucumber Sauce
page 68

Bacon Wands
page 36

Date Nut Bread
with Cream Cheese
page 165

Parisian
Mocha
page 56

The day before:
Prepare Holiday Fruit Pudding. Cool. Refrigerate.
Bake Salmon Loaf. Cool. Refrigerate.

Mix and refrigerate cucumber sauce.

Prepare and refrigerate quiche shell.

Bake Date Nut Bread.

Mix dry ingredients for Parisian Mocha.

Morning of the Brunch:
Bake quiche shell.

Slice Date Nut Bread and spread with softened cream cheese. Arrange on plate. Cover with plastic wrap.

Wrap bread sticks with bacon. Refrigerate.

20 minutes before serving:
Mix quiche filling. Bake quiche.

While quiche is baking, garnish salmon loaf with cucumber sauce. Do not warm sauce.

Cook Bacon Wands.

Fry sausages conventionally while Bacon Wands are cooking.

Make Parisian Mocha while guests are at buffet.

"Souper" Lunch

New England
Clam Chowder
page 56

Onion Herb Bread
page 164

Mixed Green Salad with
Tomato Wedges, Radish Slices,
French Dressing

Bundt Cake
page 169

Early in the day:
Bake cake.

Prepare and refrigerate salad ingredients.

Melt butter for Herb Butter.

20 minutes before serving:
Cook chowder.

Prepare Herb Bread while chowder is cooking.

Toss salad during final heating of chowder.

Heat bread.

Children's Luncheon

Chili
page 113

Peanut Butter Kidwiches
page 47

S'Mores
page 14

20 minutes before serving:
Prepare chili.
While chili is cooking, assemble Kidwiches and
S'Mores.
Ladle chili into bowls. Heat sandwiches.
After lunch, let children heat S'Mores and watch
them puff.

Ladies' Luncheon

Luncheon Shrimp
page 63

Grapefruit & Avocado Salad

Assorted Relishes

Buttermilk
Bran Muffins
page 164

Lemon Butter
Dessert Squares
page 184

Early in the day:
Prepare grapefruit sections. Refrigerate.
Bake Lemon Butter Dessert Squares.
Prepare and refrigerate muffin batter.
25 minutes before serving:
Prepare and bake Luncheon Shrimp.
While shrimp is cooking, arrange relish plate.
Spoon muffin batter into paper baking cups.
Peel and slice avocado. Assemble salad.
Bake muffins while shrimp dish is standing.

Veal Paprika Dinner

Creamy Velvet Veal
page 85

Poppy Seed Noodles

Stuffed Tomatoes
page 145

Spinach Salad

Pumpkin Bars
page 184

Early in the day:
Make Pumpkin Bars.
Prepare spinach leaves for salad, Refrigerate.
About 30 minutes before serving:
Cook noodles conventionally.
While water is coming to a boil, brown veal.
Cook tomato stuffing. Mix veal sauce.
Cook veal.
Stuff tomatoes while veal is cooking.
Bake tomatoes.

While tomatoes are cooking, toss salad and dress noodles with butter and 2 teaspoons poppy seed.

"I Forgot to Defrost the Meat" Dinner

Freezer to Table
Swiss Steak
page 83

Cheese Stuffed Potatoes
(half recipe)
page 141

Cole Slaw

Cranberry Crisp
page 175

About 40 minutes before serving time:
Bake two potatoes, page 150. Wrap in foil and let stand.
Cook Swiss Steak
While Swiss steak is cooking, make cole slaw. Stuff potatoes. Prepare ingredients for cranberry crisp, but do not sprinkle topping on berries.
While Swiss steak is standing, heat potatoes. Top berries.
Bake Cranberry Crisp while eating dinner.

Leftover
Lamb Dinner

Lamb Pilaf
page 95

Zucchini Parmesan
page 145

Tossed Green Salad with
Tomato Wedges
Pitted Black Olives

Fruit Cocktail Torte
page 177

34 to 45 minutes before serving time:
Cook rice conventionally
While rice is cooking, bake Torte. Cook lamb mixture. Prepare zucchini for cooking.
While zucchini is cooking, layer lamb casserole.
Heat casserole. Prepare salad.
Reheat zucchini, if necessary.

Family Style
Meat Loaf Dinner

Meat Loaf
page 81

Sour Cream & Potato
Casserole
page 143

Spicy Carrots
page 137

Lettuce Wedges

Cherry Crumble
page 175

Early in the day:
Bake Cherry Crumble.
About 1 hour before serving time:
Mix and bake meat loaf.
While meat loaf is baking, mix Sour Cream and Potato Casserole.
Bake Casserole. Prepare carrots for cooking.
Cut lettuce wedges.
While carrots are cooking, slice meat loaf.
Arrange on plate. Cover with waxed paper.
Reheat meat loaf, if necessary.

Busy Day Supper

Orangeberry-glazed
Luncheon Meat
page 97

Instant Mashed Potatoes
with Parmesan Cheese

Canned Green Bean Salad
with Italian Dressing

Hot Fudge Sundae with
Bottled Ice Cream Topping

Early in the day:
Place can of green beans in refrigerator to chill.

About 10 minutes before serving time:
Slice and fill luncheon meat with cranberry relish.

In 1-quart measure prepare mashed potatoes as directed on package. Stir in 2 tablespoons parmesan cheese. Let stand, covered, while heating meat.

While meat is cooking, drain beans and toss salad.

After dinner, heat fudge topping while dishing ice cream.

NOTE: Children can help spread relish on luncheon meat. An older child could prepare the entire dinner.

Company Chicken Dinner

Zippy Madrilene
(double recipe)
page 56

Chicken Saltimbocca
page 103

Stuffed Mushrooms
page 43

Endive, Orange & Onion Salad
with Oil & Vinegar Dressing

Assorted
Dinner Rolls

Mocha Torte
page 167

Early in the day:
Bake and refrigerate Mocha Torte.
Prepare and refrigerate salad ingredients.

45 minutes to 1 hour before guests arrive:
Prepare mushroom stuffing.
Bake chicken breasts.
While chicken is cooking, stuff mushrooms.
Combine soup ingredients.
Assemble chicken for final heating.

At serving time:
Heat and serve Zippy Madrilene.
Heat Chicken Saltimbocca. Toss salad while chicken is heating.
Bake mushrooms.
Warm rolls while serving chicken, mushrooms and salad.

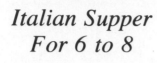

Italian Supper For 6 to 8

Antipasto Relish
page 188

Noodles Bolognese
page 113

Broccoli Italian Style
(double recipe)
page 136

Garlic Bread
page 164

Fantastic Chocolate Fondue
page 179

A day or two before:
Make Antipasto Relish. Refrigerate.

Early in the day:
Prepare fruits. Dip banana slices in lemon juice to prevent darkening. Refrigerate berries and pineapple.
Prepare garlic bread. Set aside.

40 minutes before serving, or earlier:
Prepare fondue sauce. Set aside to reheat.
Cook and drain noodles. Make meat sauce.
Cook two packages broccoli, page 148, for 12 to 14 minutes. Assemble Noodles Bolognese. Drain. Set broccoli aside, covered.
Place Antipasto in serving dish.
Bake the Noodles Bolognese while serving the Antipasto.
Finish and warm broccoli, if necessary.
Heat Garlic Bread.
After dinner, reheat Fondue Sauce while clearing the table.

No Time To Cook For Company Dinner

Ham Roll Ups
page 37

Salmon Piquante
with Cucumber Sauce
page 68

Peas and Onions
page 17

Small Potatoes (canned)
in Dill-butter Sauce

Bananas Foster
with Ice Cream
page 178

30 minutes before guests arrive:
Prepare Ham Roll Ups.
Prepare Salmon Piquante for cooking. Make cucumber sauce. Refrigerate.
Prepare banana for cooking.
Drain and rinse canned potatoes. Combine with butter. Sprinkle with dill.

When guests arrive:
Heat and serve Ham Roll Ups.

20 to 25 minutes before serving time:
Bake salmon. Let stand, covered.
Heat potatoes. Cook peas.
After dinner, bake Bananas Foster while dishing ice cream. Ignite at table.

Get Together Buffet

Hot Cheese-Clam Dip
page 41

Crackers and Chips

Baked Ham   *Chicken Barbecue*
page 91   *page 103*

German Potato Salad
page 142

Cole Slaw with
Old-Fashioned Cooked Dressing
page 158

Hot Cheese Frenchies
page 165

Assorted   *Strawberry Macaroon Torte*
Relishes   *page 171*

Early in the day:
Make salad dressing. Cool and refrigerate.
Bake Strawberry Macaroon Torte.
Prepare relishes. Refrigerate.
Make cole slaw. Refrigerate.
Make Chicken Barbecue. Cool and refrigerate.
Prepare German Potato Salad. Cool. Refrigerate.
Make Cheese-Clam Dip.

When guests arrive:
Heat and serve dip.
Bake ham. Halfway through the cooking time, turn ham and return to guests.
While ham is standing, reheat chicken. Set aside, covered. Reheat potato salad. Prepare bread for heating.
Carve ham.
Heat bread.

Thanksgiving Dinner

Carrot Curls,   *Pickles & Olives*
Celery Sticks,
Green Onions   *Rolls*

Roast Turkey with Gravy

Stuffing Supreme   *Cranberry Sauce*
page 104   *page 104*

Speedy Orange-glazed Yams
page 145

Asparanuts   *Perfection Salad*
page 134

Pumpkin Pie
page 174

Day before:
Prepare cranberry sauce. Make and refrigerate salad.

Early in the day:
Defrost turkey if necessary.
Prepare and cool Stuffing Supreme.
Stuff turkey just before roasting. Roast Conventionally.
Prepare carrots, celery, onions. Refrigerate in ice water to crisp.
Prepare and bake pastry shell.

45 minutes before serving time:
Fill and bake Pumpkin Pie.
Remove turkey from oven. Let stand, tented with foil.
Make gravy.
Heat yams. Let stand, covered.
Cook Asparanuts.
Reheat gravy and yams if necessary.
Warm rolls.

Appetizers

Hot appetizers add excitement to a party, and microwave cooking makes them quick and easy. Many can be assembled in advance for a brief last-minute heating, while others can be made on the spur of the moment from ingredients kept on hand in the pantry.

The recipes in this section cover three categories: Bite-size morsels served on cocktail picks, Canapes and Dips. They heat so quickly you can serve an assortment, perhaps one or more of each type.

BUTTERFLIED WIENERS ▦

2½ cups sauce
1½-quart casserole

1 *pound wieners*   1 *bottle (18-ounces) barbecue sauce*
¼ *cup honey*

Cut wieners crosswise in 3 pieces. Cut each piece in half lengthwise to make 6 pieces. Slit each piece through ends, leaving a ¼-inch join in center. Set aside.

Mix honey and barbecue sauce in 1½-quart casserole. Cover lightly with plastic wrap or waxed paper. MICROWAVE 1 MINUTE on HIGH. Stir.

Add wieners. Cover lightly. MICROWAVE 3 MINUTES on HIGH, or until ends of wieners curl. Serve with cocktail picks.

RAREBIT DIP ▦

2 cups

1 *jar (16-ounces) pasteurized*   ¼ *cup beer*
   process cheese spread

Remove cap from jar. MICROWAVE 3 MINUTES on '5', or until cheese melts. Pour into serving bowl. Stir. MICROWAVE 1 to 2 MINUTES on '5', or until hot. Add beer and stir until foam subsides. Serve with pretzels.

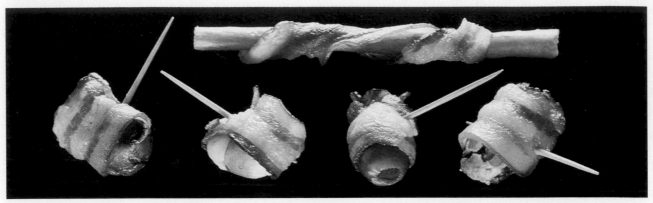

Left to right: Rumaki, Shrimp in Bacon, Olives in Bacon Blankets, Bacon Oysters. Rear: Bacon Wands

RUMAKI

3 dozen
Plate lined with paper towels

1 *can (6-ounces) water chestnuts, drained*
8-*ounces chicken livers, fresh or frozen and defrosted*
Soy sauce
12 *slices bacon, cut in thirds*

Slice drained water chestnuts in thirds. Cut chicken livers in 1-inch pieces. Dip in soy sauce. Place 1 slice water chestnut and 1 piece chicken liver on 1 piece bacon. Roll up and secure with wooden pick. Place 10 at a time on paper towel-lined plate. Cover with paper towel. MICRO-WAVE 6 to 7 MINUTES on HIGH, or until bacon is crisp.

NOTE: Bacon right from refrigerator is easier to handle.

NOTE: Rumaki and variations can be cooked on a micro-wave roasting rack, covered loosely with a paper towel.

SHRIMP IN BACON

18 pieces
Plate lined with paper towel

18 *large shrimp, fresh or frozen, defrosted*
6 *slices bacon, cut in thirds*

Wrap shrimp as in Rumaki. Place on paper towel-lined plate. MICROWAVE 5 to 6 MINUTES on HIGH, or until bacon is crisp and shrimp pink.

OLIVES IN BACON BLANKETS

18 pieces
Plate lined with paper towel

18 *large stuffed olives, drained*
6 *slices bacon, cut in thirds*

Wrap olives as in Rumaki. Place on paper towel-lined plate. MICROWAVE 5 to 6 MINUTES on HIGH, or until bacon is crisp.

BACON OYSTERS

24 pieces
Plate lined with paper towel

1 *can (8-ounces) oysters, drained*
12 *slices bacon, cut in half*

Wrap oysters as in Rumaki. Place 8 at a time on paper towel-lined plate. MICROWAVE 4 MINUTES on HIGH, or until bacon is crisp.

BACON WANDS

12 pieces
Plate lined with paper towels

12 *very thin bread sticks*
12 *slices bacon*

Wrap each bread stick with a bacon slice, in a spiral. Place 6 at a time on paper towel-lined plate. Cover with paper towel. MICROWAVE 6 MINUTES on HIGH, or until bacon is crisp, turning once.

BOURBON WIENERS

8 to 10 servings
1½-quart casserole

1 *pound wieners*
1 *cup catsup*
¾ *cup bourbon*
½ *cup firmly packed brown sugar*

Cut each wiener in four pieces cross-wise.

Combine catsup, bourbon and brown sugar. Mix well. Cover with waxed paper. MICROWAVE 3 MINUTES on HIGH, or until mixture begins to boil.

Add wieners. MICROWAVE 4 to 5 MINUTES on HIGH, or until wieners are hot.

MINI MEATBALLS

About 40 pieces
Plate lined with paper towels

1 *pound lean ground beef*
1 *tablespoon instant minced onion*
1 *tablespoon parsley flakes*
1½ *teaspoons salt*
⅛ *teaspoon allspice*
Pinch of cloves
¼ *teaspoon garlic salt*
½ *cup dry bread crumbs*
1 *egg*
2 *tablespoons milk*

Combine all ingredients in a large mixing bowl. Form into one-inch meatballs. Place 8 to 10 on a paper towel-lined plate. Cover with paper towel to prevent spatters. Meatballs may be refrigerated and cooked just before serving.

To cook: MICROWAVE 3 MINUTES on HIGH. Serve hot with cocktail picks.

NOTE: Meatballs may be frozen on baking sheets, then stored in freezer containers. To cook, arrange meatballs on plate, as above, and MICROWAVE 5 MINUTES on HIGH, or until meatballs are no longer pink, turning over once.

HAM ROLL UPS

16 pieces
Plate

4 *slices Danish ham*
16 *strips Swiss cheese, ¼ x ¼ x 1-inch*
Cranberry-orange relish

Cut each ham slice in 4 pieces. Place 1 strip Swiss cheese and ½ teaspoon cranberry-orange relish on each piece and roll up. Secure with wooden pick. Arrange on plate. MICROWAVE 30 SECONDS to 1 MINUTE on HIGH, or until cheese begins to melt. Serve hot.

BABY BURGERS

12 pieces
Paper plate

½ *pound lean ground beef*
½ *teaspoon salt*
⅛ *teaspoon pepper*
Kitchen Bouquet
12 *cocktail buns, split*

Combine ground beef, salt and pepper in small mixing bowl. Mix well. Form into 12 patties, about ¼-inch thick. Place on paper plate. Brush with Kitchen Bouquet. MICROWAVE 1 MINUTE on HIGH.

Turn patties. Brush with Kitchen Bouquet. MICROWAVE 1 MINUTE on HIGH, or until burgers appear medium rare. Serve on cocktail buns.

HAM AND PINEAPPLE KABOBS

24 pieces
2-cup measure
Plate lined with paper towel

¼ *cup honey*
¼ *cup firmly packed brown sugar*
¼ *cup barbecue sauce*
24 *1-inch cubes cooked ham*
1 *can (8-ounces) pineapple chunks, drained*

Combine honey and brown sugar in 2-cup measure. Stir to soften sugar. MICROWAVE 1 MINUTE on HIGH, or until boiling. Add barbecue sauce. MICROWAVE 30 SECONDS on HIGH, or until boiling.

Alternate ham cubes and pineapple chunks on wooden picks. Dip in sauce. Arrange on paper towel-lined plate. MICROWAVE 1 MINUTE on HIGH, or until hot.

NOTE: Leftover sauce may be saved and used again.

MUSHROOM KABOBS

15 to 20 pieces
Custard cup
Plate lined with paper towel

8 *ounces fresh mushrooms, 1-inch diameter*
2 *tablespoons butter or margarine*
2 *medium green peppers, cut in 1-inch squares*

Remove mushroom stems. (Save for casseroles.) Place butter in custard cup. MICROWAVE on HIGH until butter melts. Dip mushrooms in butter. Place on wooden pick between two pieces of green pepper. Arrange on paper towel-lined plate. MICROWAVE 1 MINUTE, 30 SECONDS to 2 MINUTES on HIGH, or until hot.

NOTE: Remove paper towel, serve on same plate which is already warm.

Variation:
Add cubes of pineapple or water chestnuts.

ITALIAN SHRIMP ✿

6 servings
8-inch cake dish

½ *cup butter or margarine*
12 *ounces frozen, uncooked, peeled and deveined shrimp, defrosted*
Garlic salt
Paprika
Parsley

Place butter in (8-inch) cake dish. MICROWAVE on HIGH, until butter melts.

Add remaining ingredients. Stir to coat shrimp. Cover with plastic wrap. MICROWAVE 3 to 5 MINUTES on HIGH, or until shrimp are pink, stirring once. Serve with cocktail picks.

NOTE: Small shrimp cook faster than large ones. Over cooking will toughen the shrimp.

ESCARGOT

4 to 6 servings
Ceramic escargot dish or small plate

½ cup butter or margarine
½ teaspoon garlic powder
1 teaspoon parsley flakes
1 tablespoon finely chopped shallots or onion
1 can (4½-ounces) snails with shells

Soften butter slightly in measuring cup or small bowl. Add garlic powder, parsley flakes and shallots and cream well.

Wash and drain snails. Place ¼ teaspoon butter mixture in each shell. Place snails in shells. Pack remaining butter mixture into shells to seal.

Place 6 at a time in escargot dish or on small plate. MICROWAVE 3 MINUTES on '5', or until butter begins to bubble.

Serve with crusty bread.

NOTE: Make ahead and refrigerate until needed.

HERBED SCALLOPS

6 servings
1-quart casserole

½ pound scallops, washed and drained
¼ cup butter or margarine
¼ teaspoon chopped chives
¼ teaspoon tarragon, crumbled
½ teaspoon chopped parsley
Dash pepper

Cut scallops in half, if large. Place butter in 1-quart casserole. MICROWAVE 1 to 2 MINUTES on HIGH, or until melted and hot. Stir in scallops and remaining ingredients. Cover. MICROWAVE 3 to 5 MINUTES on '6', or until scallops are tender, stirring after 2 minutes. Be careful not to over cook. Serve on cocktail picks.

For ovens without solid state heat control, MICROWAVE 3 MINUTES, 30 SECONDS to 6 MINUTES on '5'.

MARINATED CHICKEN WINGS

16 to 20 pieces
2-cup measure
10 x 8-inch utility dish

8 to 10 chicken wings
2 tablespoons firmly packed brown sugar
2 tablespoons soy sauce
1 tablespoon Worcestershire sauce
1 tablespoon white vinegar
1 teaspoon sliced crystallized ginger or ½ teaspoon ground ginger
2 teaspoons lemon juice
¼ cup water

Disjoint chicken wings, discarding tips. Arrange chicken wings in a single layer in (10 x 8-inch) utility dish. Set aside.

Combine sugar, soy sauce, Worcestershire sauce, vinegar, ginger, lemon juice and water in 2-cup measure. MICROWAVE 2 MINUTES on HIGH. Pour hot marinade over chicken wings. Cover. Marinate at least 3 to 4 hours at room temperature, preferably overnight in refrigerator.

10 minutes before serving time, drain marinade. Cover tightly. MICROWAVE 3 to 4 MINUTES on HIGH, or until fork tender. Let stand 3 minutes.

PARTY APPETIZER PIE

2 cups
8-inch pie plate

1 package (8-ounces) cream cheese, softened
2 tablespoons milk
1 jar (2½-ounces) diced dried beef, finely chopped
2 tablespoons instant minced onion
2 tablespoons finely chopped green pepper
⅛ teaspoon pepper
½ cup dairy sour cream
¼ cup coarsely chopped walnuts

Blend cream cheese and milk in 1-quart mixing bowl. Add dried beef, onion, green pepper and pepper. Mix well. Stir in sour cream. Spread evenly on 8-inch pie plate. Cover with waxed paper. MICROWAVE 2 MINUTES, 15 SECONDS on HIGH, or until entire mixture is hot.

Let stand 2 minutes to firm slightly. Sprinkle with walnuts. Serve with assorted crackers.

Variation:
Substitute 5 slices bacon, cooked crisp and crumbled, for dried beef.

COCKTAIL NIBBLES

8 cups
3 to 4-quart casserole

¾ cup butter or margarine
3 tablespoons Worcestershire sauce
1½ teaspoons onion salt
1¼ teaspoons garlic salt
1 teaspoon celery salt
1 can (6¾-ounces) cocktail peanuts
1 package (9 to 10-ounces) thin pretzel sticks
2 cups bite-size shredded wheat cereal
2 cups bite-size shredded rice cereal
2 cups puffed oat cereal

Combine butter, Worcestershire sauce and salts in 3-quart casserole. MICROWAVE on HIGH until butter is melted. Add remaining ingredients, tossing thoroughly until well coated. MICROWAVE 8 MINUTES on HIGH, tossing every 2 minutes to distribute seasoned butter. Cool and store in air-tight container.

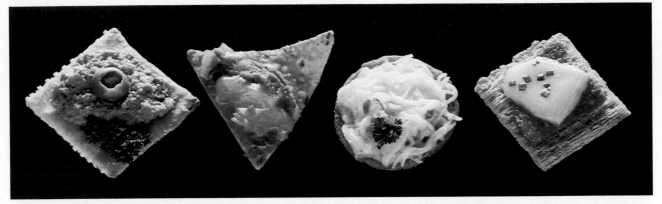

Left to right: Liverwurst Pate, Cheese Nachoes, Seafood Tantalizers, Easy-Does-It Canapes

LIVERWURST PATE ON TOAST

30 pieces
1-quart bowl
Plate lined with paper towel

3 *ounces liverwurst*
1 *package (3-ounces) cream cheese*
1 *tablespoon dairy sour cream*
¼ *teaspoon salt*
⅛ *teaspoon pepper*
Melba toast rounds or soda crackers

Place liverwurst and cream cheese in 1-quart bowl. MICROWAVE 1 to 2 MINUTES on '5', or until softened. Mix together with a fork until well combined. Mix in sour cream, salt and pepper.

Mound pate on Melba toast. Place 8 at a time on paper towel-lined plate. MICROWAVE 30 SECONDS to 1 MINUTE on HIGH, or until bubbly. Can be garnished with parsley before heating, if desired.

CHEESE NACHOES

30 pieces
Paper plate

1 *can (3⅛-ounces) jalapeno bean dip*
1 *bag (5½-ounces) Taco chips*
1 *bag (6-ounces) shredded cheddar cheese*

Spread bean dip lightly on taco chips. Top with cheese. Place 8 to 10 chips at a time on paper plate. MICRO-WAVE 30 SECONDS on '5', or until cheese begins to melt.

NOTE: Filling for cracker canapés can be made ahead and spread on at time of serving. Crackers will get soft if spread with filling ahead of time.

SEAFOOD TANTALIZERS

16 pieces
Plate lined with paper towel

1 *can (6½-ounces) crab, shrimp or tuna, drained and broken up with a fork*
½ *cup finely chopped celery*
2 *teaspoons prepared mustard*
4 *teaspoons chopped sweet pickle*
½ *cup mayonnaise*
Crisp crackers or Melba toast

In a 1-quart bowl, combine seafood, celery, mustard, pickle and mayonnaise well.

Spread on crackers or Melba toast. Place 10 to 12 at a time on a plate lined with a paper towel.

MICROWAVE 30 SECONDS to 1 MINUTE on HIGH, or until hot.

EASY-DOES-IT CANAPÉS

Plate lined with paper towel

Crisp crackers
Luncheon meat cut in quarters or squares
Triangles of cheese or generous pinches grated cheese

Place a piece of meat on each crisp cracker. Top with cheese. Garnish with any of the following: parsley, chives, crumbled bacon bits, sliced olives or pickles.

Place 10 at a time on a paper towel-lined plate, MICRO-WAVE 30 SECONDS to 1 MINUTE on HIGH, or until cheese begins to melt.

NOTE: One piece of sliced luncheon meat makes 4 canapes.

CHICKEN 'N BACON BITS

Makes 1 cup
Plate lined with paper towel

8 *slices bacon, cooked crisp and crumbled*
1 *can (5-ounces) boned chicken, or 1 cup finely
    chopped leftover chicken*
1 *tablespoon finely chopped pimiento*
¼ *cup mayonnaise*
Salt and pepper to taste
Crisp crackers or Melba toast

In a 1-quart bowl, combine crumbled bacon, chicken, pimiento, mayonnaise, salt and pepper. Spread on crackers or Melba toast. Place 10 at a time on a paper towel-lined plate. MICROWAVE 1 MINUTE on HIGH, or until hot.

PATIO DIP

1½ cups
1-quart casserole or bowl

½ *cup orange marmalade*
2 *tablespoons firmly packed brown sugar*
1 *tablespoon vinegar*
½ *teaspoon Worcestershire sauce*
½ *teaspoon salt*
¼ *teaspoon curry powder*
1 *cup dairy sour cream*
*Assorted raw fruits and vegetables, cut in bite-size
    pieces, oranges, apples, pears, raw beans, broccoli,
    cauliflower*

Combine marmalade, brown sugar, vinegar, Worcestershire sauce, salt and curry powder in 1-quart casserole. MICROWAVE 1 to 2 MINUTES on HIGH, or until mixture boils. Stir. MICROWAVE 2 MINUTES on HIGH, or until sugar is dissolved. Stir to blend.

Refrigerate 10 minutes. Blend in sour cream. Serve with fruit and vegetables for dipping.

SAUCY SHRIMP HORS D'OEUVRE

16 pieces
Plate lined with paper towel

1 *package (8-ounces) small frozen, pre-cooked shrimp,
    defrosted*
2 *English muffins, split and toasted*
¼ *cup chili sauce*
½ *teaspoon Worcestershire sauce*

Layer shrimp on toasted English muffin halves. Mix together chili and Worcestershire sauce. Spoon over shrimp. Arrange on plate lined with paper towel. MICROWAVE 2 to 3 MINUTES on '6', or until sauce is hot and bubbly. Cut each one in quarters to serve.

*For ovens without solid state heat control, MICROWAVE
2 MINUTES, 30 SECONDS to 3 MINUTES, 30 SEC-
ONDS on '5'.*

BACON-BLEU CHEESE HORS D'OEUVRE

16 to 20 pieces
Small bowl
Plate lined with paper towel

1 *package (3-ounces) cream cheese*
3 *tablespoons crumbled bleu cheese*
3 *slices bacon, cooked crisp and crumbled*
½ *teaspoon Worcestershire sauce*
Dash hot pepper sauce
Crisp crackers or Melba toast

Place cream cheese and bleu cheese in small bowl. MICROWAVE 1 MINUTE on '5'. Blend in remaining ingredients. Spread mixture on crackers or Melba toast, using 1 teaspoon per cracker.

Place 10 at a time on paper towel-lined plate. MICROWAVE 1 to 2 MINUTES on '6', or until cheese begins to bubble.

*For ovens without solid state heat control, MICROWAVE
2 MINUTES, to 2 MINUTES, 30 SECONDS on '5'.*

SEA SALAD CANAPÉS

20 pieces
Plate lined with paper towel

1 *can (6½-ounces) tuna, salmon or crab, drained and
    broken up with fork*
¼ *cup mayonnaise*
2 *tablespoons catsup*
2 *teaspoons finely chopped onion*
2 *teaspoons horseradish*
1 *teaspoon Worcestershire sauce*
½ *teaspoon dry mustard*
½ *teaspoon lemon juice*
Toast squares or crisp crackers
Parsley flakes

Combine tuna, mayonnaise, catsup, onion, horseradish, Worcestershire sauce, mustard and lemon juice in 1-quart mixing bowl. Mix well. Spoon 2 teaspoons mixture on each toast square. Sprinkle with parsley flakes. Place on paper towel-lined plate.

8 canapés: MICROWAVE 30 SECONDS to 1 MINUTE on HIGH, or until hot.
12 canapés: MICROWAVE 45 SECONDS to 1 MINUTE, 30 SECONDS on HIGH, or until hot.

QUICK AND EASY CLAM DIP

2 cups
1-quart casserole or bowl

1 *package (8-ounces) cream cheese*
2 *cans (6½-ounces each) minced clams*
1 *teaspoon horseradish*
1 *small onion, finely chopped*
Salt and pepper to taste

Place cheese in 1-quart casserole or bowl. MICROWAVE 1 to 2 MINUTES on '6', or until softened. Drain clam liquid into casserole. Add horseradish and onion, mix thoroughly. MICROWAVE 1 to 2 MINUTES on HIGH, or until hot.

For ovens without solid state heat control, MICROWAVE 2 MINUTES to 2 MINUTES, 30 SECONDS on '5'.

HOT CHEESE DIP

2 cups
1-quart casserole or bowl

2 *jars (5-ounces each) sharp cheese spread*
1 *can (6½-ounces) minced clams, drained*
¼ *large green pepper, finely chopped*
4 *green onions, including green top, finely chopped*
2 *dashes hot pepper sauce*
Garlic salt to taste

Combine all ingredients in casserole. MICROWAVE 3 to 4 MINUTES on '8', or until cheese melts, stirring twice.

Serve very hot with crisp corn chips. Can be reheated as needed, or kept warm in a fondue pot.

For ovens without solid state heat control, MICROWAVE 2 MINUTES, 30 SECONDS to 3 MINUTES on HIGH.

HOT CHEESE DIP WITH FRUIT

3 to 4 cups
1-quart glass bowl

1 *can (6-ounces) evaporated milk*
1 *cup shredded sharp American cheese*
1 *cup shredded Swiss cheese*
1 *tablespoon prepared mustard*
1 *teaspoon Worcestershire sauce*
Dash bottled hot pepper sauce
¼ *cup finely chopped pimiento*
6 *to 8 firm fresh apples or pears, cut in wedges*

Combine milk, cheese, mustard, Worcestershire sauce and pepper sauce in bowl. MICROWAVE 6 MINUTES on '6', or until cheese melts. Stir once half way through, and again when removed from oven. Stir in pimiento and serve hot, as a dip for apple or pear wedges. Can be reheated.

For ovens without variable heat control, MICROWAVE on DEFROST and allow to stand 20 seconds after the first stirring.

HOT CHEESE-CLAM DIP

3 cups
1-quart casserole or bowl

4 *tablespoons butter or margarine*
1 *medium onion, finely chopped*
1 *medium green or sweet red pepper, finely chopped*
1 *can (6½-ounces) minced clams, drained*
1 *pound American process cheese, diced*
1 *teaspoon sherry*
½ *cup catsup or barbecue sauce*
1 *tablespoon Worcestershire sauce*
¼ *teaspoon pepper*

Place butter in 1-quart casserole. MICROWAVE on HIGH until butter is melted. Add onion and pepper. Stir to coat with butter. MICROWAVE 3 to 4 MINUTES on HIGH, or until onion is transparent.

Add clams, cheese, wine, catsup, Worcestershire sauce and pepper. Stir thoroughly. MICROWAVE 4 to 5 MINUTES on '8', or until cheese melts, stirring three times during cooking. Serve hot, with crackers or chips. Can be reheated, if necessary.

For ovens without solid state heat control, MICROWAVE 4 MINUTES on HIGH, stirring three times. Let stand 30 seconds. MICROWAVE 1 MINUTE on HIGH.

MUSHROOM-CHEDDAR CANAPÉS

1 cup
Plate lined with paper towel

1 *tablespoon butter or margarine*
Pinch of chili powder
1 *tablespoon flour*
2 *tablespoons heavy cream or evaporated milk*
1 *can (4-ounces) mushrooms, drained and finely chopped, reserve liquid*
⅓ *cup liquid from can of mushrooms*
1 *cup grated cheddar cheese*
1 *tablespoon parsley flakes*
Melba toast

Place butter and chili powder in 1-quart casserole. MICROWAVE on HIGH until butter is melted. Blend in flour. Stir in cream and mushroom liquid. MICROWAVE 1 MINUTE on HIGH. Add cheese. MICROWAVE 1 to 2 MINUTES on HIGH, or until cheese is melted. Stir in mushrooms.

Spread mixture on Melba toast and garnish with parsley. Place 10 at a time on a paper towel-lined plate. MICROWAVE 40 SECONDS on HIGH, or until hot.

11 Ways to Stuff a Mushroom

BASIC RECIPE

6 to 8 servings
Small bowl
Plate

8 ounces fresh, uniform size mushrooms, cleaned
1 small onion, finely chopped
2 tablespoons butter or margarine
¼ cup seasoned bread crumbs

Remove stems from mushrooms. Chop stems finely. Combine butter, chopped stems and onions in small bowl. MICROWAVE 1 to 2 MINUTES on HIGH, or until onions are transparent and mixture is hot, stirring once.

Spoon mixture into caps with teaspoon. Place 10 to 12 on plate. Depending on size of mushrooms, MICROWAVE 1 MINUTE 30 SECONDS to 3 MINUTES on '8', or until mushrooms and filling are hot.

For ovens without solid state heat control, MICROWAVE 1 to 2 MINUTES 30 SECONDS on HIGH, watching carefully.

Variations:

SHRIMP

1 can (6-ounces) shrimp
1 teaspoon cream
Basic filling

Finely chop enough shrimp to make 1 tablespoon. Add chopped shrimp and cream to basic filling with crumbs. Fill caps, top with additional shrimp. Heat as above.

MEXICAN

¼ pound crumbled ground beef, cooked and drained
1 tablespoon taco sauce
1 small tomato, chopped
Grated cheddar cheese

Combine hamburger and taco sauce. Fill mushroom caps. Spread chopped tomatoes on filling, top with grated cheese. Heat as above, or until mushrooms are hot and cheese melts.

CHESTNUT-CELERY

½ teaspoon cream sherry
Basic filling
16 slices celery, ⅛-inch thick
5 chestnuts, cut in triangles

Add sherry to basic filling after heating. Fill caps. Garnish with celery slices and chestnut triangles. Heat as above.

BLEU CHEESE

¼ cup crumbled bleu cheese
Basic filling

Mix 1 tablespoon cheese into basic filling. Fill caps. Top with remaining cheese. Heat as above.

CRAB OR LOBSTER

1 can (6½-ounces) crab or lobster, drained and flaked
1 tablespoon mayonnaise
1 package (3-ounces) cream cheese, softened
½ teaspoon lemon juice
Dash prepared mustard

Mix above ingredients well. Fill caps. Garnish with parsley. Heat as above.

POLYNESIAN

1 can (8-ounces) pineapple chunks, drained
1 can (5-ounces) chicken
2 tablespoons mayonnaise
½ teaspoon lemon juice
16 walnut halves

Combine pineapple, chicken, mayonnaise and lemon juice. Fill caps. Garnish with walnut halves. Heat as above.

FLORENTINE

1 package (3-ounces) cream cheese
1 can (8-ounces) spinach, drained and chopped
2 slices bacon, cooked and crumbled

Soften cream cheese. Mix in spinach. Fill mushroom caps. Garnish with small bacon pieces. Heat as above.

BACON

1 package (3-ounces) cream cheese
½ teaspoon finely chopped onion
6 slices bacon, cooked and crumbled

Soften cream cheese. Cream in onion. Form in balls. Roll balls in crumbled bacon. Fill caps. Heat as above.

ITALIAN

½ pound ground sausage, cooked and drained
2 tablespoons catsup
⅛ teaspoon oregano
Dash garlic powder
2 tablespoons fresh parsley, torn in small pieces
Grated mozzarella cheese

Mix cooked sausage, catsup, oregano and garlic powder in measure or small bowl. MICROWAVE 1 MINUTE on HIGH. Fill caps. Sprinkle parsley on filling. Top with grated cheese. Heat as above, or until mushrooms are hot and cheese melts.

STROGANOFF

¼ pound crumbled ground beef, cooked and drained
1 packet (.18-ounce) single serving instant beef broth, diluted with 1½ teaspoons water
2 tablespoons dairy sour cream

Combine ground beef and beef broth in small bowl. MICROWAVE 1 MINUTE on HIGH. Stir in sour cream. Fill caps. Heat as above.

NOTE: Stuffed mushrooms also make a good vegetable side dish.

Clockwise from spoon: Mexican, Polynesian, Florentine, Chestnut-Celery, Crab, Bacon, Bleu Cheese. Center: Italian.

Sandwiches

Hot sandwiches are just seconds away by microwave. Most of them cook on a napkin, so there's no clean-up. Be creative. A touch of microwave magic and a new ingredient transform the common sandwich into a taste sensation.

ALL-AMERICAN CHEESEBURGER

4 servings
2-cup measure
Paper towel

1 *tablespoon butter or margarine*
1 *medium onion, sliced and separated into rings*
4 *hamburger patties, cooked (page 16)*
4 *sesame buns, split*
4 *slices American process cheese*

Place butter in 2-cup measure. MICROWAVE on HIGH, until melted. Stir onion rings into hot butter until coated.

Place hamburger patties on bottom half of buns. Top with cheese slices and onion rings. Arrange on paper towel. MICROWAVE 30 SECONDS to 1 MINUTE on HIGH, or until cheese starts to melt. Cover with tops of buns.

FRANKFURTER SPECIAL

4 servings
Plate
Paper towel

4 *large old-fashioned frankfurters*
4 *slices Swiss cheese, cut in thirds*
4 *large frankfurter buns, split*
Prepared mustard

Make 3 diagonal slashes in each frankfurter. Place on plate. MICROWAVE 2 to 3 MINUTES on HIGH, or until hot.
Place hot frankfurters in buns with slashes toward outside. Lay one strip of cheese across each slash. Arrange on paper towel. MICROWAVE 30 SECONDS to 1 MINUTE on HIGH, or until cheese melts. Serve with mustard.

GRILLED CHEESE SANDWICH

1 serving
Browning dish

2 *slices American process cheese*
2 *slices bread*
Butter or margarine

Place cheese slices between bread slices. Spread butter on outsides of sandwich. To preheat browner, MICROWAVE 4 MINUTES on HIGH. With oven door open, place sandwich in browner for 30 seconds. Turn to brown other side 30 seconds. MICROWAVE 30 SECONDS on HIGH, if necessary, to melt cheese.

45

SANDWICH BASICS

Sandwiches heat very quickly. Be careful not to over cook. Heat bread until warm, not hot, cheese just until it begins to melt.

The best sandwiches are made with day-old or toasted bread; breads rich in eggs or shortening; full-bodied breads such as rye or whole wheat.

Several thin slices of meat heat better than one thick slice.

Always heat sandwiches on paper napkins or towels to absorb steam which can make the bread soggy, except when grilling cheese or Reuben sandwiches in the micro-browner.

HAMBURGERS

3 to 4 hamburgers
Microwave roasting rack

1 *pound lean ground beef*
½ *teaspoon Kitchen Bouquet, mixed with 2*
  tablespoons water
Salt and pepper to taste

Combine all ingredients in medium bowl. Mix well. Form into 3 to 4 patties. Place on roasting rack. MICROWAVE 2 MINUTES, 30 SECONDS to 4 MINUTES on HIGH, or until desired doneness, turning once.

NOTE: Hamburger is medium-rare when juice begins to ooze to surface, medium when surface appears juicy, and well done when no pink remains.

Variations:
Mix one or more of the following with meat before forming patties:
Chopped onion
Chopped olives
Chopped mushrooms
1 teaspoon horseradish
1 tablespoon steak sauce
1 tablespoon chili sauce
Finely diced cheese
Crumbled bleu cheese

NOTE: Above variations may be used for browning-dish hamburgers, (page 16).

BURGER-DOGS

4 to 8 servings
Microwave roasting rack

1 *pound lean ground beef*
½ *cup crushed rice cereal*
½ *cup chopped onion*
1 *egg, slightly beaten*
¼ *cup prepared mustard*
1 *tablespoon Worcestershire sauce*
½ *teaspoon salt*
⅛ *teaspoon pepper*
8 *wiener buns, split*

Combine beef, cereal, onion, egg and seasonings in medium bowl. Mix well. Form into 8 long rolls, resembling hot dogs. Place 4 at a time on roasting rack. MICROWAVE 4 to 6 MINUTES on '8', or until meat loses color. Turn halfway through cooking period.

For ovens without solid state heat control, MICROWAVE 3 to 5 MINUTES on HIGH, turning once.

FRENCH RIVIERAS

6 sandwiches
Paper napkin

¼ *cup butter or margarine, softened*
1 *tablespoon prepared mustard*
6 *large hard rolls, split*
6 *slices bologna*
6 *slices cooked ham*
6 *slices salami*
6 *slices cheese, Swiss, cheddar or American process*

Blend butter with mustard in small bowl. Spread inside rolls. For each sandwich, layer 1 slice bologna, 1 slice ham, 1 slice salami and 1 slice cheese on half of roll and cover with other half. Secure top with toothpick and place on paper napkin. MICROWAVE 45 SECONDS on '8', or until cheese melts.

For ovens without solid state heat control, use HIGH and watch carefully.

NOTE: Long loaf sandwiches are easy for entertaining. Cut French bread in half lengthwise, layer with your favorite cold cuts and cheese. Garnish with fresh tomatoes and cucumbers. Follow above directions for heating.

BARBECUES

4 servings
1-quart casserole

½ *pound lean ground beef*
½ *cup chopped onion*
½ *cup catsup*
2 *tablespoons vinegar*
1 *tablespoon brown sugar*
½ *teaspoon salt*
¼ *teaspoon dry mustard*
4 *split hamburger buns*

Combine ground beef and onion in 1-quart casserole. Cover. MICROWAVE 2 to 3 MINUTES on HIGH. Add catsup, vinegar, brown sugar, salt and mustard. Cover.

MICROWAVE 5 MINUTES on '8', or until bubbly. Serve on hamburger buns.

For ovens without solid state heat control, MICROWAVE 4 MINUTES on HIGH, stirring after 2 minutes.

DENVER SANDWICH

1 serving
1-cup measure
Small plate

1 *egg*
1 *tablespoon chopped green pepper*
2 *tablespoons chopped onion*
3 *tablespoons diced ham*
Toasted bun

Beat all ingredients together with fork in 1-cup measure. Pour onto small plate. MICROWAVE 45 SECONDS to 1 MINUTE on '8', or until egg is set. Place on toasted bun and serve.

For ovens without solid state heat control, MICROWAVE on HIGH, watch carefully.

SWISS HAM SANDWICHES

3 to 6 servings
Paper napkins

¼ *cup butter or margarine, softened*
2 *tablespoons finely chopped onion*
1 *teaspoon prepared mustard*
1 *teaspoon poppy seed*
6 *large hard rolls, split*
6 *thin slices cooked ham*
6 *slices Swiss cheese*

Combine butter, onion, mustard and poppy seed in small bowl. Spread seasoned butter inside each roll. Top with 1 slice each ham and cheese. Cover with other half of roll. Place three buns on paper napkins. MICROWAVE 1 to 1½ MINUTES on '8', or until cheese melts.

For ovens without solid state heat control, use HIGH and watch carefully.

HOT DOGS

2 to 4 servings
Paper towel or napkin

4 *wieners*
4 *wiener buns, split*

Place wieners on open buns. Arrange on paper towel. For 1 wiener on bun, MICROWAVE 30 SECONDS on '8'. For 4 wieners on buns, MICROWAVE 1 MINUTE, 30 SECONDS, or until wiener feels warm. Let stand 1 minute.

For ovens without solid state heat control MICROWAVE 30 SECONDS on HIGH.

GROUND BEEF GUMBOS

4 servings
1-quart casserole

½ *pound lean ground beef*
1 *medium onion, chopped*
1 *can (10¾-ounces) condensed chicken gumbo soup, drained of excess liquid*
2 *tablespoons catsup*
2 *tablespoons prepared mustard*
½ *teaspoon salt*
4 *English muffins, split and toasted*

Crumble ground beef into 1-quart casserole. Add onion. Cover with paper towel. MICROWAVE 2 MINUTES on HIGH, or until meat is set.

Stir in soup, catsup, mustard and salt. Mix well. MICROWAVE 4 MINUTES on '8', or until bubbly hot. Spoon over muffins.

NOTE: Hamburger buns may be substituted for muffins.

For ovens without solid state heat control use HIGH, stirring after 2 minutes.

PEANUT BUTTER KIDWICHES 🔲

The children's favorite sandwich filling forms the base for hot and bubbly sandwiches they can microwave themselves.

1 *slice toast*
Peanut butter

Spread toast with peanut butter. Top with one of the following combinations:

Jelly
Marshmallow

Cheese
Bacon bits

Tomato slice
Cheese

Place sandwich on napkin. MICROWAVE 15 SECONDS to 30 SECONDS on HIGH, or until melty.

CHEESE 'N TUNA BUNS

8 to 12 servings
Paper napkins

1 *can (6½-ounces) tuna, drained and flaked*
1 *cup grated sharp cheddar cheese*
½ *cup mayonnaise*
3 *hard cooked eggs, finely chopped*
¼ *cup finely chopped onion*
¼ *cup finely chopped stuffed green olives*
¼ *cup sweet pickle relish*
8 *hamburger buns, split*

Combine tuna, cheese, mayonnaise, eggs, onion, olives and relish in medium bowl. Mix well. Spoon mixture into buns. Wrap each bun in paper napkin. Place 2 at a time in oven. MICROWAVE 1 to 2 MINUTES on '8', or until cheese has softened into mixture.

NOTE: Tuna mixture can be made ahead and refrigerated. Allow extra time for cooking from refrigerated temperature.

For ovens without solid state heat control, use HIGH and watch carefully.

OPEN FACE BEANS AND WIENER SANDWICH

4 servings
Paper towel

1 *can (12-ounces) baked beans*
4 *slices bread, toasted*
4 *wieners, split in half lengthwise*
½ *cup catsup*
¼ *cup chopped onion*

Spread ¼ cup beans on each toast slice. Arrange on paper towel. Cover with paper towel to prevent spatters. MICROWAVE 4 MINUTES on '6', or until beans are hot.

Place wieners on beans. Top with catsup and onion. MICROWAVE 2 to 3 MINUTES on '6', or until wiener is hot and sauce is bubbly.

For ovens without solid state heat control, MICROWAVE 2 MINUTES, 30 SECONDS to 3 MINUTES, 30 SECONDS on '5'.

FISHBURGER

1 serving
Paper towel

1 *frozen fish patty*
1 *tablespoon mayonnaise*
1 *sweet pickle, sliced*
1 *hamburger bun, split*

Place frozen fish patty on paper towel. Top with mayonnaise and sliced pickle. MICROWAVE 1 MINUTE, 30 SECONDS on HIGH, or until hot.

Serve on bun. Garnish with tartar sauce or chili sauce.

SOUTH OF THE BORDER BUNS

8 sandwiches
2-quart casserole

1 *pound lean ground beef*
1 *medium onion, chopped*
1 *small green pepper, chopped*
1 *clove garlic, pressed or finely chopped*
1 *can (8-ounces) tomato sauce*
1 *teaspoon Worcestershire sauce*
½ *teaspoon salt*
¼ *teaspoon chili powder*
Dash hot pepper sauce
8 *hamburger buns, split*
Tomato slices
Shredded lettuce
Grated cheddar cheese

Crumble ground beef into 2-quart casserole. Add onion, pepper and garlic. MICROWAVE 4 to 5 MINUTES on HIGH, or until beef loses its pink color.

Stir in tomato sauce, Worcestershire sauce, salt, chili powder and pepper sauce. Cover. MICROWAVE 5 to 6 MINUTES on HIGH, or until sauce is thickened and very hot. Serve in hamburger buns. Garnish with tomato slices, shredded lettuce and grated cheese.

CONEY ISLANDS

10 to 12 servings
1-quart casserole
Paper towel

1 *can (15-ounces) chili without beans*
1 *package (1-pound) wieners*
6 *wiener buns, split*
½ *cup chopped onion*
Grated cheddar cheese

Place chili in 1-quart casserole. MICROWAVE 2 MINUTES on HIGH, or until hot and bubbly, stirring once. Set aside.

Place wieners on open buns. Arrange on paper towel. MICROWAVE 2 to 3 MINUTES on '8', or until wiener feels warm.

Spoon chili over wieners. Sprinkle with raw onion. Top with grated cheddar cheese. MICROWAVE 10 SECONDS on HIGH, or until cheese begins to melt.

For ovens without solid state heat control, when heating wieners, MICROWAVE 2 MINUTES, 10 SECONDS on HIGH.

REUBEN SANDWICH

1 serving
Browning dish

1 *tablespoon mayonnaise or salad dressing*
1 *teaspoon prepared mustard*
2 *slices pumpernickel or other dark bread*
3 *to 4 thin slices corned beef*
2 *teaspoons drained sauerkraut*
1 *slice Swiss cheese*
Butter or margarine

Mix mayonnaise and mustard together. Spread on bread slices. Layer corned beef, sauerkraut and Swiss cheese between bread slices. Butter both sides of sandwich.

Place browning dish in oven. MICROWAVE 4 MINUTES on HIGH.

Add sandwich. MICROWAVE 2 MINUTES on HIGH, or until cheese starts to melt, turning sandwich over after 1 minute.

BARBECUED CRAB SANDWICHES

6 servings
1-quart casserole

3 *tablespoons butter or margarine*
½ *cup finely chopped celery*
¼ *cup finely chopped onion*
1 *teaspoon instant chicken bouillon*
½ *cup tomato sauce*
2 *teaspoons Worcestershire sauce*
2 *teaspoons soy sauce*
2 *whole cloves*
2 *bay leaves*
¼ *teaspoons salt*
⅛ *teaspoon pepper*
1 *can (6½-ounces) crab meat, broken up with fork*
1 *teaspoon parsley flakes*
6 *large rolls, split and buttered*

Combine butter, celery and onion, in 1-quart casserole. MICROWAVE 3 MINUTES on HIGH, or until onion is transparent.

Add instant bouillon, tomato sauce, Worcestershire sauce, soy sauce, cloves, bay leaves, salt and pepper. Mix well. MICROWAVE 2 MINUTES on HIGH, or until bubbly. Remove bay leaves and cloves.

Stir in crab meat and parsley. MICROWAVE 2 MINUTES on '6' to heat crab meat. Spoon hot mixture into rolls.

NOTE: For party sandwiches, spoon mixture on warm biscuits. Garnish with stuffed olives.

For ovens without solid state heat control MICROWAVE 2 to 3 MINUTES on '5' to heat crab.

HOT MEAT AND GRAVY SANDWICHES

4 servings
2-cup measure
Paper towel

4 *slices bread or toast*
8 *slices meat or meat loaf*
1½ *cups gravy, leftover or prepared from mix or sauce*

Choose meat and topping from the following suggestions:

Roast beef
Gravy or canned mushroom sauce

Roast pork
Gravy or barbecue sauce or applesauce

Roast lamb
Gravy or canned mushroom sauce or curry sauce or mint sauce

Roast chicken or turkey
Giblet gravy or chicken gravy or canned mushroom sauce

Meat loaf
Gravy or tomato sauce or cheese sauce or cranberry sauce

Measure leftover gravy or sauces into 2-cup measure. MICROWAVE 3 to 4 MINUTES on HIGH, or until hot. Set aside.

If using gravy mix, prepare according to package directions in 2-cup measure. MICROWAVE 3 MINUTES, 30 SECONDS to 4 MINUTES, 30 SECONDS on HIGH, or until thickened. Set aside.

Line oven shelf with paper towel. Top bread slices with 2 slices meat each. Arrange sandwiches on paper towel. MICROWAVE 3 to 4 MINUTES on HIGH, or until meat is hot.

Place sandwiches on plates. Pour hot sauce or gravy over meat. Serve immediately.

TURKEY DIVAN SANDWICH

4 to 6 servings
1-quart mixing bowl

1½ *cups chopped, cooked turkey*
1 *jar (8-ounces) American process cheese spread*
1 *package (10-ounces) frozen broccoli spears, cooked and drained (page 148)*
4 *English muffins, split, toasted and buttered*

Blend turkey and cheese spread in 1-quart bowl until smooth. MICROWAVE 3 to 5 MINUTES on '6', or until hot.

Place cooked broccoli spears on English muffins. Top with hot turkey sauce. If necessary, MICROWAVE 30 SECONDS on HIGH to reheat.

For ovens without solid state heat control, MICROWAVE 4 to 6 MINUTES on '5'.

Magic Meltwiches

A microwave show-off, Magic Meltwiches are easy to assemble, quick to heat and delicious to eat. They team up two appliances, the toaster and the microwave oven. Make them for a quick lunch, a snack or a party, to serve one person or fifty. Follow the suggestions below, or invent your own combinations.

Ingredients are listed in order used. Start with a piece of toast, add meat or fish, a vegetable or fruit garnish, sauces or cheese. MICROWAVE 15 to 30 SECONDS. Watch through the oven door for melting or bubbling since timing varies with the amount and type of filling used. Sandwiches topped with cheese heat rapidly.

15-SECOND PIZZA (top left)

Half toasted English muffin
Pepperoni slices
Canned pizza sauce
Grated mozzarella cheese
Oregano leaves
Chopped onions
Garnish with ripe olives or chopped mushrooms if desired

INSTANT CHEESEBURGER (top right)

Toasted whole wheat bread
Pre-cooked ground beef
Salt and pepper
Onion rings
Sliced American process cheese

ROAST BEEF SPECIAL (middle left)

Toasted pumpernickel bread
Lettuce
Thinly sliced roast beef
Sliced Swiss process cheese
Green pepper ring

WIDE-OPEN REUBEN (middle right)

Toasted pumpernickel bread
Shaved corned beef
Sauerkraut
Mustard
Swiss cheese triangles

CHEESY B.L.T. (bottom left)

Toasted rye bread
Mayonnaise
Lettuce
Tomato slices
Cooked bacon
American or cheddar cheese

ROMA

Toasted French or Italian bread
Sautéed mushrooms
Mozzarella cheese

KEY WEST (bottom right)

Toasted bread
Crab meat mixed with softened cream cheese and seasoned with lemon juice and salt
Avocado slices
Tomato wedges
Garnish with watercress after heating

SOUTH-OF-THE-BORDER

Toasted corn bread
Avocado slices
Thin tomato slices
Taco sauce
Crumbled cooked bacon
Chopped ripe olives
Grated Monterey jack cheese

ORIENTAL BEEF OR PORK

Toasted white bread
Pinch of dry mustard
Thin slices of rare roast beef or roast pork
Marmalade mixed with softened cream cheese

HOT LOX AND BAGEL

Half toasted bagel
Cream cheese
Thinly sliced smoked salmon
Onion rings
Garnish with chopped or sliced ripe olives

BOLOGNESE

Toasted French or Italian bread
Sliced chicken or turkey
Thin slice ham or prosciutto
Slice mozzarella cheese

HANS CHRISTIAN ANDERSEN

Toasted white bread
Liver pate
2 slices crisp cooked bacon
Thin tomato slices
Sprinkle with fresh parsley after heating

Magic Meltwiches are a great idea for an informal party, easy on the hostess and entertaining for the guests. Arrange a buffet on a counter near your microwave oven.
Selection of toasted breads: white, dark and light rye, whole wheat, English muffins
Assorted sliced meats, cheese, seafood
Bowls of sandwich filling: crab and cream cheese or tuna salad
Garnishes: onion and green pepper rings, fresh tomato slices, sliced or chopped canned mushrooms, avocado wedges, orange segments, sliced ripe or stuffed green olives, chopped pickle
Condiments: tomato sauce, catsup, mustard, mayonnaise

Let each guest assemble a sandwich on a paper napkin and heat it in the microwave oven. For a complete supper, add cole slaw, potato salad, or a tossed green salad.
NOTE: Breads may be toasted in advance, cooled and covered tightly with plastic wrap.

Soups & Beverages

Versatile soups can be a quick pick-me-up, or a hearty meal. Microwave a mug full of water for an instant cup of soup. Canned soups can be heated right in the bowl to eliminate clean-up. Prepare dehydrated soups in a 4-cup measure for easy pouring.

Made from scratch soups take more time, but with heat control, soup meat cooks tender and flavors blend in less time than it takes conventionally. If you have favorite "short-cut" recipes for old favorites, such as chowder, French onion, or borscht, try them in the microwave oven. The time will be cut shorter than ever.

Microwave works wonders with 2 to 3 quarts of soup, for more than that, cook soup conventionally and microwave the rest of the meal.

BORSCHT

4 to 6 servings
3-quart casserole

½ *pound beef stew meat, cut in* ½-*inch cubes*
1 *onion, thinly sliced*
1 *clove garlic, pressed or finely chopped*
7 *cups water*
1 *bay leaf*
1 *teaspoon dried thyme*
½ *teaspoon pepper*
2 *cups finely shredded cabbage*
1 *carrot, thinly sliced*
1 *turnip, thinly sliced*
2 *medium tomatoes, peeled and chopped*
1 *tablespoon salt*
2 *large beets, cooked, peeled, cut in julienne strips*
1 *carton (8-ounces) dairy sour cream*

Combine meat, onion, garlic, water, bay leaf, thyme and pepper in 3-quart casserole. Cover. MICROWAVE 10 MINUTES on HIGH.

Reduce setting. MICROWAVE 30 MINUTES on '6'.

Stir in cabbage, carrot, turnip, tomatoes and salt. Cover. MICROWAVE 10 MINUTES on '6'.

Add beets. Cover. MICROWAVE 5 MINUTES on '6', or until beets are heated through and vegetables tender crisp. Let stand 5 minutes, covered.

Remove bay leaf before serving. Top each serving with sour cream.

NOTE: Beets lose their color if allowed to stand in soup. To make ahead, remove soup from oven before adding beets. Cool and refrigerate. Before serving, reheat, add beets and finish cooking.

For ovens without solid state heat control, during second cooking period MICROWAVE 35 MINUTES on '5'. Follow above procedure then MICROWAVE 12 and 6 MINUTES on '5'.

FRENCH ONION SOUP

6 to 8 servings
3-quart bowl or casserole

2 *tablespoons butter or margarine*
3 *medium onions, thinly sliced*
3 *cans (10½-ounces) condensed beef broth, diluted*
  with 2¼ cups water, or 2 tablespoons instant beef
  boullion dissolved in 6 cups water
Salt to taste
French bread slices, toasted
Grated Parmesan cheese

Combine butter and onion in 3-quart bowl or casserole. Cover. MICROWAVE 8 MINUTES on HIGH, or until onions are transparent, stirring once.

Stir in broth. Cover. MICROWAVE 8 to 10 MINUTES on HIGH, or until onions are tender and soup is hot. Salt to taste.

Top each serving with slice of toasted French bread. Sprinkle generously with Parmesan cheese.

SPLIT PEA SOUP

8 to 10 servings
4-quart mixing bowl

2 *quarts boiling water*
1 *pound split dried peas*
Ham bone
1 *small onion, sliced*
5 *peppercorns*
1 *cup diced cooked ham*
½ *cup diced potato*
⅓ *cup sliced carrot*
Salt and pepper to taste

Combine water, peas, ham bone, onion and peppercorns in 4-quart mixing bowl. Cover tightly. MICROWAVE 25 MINUTES on HIGH, or until peas are tender, stirring after 15 minutes.

Remove ham bone. Cut away any meat and add to soup. Add diced ham, potatoes and carrots. Cover. MICRO-WAVE 15 to 20 MINUTES on HIGH, or until vegetables are tender-crisp. Taste for seasoning and correct.

CREAMY TOMATO SOUP

4 to 6 servings
2-quart casserole

¼ *cup butter or margarine*
1 *tablespoon finely chopped onion*
3 *tablespoons flour*
2 *tablespoons sugar*
1 *teaspoon salt*
Pepper to taste
1 *can (16 to 18-ounces) tomato juice*
2 *cups milk*

Combine butter and onion in 2-quart casserole. MICRO-WAVE 2 MINUTES on HIGH, or until butter is melted. Blend in flour, sugar, salt and pepper. Gradually stir in

tomato juice. MICROWAVE 4 MINUTES on HIGH, or until hot, stirring after 2 minutes.

Gradually stir in milk. MICROWAVE 8 to 10 MINUTES on '8', or until mixture is about to boil, stirring every 2 minutes. Serve hot, garnished with croutons or oyster crackers, if desired.

For ovens without solid state heat control, MICROWAVE 6 to 8 MINUTES on HIGH, stirring after every minute.

CHEESE SOUP CANADIENNE

5 to 6 servings
2-quart casserole

1 *cup hot tap water*
1 *cup finely chopped onion*
1 *cup finely chopped potatoes*
¼ *cup finely chopped carrots*
¼ *cup finely chopped celery*
1 *can (10¾-ounces) chicken broth, diluted with ¾ cup*
  water or 2 teaspoons instant bouillon dissolved in
  2 cups water
1 *cup grated sharp cheddar cheese*
½ *cup whipping cream*
3 *peppercorns*
2 *tablespoons snipped fresh parsley*

Combine water and vegetables in 2-quart casserole. Cover. MICROWAVE 7 to 8 MINUTES on HIGH, or until vegetables are tender-crisp.

Stir in broth, cheese, cream and peppercorns. Cover. MICROWAVE 5 MINUTES on '8', or until hot. Remove peppercorns and stir. Garnish with parsley.

For ovens without solid state heat control, MICROWAVE 4 MINUTES on HIGH, stirring after 2 minutes.

CHILI CON QUESO SOUP

4 to 6 servings
1½-quart bowl or casserole

3 *tablespoons butter or margarine*
1 *cup finely chopped onion*
1 *can (14½-ounces) stewed tomatoes*
1 *can (4-ounces) chopped green chilies, rinsed of*
  seeds
1 *jar (2-ounces) chopped pimiento*
1 *teaspoon salt*
½ *teaspoon pepper*
1 *pound Monterey jack or cheddar cheese, finely diced*
Beer

Combine butter and onion in 1½-quart bowl. MICRO-WAVE 3 MINUTES on HIGH, or until onion is transparent.

Stir in tomatoes, chilies, pimiento, salt and pepper. MICROWAVE 3 MINUTES on HIGH, or until very hot. Gradually add cheese, stirring after each addition until melted. After last addition, MICROWAVE 1 MINUTE on '5', if necessary to complete melting. If soup is too thick, thin with beer to desired consistency.

CREAM OF TURKEY SOUP

6 servings
3-quart casserole

3 cups turkey stock
1 cup finely chopped potatoes
2 teaspoons finely chopped onion
1 can (10¾-ounces) condensed cream of celery soup,
   undiluted
½ cup diced, cooked turkey
6 slices bacon, cooked crisp and crumbled, (page 96)
2 tablespoons snipped parsley
½ teaspoon salt
Pepper

Combine turkey stock, potatoes and onion in 3-quart casserole. Cover. MICROWAVE 14 MINUTES on HIGH, or until potatoes are tender.

Add remaining ingredients. Mix well. MICROWAVE 6 MINUTES on HIGH, or until hot.

CHICKEN SOUP WITH LITTLE DUMPLINGS

4 servings
2-quart casserole

3½ cups chicken stock or 2 cans (13¾-ounces each)
   chicken broth
1 small onion, quartered
1 stem celery, cut in 4 pieces
¼ teaspoon thyme
1½ teaspoons dried parsley flakes
½ teaspoon salt
1 egg
¼ cup all-purpose flour
⅛ teaspoon salt

Combine chicken broth, onion, celery, thyme, parsley and salt in 2-quart casserole. Cover. MICROWAVE 8 to 10 MINUTES on HIGH, or until mixture begins to boil.

Reduce setting. MICROWAVE 5 MINUTES on '6', or until celery and onion are soft. Remove vegetables with slotted spoon, discard.

While soup is cooking, combine egg, flour and salt in 1-quart mixing bowl. Beat until batter is smooth.

After removing vegetables, drop batter into soup by rounded half-teasponfuls. Do not cover. MICROWAVE 2 to 3 MINUTES on '6', or until dumplings rise to the surface and firm.

For ovens without solid state heat control, after stock boils MICROWAVE 6 MINUTES on '5'. Remove vegetables and add dumplings. MICROWAVE 2 MINUTES, 25 SECONDS to 3 MINUTES, 35 SECONDS on '5'.

Variation:
For a hearty soup, add 1 can (6-ounces) boned chicken and broth to stock ingredients before first cooking period.

OYSTER STEW

6 servings
2-quart casserole

1 quart light cream
1 pint fresh oysters, drained, reserve liquor
½ teaspoon onion salt
½ teaspoon Worcestershire sauce
⅛ teaspoon pepper
6 tablespoons butter or margarine

Combine light cream and reserved oyster liquor in 2-quart casserole. Cover. MICROWAVE 10 to 12 MINUTES on '8', or until mixture is almost boiling.

Add oysters, salt, Worcestershire sauce and pepper. Do not cover.

MICROWAVE 2 MINUTES on '8', or until oysters swell and edges begin to curl.

Place 1 tablespoon of butter in each soup bowl. Ladle stew into bowls. Serve at once.

For ovens without solid state heat control MICROWAVE 8 to 10 MINUTES on HIGH, stirring after 4 minutes. Watch carefully. Add oysters and seasonings. MICROWAVE 2 MINUTES on HIGH, stirring after 1 minute.

SPICED MEATBALL SOUP

6 to 8 servings
12 x 8-inch utility dish
2-quart casserole

1 pound lean ground beef
1 egg, slightly beaten
1 teaspoon basil
1 teaspoon salt
Dash pepper
1 medium onion, finely chopped
1 clove garlic, pressed or minced
3 teaspoons instant beef bouillon dissolved in 3 cups
   hot water
1 can (6-ounces) tomato paste
1 teaspoon ground cumin

Mix together ground beef, egg, basil, salt and pepper in medium mixing bowl. Drop by rounded teaspoonfuls into (12 x 8-inch) utility dish. MICROWAVE 3 to 4 MINUTES on HIGH, or until meat is set. Drain fat, set meatballs aside.

Combine onions, garlic, beef broth, tomato paste and cumin in 2-quart casserole. Mix well. MICROWAVE 6 MINUTES on HIGH, or until mixture begins to boil.

Reduce setting. Cover. MICROWAVE 6 MINUTES on '6'. Add meatballs to simmering stock, cover. MICROWAVE 2 to 3 MINUTES on '6', or until meatballs are heated through.

For ovens without solid state heat control, after stock boils, MICROWAVE 7 MINUTES on '5'. Add meatballs, cover. MICROWAVE 2 MINUTES, 35 SECONDS to 3 MINUTES, 35 SECONDS on '5'.

FISH CHOWDER

6 to 8 servings
12 x 8-inch baking dish
2½-quart casserole

2 *pounds lean white fish fillets, fresh or frozen and defrosted*
Water, as needed
1 *can (11½-ounces) condensed green pea soup, undiluted*
1 *can (10¾-ounces) condensed tomato soup, undiluted*
1 *cup milk*
2 *tablespoons finely chopped onion*
¼ *teaspoon allspice*
¼ *teaspoon cloves*
⅛ *teaspoon pepper*
1 *teaspoon salt*
Snipped parsley

Arrange fillets in (12 x 8-inch) baking dish, thickest parts to outside. Cover tightly with plastic wrap. MICRO-WAVE 6 to 8 MINUTES on HIGH, or until fish is almost cooked. Drain and reserve liquid, adding water to make 1 cup. Break up fish with fork.

Combine soups, fish liquid, milk, onion, allspice, cloves and pepper in 2½-quart casserole. Mix well; stir in fish. Cover. MICROWAVE 8 to 10 MINUTES on '8', or until bubbly hot. Stir in salt. Let stand 5 minutes. Garnish with parsley.

For ovens without solid state heat control MICROWAVE 6 to 8 MINUTES on HIGH, stirring every 2 minutes. Let stand.

MANHATTAN CLAM CHOWDER

8 servings
3-quart casserole

3 *slices bacon, chopped*
3 *cans (6½-ounces each) minced clams*
1 *can (1-pound, 12-ounces) tomatoes*
1 *cup sliced onions*
1 *cup diced carrots*
1 *cup diced celery*
3½ *cups peeled and diced potatoes*
1 *tablespoon snipped parsley*
2 *teaspoons salt*
1½ *teaspoon thyme*

Place chopped bacon in 3-quart casserole. MICRO-WAVE 2 MINUTES on HIGH. Drain clam liquid into bacon and drippings. Set clams aside.

Stir in tomatoes, onions, carrots, celery, potatoes, salt and thyme. Cover. MICROWAVE 10 to 12 MIN-UTES on HIGH, or until vegetables are tender.

Stir in clams. MICROWAVE 2 MINUTES on HIGH, or until hot.

NEW ENGLAND CLAM CHOWDER

6 servings
2-quart casserole

3 *slices bacon, chopped*
3 *cans (6½-ounces each) minced clams*
2 *cups peeled and diced potatoes*
1 *medium onion, chopped*
¼ *cup flour*
2 *cups milk*
¾ *cup light cream*
1 *teaspoon salt*
⅛ *teaspoon pepper*

Place chopped bacon in 2-quart casserole. MICRO-WAVE 2 MINUTES on HIGH. Drain clam liquid into bacon and drippings. Set clams aside.

Stir in potatoes and onion. Cover. MICROWAVE 8 MINUTES on HIGH, or until vegetables are tender.

Blend in flour until smooth. Stir in milk. Cover. MICRO-WAVE 3 MINUTES on '8'.

Stir in clams, cream, salt and pepper. Do not cover. MICROWAVE 3 MINUTES on '8', or until piping hot.

For ovens without solid state heat control, during last 2 steps, MICROWAVE 2 MINUTES on HIGH, stirring after every minute.

QUICKIE CORN CHOWDER

4 to 6 servings
3-quart casserole

1 *tablespoon butter or margarine*
1 *small onion, finely chopped*
1 *can (10¾-ounces) condensed cream of mushroom soup, undiluted*
4 *cups milk*
1 *can (16-ounces) whole kernel corn, drained*
½ *teaspoon salt*
Pepper

Combine butter and onion in 3-quart casserole. MICRO-WAVE on HIGH until onion is transparent.

Add soup, milk, corn, salt and pepper. Stir until well blended. MICROWAVE 7 to 8 MINUTES on HIGH, or until hot.

ZIPPY MADRILENE

2 servings
1-quart measure

1 *can (13-ounces) consomme madrilene*
1 *dash hot pepper sauce*
2 *tablespoons sherry*

Combine consomme and pepper sauce in 1-quart measure. MICROWAVE 3 to 4 MINUTES on HIGH, or until just beginning to bubble. Stir in sherry and serve immediately. Garnish with lemon slices if desired.

56

SHRIMP BISQUE

4 servings
2-quart casserole

1 *tablespoon butter or margarine*
1 *small onion, finely chopped*
1 *stem celery, finely chopped*
1 *carrot, finely grated*
1 *can (13¾-ounces) chicken broth*
2 *cans (6-ounces each) shrimp, drained and mashed*
  fine with fork
⅛ *teaspoon thyme*
1 *cup heavy cream*
¼ *cup dry white wine (optional)*
Salt and pepper to taste

Combine butter, onion, celery and carrot in 2-quart casserole. MICROWAVE 4 to 5 MINUTES on HIGH, or until onion is transparent, stirring once.

Stir in chicken broth, shrimp and thyme. MICROWAVE 4 to 6 MINUTES on HIGH, or until mixture boils.

Strain mixture, pressing as much of the shrimp as possible through sieve. Return soup to casserole. Stir in cream and wine. MICROWAVE 4 to 5 MINUTES on '6', or until mixture is steaming hot. Season with salt and pepper to taste.

For ovens without solid state heat control, after adding cream and wine, MICROWAVE 5 to 6 MINUTES on '5'.

VEGETABLE SOUP ❄️

8 to 10 servings
4-quart casserole

1 *pound extra lean ground beef*
1 *medium onion, finely chopped*
1 *cup sliced celery*
1 *cup thinly sliced carrots*
1 *cup diced potatoes*
1 *bay leaf*
½ *teaspoon basil*
2 *teaspoons salt*
1 *cup shredded cabbage*
1 *can (16-ounces) tomatoes, including liquid*
3 *cups hot water*

Crumble ground beef into 4-quart casserole. MICROWAVE 4 MINUTES on HIGH, or until set. Drain fat.

Add onion, celery, carrots, potatoes, bay leaf, basil, salt, cabbage, tomatoes and water. Mix thoroughly. Cover. MICROWAVE 10 MINUTES on HIGH. Stir.

Reduce setting. MICROWAVE 20 to 30 MINUTES on '6', or until vegetables are tender crisp.

For ovens without solid state heat control MICROWAVE 25 to 35 MINUTES on '5'.

TOMATO SOUP EXCEPTIONAL

2 to 4 servings
3-quart casserole

2 *tablespoons butter or margarine*
2 *tablespoons chopped green onions, including tops*
1 *can (10¾-ounces) condensed tomato soup, undiluted*
1 *soup can milk or water*
¼ *teaspoon Worcestershire sauce*

Combine butter and onion in 3-quart casserole. MICROWAVE on HIGH until onion is transparent.

Add soup, milk and Worcestershire sauce. Stir until well blended. Cover. MICROWAVE 7 to 8 MINUTES on HIGH, or until hot.

INSTANT VICHYSSOISE

4 servings
2-quart batter bowl

4 *servings prepared instant mashed potatoes*
1 *teaspoon instant chicken bouillon*
1 *cup hot water*
1 *cup whipping cream*
1½ *teaspoons Worcestershire sauce*
1 *teaspoon onion powder*
⅛ *teaspoon white pepper*
½ *to 1 teaspoon chopped chives*

Prepare potatoes according to package directions using 2-quart batter bowl. Add instant bouillon to hot water and blend with cream, Worcestershire sauce, onion powder and pepper. Blend into instant mashed potatoes with wire whip to make a smooth soup. MICROWAVE 4 to 5 MINUTES on HIGH, or until hot and bubbly, stirring once. Garnish with chives. Serve hot or cold.

CREAMY CHICKEN 'N HAM SOUP

4 servings
3-quart casserole

1 *can (10½-ounces) condensed cream of celery soup,*
  undiluted
1 *can (10½-ounces) condensed chicken vegetable*
  soup, undiluted
1½ *soup cans milk or water*
1 *cup chopped cooked ham*
2 *teaspoons parsley flakes*
¼ *teaspoon crushed rosemary*
Salt and pepper to taste

Combine all ingredients in 3-quart casserole. Stir until well blended. Cover. MICROWAVE 7 to 8 MINUTES on HIGH, or until hot.

Parisian Mocha, left; Hot Mulled Wine, right.

PARISIAN MOCHA

2 servings
1-quart measure

2 *cups water*
3 *packages (1 ounce each) instant cocoa mix*
2 *tablespoons instant coffee*
½ *teaspoon cinnamon*
Whipped cream
Shaved chocolate curls
2 *cinnamon sticks*

Measure water into 1-quart measure. MICROWAVE 4 to 5 MINUTES on HIGH, or until almost boiling.

Combine cocoa mix, instant coffee and cinnamon. Add to water. Stir. Pour into cups. Garnish with whipped cream and chocolate curls.

Add cinnamon sticks. Serve immediately.

COFFEE HOUSE VARIETIES

Experiment with your own coffee house varieties.

Suggestions:

CAFE AU LAIT

Equal parts coffee and milk

ESPRESSO ROYALE

1 *teaspoon cognac*
Sugar cube to each cup

HOT MULLED WINE

2 servings
1-quart measure

2 *cups red wine*
4 *whole cloves*
2 *sticks cinnamon*
1 *teaspoon lemon juice*
1 *slice lemon, halved and studded with 8 whole cloves*

Combine wine, cloves, cinnamon sticks and lemon juice in 1-quart measure. MICROWAVE 3 to 4 MINUTES on HIGH, or until steaming hot. Pour into mugs. Garnish with lemon slice studded with cloves.

HOT TODDY

1 serving
Mug

1 *tablespoon sugar*
¾ *cup water*
¼ *teaspoon lemon juice*
1 *jigger (1½-ounces) light rum*
1 *teaspoon butter*
Nutmeg

Dissolve sugar in water and lemon juice in coffee mug or cup. MICROWAVE 1 to 2 MINUTES on HIGH, or until piping hot. Add rum. Float butter on top. Sprinkle with nutmeg.

HOT CHOCOLATE

4 to 6 servings
2-quart bowl or pitcher

1 *cup water*
2 *ounces unsweetened chocolate*
¼ *cup sugar*
¼ *teaspoon salt*
3 *cups milk*

Measure water into 2-quart bowl. Add chocolate. MICRO-WAVE 5 MINUTES on HIGH, or until chocolate melts. Blend well.

Mix in sugar and salt. Gradually stir in milk. MICRO-WAVE 4 to 6 MINUTES on HIGH, or until mixture begins to boil. Beat with rotary beater until frothy.

ELEGANT EGG NOG

8 to 12 servings
2-quart batter bowl or casserole

4 *eggs, separated*
3 *tablespoons sugar*
½ *cup sugar*
¼ *teaspoon salt*
3 *cups milk*
1 *teaspoon rum or vanilla*

Beat egg whites until foamy in 1-quart bowl. Beat in 3 tablespoons sugar, 1 tablespoon at a time. Continue beating until stiff and glossy. Set aside.

Combine egg yolks, ½ cup sugar and salt in 2-quart bowl. Beat until thick and lemon-colored. Stir in milk and rum or vanilla. MICROWAVE 4 MINUTES on HIGH, or until mixture is hot but not boiling.

Carefully fold egg whites into milk mixture until well blended. Fill serving cups ½ to ¾ full. Top with grated chocolate or nutmeg.

NOTE: To serve cold, cool to room temperature and then refrigerate. Egg nog cannot be reheated, as egg white will cook.

CAFE BRULOT

8 servings
2-quart casserole

2 *cinnamon sticks, broken*
6 *whole cloves*
Rind of 1 medium orange, cut in thin slivers
Rind of ½ lemon, cut in thin slivers
8 *lumps sugar*
¾ *cup cognac or brandy*
4 *cups strong, hot coffee*

Combine cinnamon, cloves, orange, lemon rinds and sugar in 2-quart casserole. Pour in cognac. MICRO-WAVE 1 MINUTE, 30 SECONDS to 2 MINUTES on HIGH, or until hot. Stir in hot coffee. Serve in demitasse or brulot cups.

SPICED CIDER

6 to 8 servings
2-cup measure
1½-quart bowl or pitcher

1 *cup water*
¼ *cup firmly packed brown sugar*
2 *sticks cinnamon*
1 *teaspoon whole cloves*
½ *teaspoon mace*
¼ *teaspoon nutmeg*
1 *quart cider*

Combine water, sugar and spices in 2-cup measure. MICROWAVE 10 to 12 MINUTES on HIGH, until mixture is reduced to ½ cup. Strain into 1½-quart bowl or pitcher. Stir in cider. MICROWAVE 4 to 5 MINUTES on HIGH, or until cider is hot.

QUICK COCOA

1 serving
Mug

1 *tablespoon cocoa*
1 *tablespoon sugar*
Milk

Combine cocoa and sugar in mug. Add enough milk to make a thin paste. Mix until smooth. Add milk to fill cup. MICROWAVE 1 MINUTE, 20 SECONDS on HIGH, or until steaming.

KILLARNEY COFFEE

1 serving
Coffee mug or Irish coffee goblet

1 *teaspoon firmly packed brown sugar*
4 *to 6 ounces strong black coffee*
1 *jigger (1½-ounces) Irish whiskey*
1 *rounded tablespoon whipped cream*

Dissolve sugar in black coffee in coffee mug or Irish coffee goblet. MICROWAVE 1 to 2 MINUTES on HIGH, or until hot. Add Irish whiskey.

Top with whipped cream.

Fish & Seafood

The classic methods of cooking fish have always been poaching and steaming. A microwave oven achieves the same delicate flavor and flaky-firm texture without elaborate procedures. No need to tie fish in cheese cloth or use a special fish-poacher. Shellfish steam tender with very little water.

Whole Lobster. Recipe on following page.

FISH AND SEA FOOD BASICS

Microwaved fish should be covered unless coated with crumbs to seal in juices. Avoid overcooking which dries and toughens fish and seafood. Fish is so delicate that, once it is hot, it almost cooks itself. Fish is done when flesh becomes opaque and flakes easily with a fork. When seafood is done, the flesh is opaque and firm. Cook fish for the minimum time. Let stand. If necessary microwave a few moments more before serving.

Most fillets cook well on a high setting. Lower heat control settings give thick steaks, whole fish and most seafood the gentle treatment they deserve.

WHOLE LOBSTER

1 to 2 servings
12 x 8-inch baking dish

Live lobster (about 1½-pounds)
¼ cup hot water

On a cutting board, place lobster on its back. To kill, sever the spinal cord by plunging the point of a sharp knife through to the back shell, where tail and body cavity are joined together.

With a sharp knife, cut lengthwise through the under shell, leaving the back shell intact. Remove small sack below the head and the intestinal vein which runs from it to the tip of the tail.

To prevent curling, peg the tail by running a wooden skewer through it lengthwise. Place lobster shell side up in (12 x 8-inch) baking dish. Pour in ¼ cup hot water. Cover tightly with plastic wrap. MICROWAVE 2 MINUTES on HIGH.

Turn lobster over. Cover. MICROWAVE 2 MINUTES on HIGH.

Turn lobster shell side up. Cover. MICROWAVE 6 to 8 MINUTES on '6', or until shell is bright red. Let stand 5 minutes, covered.

Serve with melted butter and lemon wedges.

For ovens without solid state heat control, during last cooking period, MICROWAVE 7 to 9 MINUTES, 30 SECONDS on '5'.

LOBSTER TAILS

2 servings
12 x 8-inch baking dish

2 lobster tails (7 to 8-ounces each), defrosted
2 tablespoons butter, or margarine melted

Split each lobster tail through top shell and release meat, leaving it connected to shell at one end. Pull meat through slit and place on top of shell. Arrange tails in baking dish and brush with butter. Cover with plastic wrap.

MICROWAVE 5 to 6 MINUTES on HIGH, or until meat is opaque and shell turns red. To cook one tail, MICROWAVE 3 MINUTES on HIGH, or until meat is opaque. Let stand to complete cooking if necessary. Over cooking causes meat to toughen.

CANTONESE SHRIMP AND PEA PODS

6 servings
3-quart casserole

1 small onion, thinly sliced
1 clove garlic, pressed or finely chopped
1 tablespoon salad oil
1½ teaspoons instant chicken bouillon, dissolved in 1 cup boiling water
1½ pounds fresh or frozen defrosted shrimp, uncooked and cleaned (or frozen pre-cooked, see note)
½ teaspoon ginger
Dash pepper
2 tablespoons corn starch
2 tablespoons cold water
1 package (9-ounces) frozen pea pods or cut green beans, defrosted
1 teaspoon salt

Combine onion, garlic and oil in 3-quart casserole. MICROWAVE 3 MINUTES on HIGH, or until onion is transparent.

Add chicken broth, shrimp, ginger and pepper. Cover. MICROWAVE 3 MINUTES on '7'.

Blend corn starch and water. Stir into shrimp mixture. Cover. MICROWAVE 5 MINUTES on '7'.

Add pea pods and MICROWAVE 6 to 8 MINUTES on '7', or until pea pods are cooked and sauce is thick. Add salt during last 2 minutes of cooking.

NOTE: When using pre-cooked shrimp, stir in after adding corn starch to prevent over cooking.

For ovens without solid state heat control, MICROWAVE 2 MINUTES, 20 SECONDS; 3 MINUTES, 30 SECONDS and 4 to 6 MINUTES on HIGH. Stir twice during cooking time.

SEA FOOD NEWBURG

4 servings
1½-quart casserole

2 cups (12-ounces) cooked lobster, crab or shrimp
¼ cup butter or margarine, melted
3 egg yolks, beaten
1 cup whipping cream
1 teaspoon paprika
Salt to taste

Combine lobster and butter in 1½-quart casserole. MICROWAVE 2 MINUTES on '7'.

Add beaten egg yolks to cream. Combine with lobster. Add paprika. MICROWAVE 5 MINUTES on '7', or until sauce is heated but not boiling, stirring after every 2 minutes. Add salt. Serve over rice or buttered toast points.

For ovens without solid state heat control, following above procedure, set oven on '5' and use cooking times of 3 minutes and 7 minutes.

SHRIMP CREOLE

5 to 6 servings
1½-quart casserole

1 clove garlic, pressed or finely chopped
1 cup chopped onion
1 green pepper, chopped
½ cup chopped celery
3 tablespoons butter or margarine
1 can (12-ounces) tomato sauce
½ cup dry red wine, or water
2 small whole bay leaves
2 tablespoons snipped parsley
¼ teaspoon thyme
½ teaspoon salt
Dash cayenne pepper
1 package (12-ounces) frozen, uncooked, cleaned
   shrimp, defrosted
3 cups hot cooked rice

Combine garlic, onion, green pepper, celery and butter in a 1½-quart casserole. MICROWAVE 3 MINUTES on HIGH, or until onion is transparent.

Stir in tomato sauce, wine, bay leaves, parsley, thyme, salt and pepper. Cover with waxed paper. MICROWAVE 5 minutes, covered, to finish cooking. Remove bay leaf.

Add shrimp, stir. Cover with waxed paper. MICRO-WAVE 4 MINUTES on HIGH. Let stand 5 minutes. Serve over rice.

LUNCHEON SHRIMP

6 servings
1½-quart casserole

12 ounces cooked shrimp
3 tablespoons butter or margarine
¼ cup finely chopped onion
1 green pepper, finely chopped
1 clove garlic, pressed or finely chopped
1 cup uncooked converted rice
8 ounces fresh mushrooms, sliced
1 jar (2-ounces) chopped pimiento, drained
1 bay leaf
1½ cups hot tap water
1 teaspoon salt

Cut shrimp in half, if large. Combine butter, onion, green pepper and garlic in 1½-quart casserole. MICROWAVE 3 to 5 MINUTES on HIGH, or until onion is transparent.

Add shrimp, rice, mushrooms, pimiento, bay leaf and water. Mix well. Cover. MICROWAVE 10 MINUTES on '8', or until rice is almost tender. Stir in salt. Let stand 5 minutes, covered, to finish cooking.

NOTE: If using frozen shrimp, defrost partially.

For ovens without solid state heat control, MICROWAVE 12 to 14 MINUTES on HIGH during second cooking period.

SPAGHETTI WITH CRAB SAUCE

6 servings
2 to 2½-quart casserole

½ cup chopped onion
½ cup chopped celery
2 cloves garlic, pressed or finely chopped
2 tablespoons chopped parsley
¼ cup butter or margarine
1 can (14½-ounces) stewed tomatoes
1 can (8-ounces) tomato sauce
¼ teaspoon oregano
¼ teaspoon salt
Dash pepper
2 cans (6½-ounces each) crab meat, drained
3 cups cooked spaghetti
Grated parmesan cheese

Combine onion, celery, garlic, parsley and butter in 2 to 2½-quart casserole. MICROWAVE 3 to 4 MINUTES on HIGH, or until onion is transparent.

Add tomatoes, sauce, oregano, salt and pepper. Cover. MICROWAVE 10 MINUTES on HIGH, or until bubbly, stirring after 5 minutes.

Add crab meat. Cover. MICROWAVE 1 to 2 MINUTES on HIGH, or until crab meat is hot. Serve over cooked spaghetti, sprinkle with parmesan cheese.

COQUILLES SAINT JACQUES

6 to 8 servings
2-quart casserole
1-cup measure
2-cup measure
6 to 8 shells or individual ramkins

1 *pound scallops, fresh or frozen, defrosted*
2 *tablespoons butter or margarine*
1 *small onion, finely chopped*
1 *package (8-ounces) fresh mushrooms, sliced*
2 *tablespoons lemon juice*
1 *cup dry white wine*
1 *bay leaf*
¼ *teaspoon savory*
½ *teaspoon salt*
⅛ *teaspoon pepper*
3 *tablespoons butter or margarine*
3 *tablespoons flour*
1 *cup light cream*
½ *cup dried bread crumbs*
Lemon wedges
Parsley sprigs

Cut scallops in half. Spread on bottom of 2-quart casserole. Set aside.

Combine butter and onions in 1-cup measure. MICROWAVE 3 MINUTES on HIGH, or until onions are transparent. Stir in mushrooms and lemon juice. Pour over scallops. Add wine, bay leaf, savory, salt and pepper. Cover. MICROWAVE 4 to 6 MINUTES on '8', or until scallops are tender. Remove bay leaf. Drain and reserve liquid.

Place 3 tablespoons butter in 2-cup measure. MICROWAVE on HIGH until melted. Blend in flour to make a smooth paste. Stir in reserved liquid and cream. Pour over scallops. MICROWAVE 3 to 4 MINUTES on '8', or until sauce thickens.

Spoon mixture into serving shells or individual ramkins. Sprinkle with bread crumbs. Place 3 to 4 shells at a time in oven. MICROWAVE 1 to 2 MINUTES on '8', per serving, or until piping hot. Garnish with lemon wedges and parsley sprigs.

NOTE: Watch carefully during final heating. Shells and ramkins differ in size and shape, which affects heating time.

For ovens without solid state heat control, after adding scallops, MICROWAVE 3 to 4 MINUTES on HIGH, stirring once. Add sauce. MICROWAVE 2 to 3 MINUTES on HIGH, stirring once. Heat filled shells, MICROWAVE 45 SECONDS to 1 MINUTE, 30 SECONDS on HIGH.

Coquilles Saint Jacques

CRAB MORNAY

5 to 6 servings
8 x 8-inch baking dish

2 *cups (12-ounces) cooked crab meat*
2 *cups white sauce (page 157)*
½ *pound Swiss or cheddar cheese, grated*

Layer half of crab meat, half of sauce and half of cheese in (8 x 8-inch) baking dish. Repeat with second layers. MICROWAVE 10 MINUTES on '7'. Garnish with parsley and paprika, if desired.

NOTE: 2 cans (6½-ounces) each crab meat or 12-ounces cooked langouste may be substituted for crab.

For ovens without solid state heat control, MICROWAVE 14 MINUTES on '5'.

SCALLOPS LORRAINE

6 servings
8-inch pie plate

Pastry for 8-inch pie shell
3 eggs, beaten
¾ cup light cream
½ pound cooked scallops, cut in 1-inch pieces
2 tablespoons sherry
2 tablespoons snipped parsley
1 teaspoon salt
½ teaspoon celery salt
Dash pepper
Paprika

Line 8-inch pie plate with pastry. Prick with fork. MICROWAVE 2 MINUTES, 30 SECONDS to 3 MINUTES on HIGH, or until pastry begins to bake.

Combine eggs and cream. Add scallops, sherry, parsley, salts and pepper. Pour mixture into pie shell and sprinkle with paprika. Cover with waxed paper. MICROWAVE 7 MINUTES, 30 SECONDS to 8 MINUTES on '8', or until pie is firm in center. Let stand 5 minutes, covered.

For ovens without solid state heat control, MICROWAVE 6 to 7 MINUTES on HIGH, turning dish twice during cooking time. Let stand 5 minutes, covered. If center is not firm after 5 minutes standing time, MICROWAVE 1 MINUTE on HIGH, let stand 3 minutes.

SCALLOP CURRY

4 servings
1½-quart casserole

1 pound fresh or frozen scallops, defrosted
1 tablespoon butter or margarine
¼ cup sliced green onions
1½ teaspoons corn starch
1½ teaspoons curry powder
¼ teaspoons salt
2 cups hot cooked rice

Rinse scallops in cold water and drain.

Place butter in 1½-quart casserole. MICROWAVE on HIGH until melted. Add onions and scallops. MICROWAVE 4 MINUTES on '8', stirring after 2 minutes.

Place 2 tablespoons butter-scallop liquid in small cup. Stir in corn starch, curry powder and salt until dissolved. Add to scallop mixture. Stir until well blended. MICROWAVE 2 MINUTES on HIGH.

Add cooked rice. Mix lightly with fork. MICROWAVE 30 SECONDS to 1 MINUTE, or until heated through. Serve with tomato slices and chutney.

For ovens without solid state heat control, MICROWAVE 3 MINUTES on HIGH.

QUICK PAELLA

4 servings
2-quart casserole

Spanish Sauce (below)
½ pound medium shrimp, fresh, or frozen and defrosted
1 cup cubed, cooked chicken (large chunks)
1 can (6½-ounces) clams, drained
2 cups hot cooked rice

Prepare Spanish Sauce in 2-quart casserole. Add shrimp, chicken and clams to sauce when adding tomatoes, mushrooms and seasonings before final cooking period. If necessary, microwave a little longer to finish cooking shrimp. Serve over rice. Garnish with lemon wedge, if desired.

Variations:
For a more elaborate Paella, add one or more of the following:
Cut up lobster meat
Cooked cubed ham
Cooked cubed veal
Cooked cubed beef
Cooked cubed pork
Cooked sliced sausage

Any of the above may be substituted for chicken in basic recipe.

SPANISH SAUCE

2 to 3 cups
1-quart casserole

1 large green pepper, chopped
1 medium onion, chopped
½ clove garlic, pressed or minced
2 tablespoons bacon fat or salad oil
1 can (15½-ounces) stewed tomatoes
1½ teaspoons Worcestershire sauce
½ teaspoon dry mustard
Dash cayenne pepper
½ teaspoon salt
1 can (2-ounces) mushroom stems and pieces

Combine peppers, onion, garlic and fat in 1-quart casserole. MICROWAVE 1 MINUTE, 30 SECONDS to 3 MINUTES on HIGH, or until onions are transparent.

Stir in remaining ingredients. Cover with waxed paper. MICROWAVE 5 to 6 MINUTES on HIGH, or until sauce reaches desired consistency, stirring after 2½ minutes.

Serve as a sauce for Spanish omelet, meat loaf, rice or pasta.

NOTE: This recipe can be easily doubled using a 2-quart casserole and increasing the time of the final cooking period by 4 to 5 minutes.

FISH SURPRISE

3 to 4 servings
2-quart casserole

1 bay leaf
6 whole cloves
1 slice lemon
1 slice onion
½ teaspoon salt
1 tablespoon vinegar
½-inch red pepper
1 pound halibut, cut in serving pieces, fresh or frozen
    and defrosted
½ cup water
2 cups medium white sauce (page 157)
½ cup blanched almonds or salted cashews, finely
    chopped
½ cup toasted bread crumbs

Place bay leaf, cloves, lemon, onion, salt, vinegar, red pepper and fish in 2-quart casserole. Pour in water. Cover. MICROWAVE 3 to 5 MINUTES on HIGH, or until fish flakes easily. Let stand, covered, while preparing white sauce.

Remove fish, drain broth and discard. Break fish into 1-inch pieces. Return to casserole. Stir nuts into white sauce. Pour over fish. Top with bread crumbs. MICROWAVE 3 to 4 MINUTES on '6', or until sauce bubbles.

For ovens without solid state heat control, MICROWAVE 3 MINUTES, 30 SECONDS to 5 MINUTES, 30 SECONDS on '5'.

ITALIAN POACHED FISH

4 servings
8 x 8-inch baking dish

2 tablespoons chopped parsley
1 clove garlic, pressed or finely chopped
1 to 1½ tablespoons olive oil
¼ cup hot water
1 pound white fish fillets, fresh or frozen defrosted
⅛ teaspoon oregano leaves
Salt and pepper to taste

Place parsley, garlic, olive oil and water in baking dish. MICROWAVE 30 SECONDS on HIGH. Arrange fillets with thickest portions to outside of dish. Sprinkle with seasonings. Cover tightly with plastic wrap. MICROWAVE 5 to 6 MINUTES on HIGH, or until fish flakes easily. Let stand 2 minutes, covered. Serve with liquid.

NOTE: Over-cooking toughens fish.

FILLETS ALMONDINE

4 servings
8 x 8-inch baking dish

¼ cup butter or margarine
¼ cup slivered almonds
1 pound white fish fillets, fresh or defrosted
2 teaspoons lemon juice
¼ teaspoon salt

Place butter and almonds in (8 x 8-inch) baking dish. MICROWAVE 5 MINUTES on HIGH, until almonds are golden, stirring once. Remove almonds and set aside. Arrange fillets in baking dish with thickest portions to outside of dish, turning to coat with butter. Sprinkle with lemon juice and salt. Cover tightly with plastic wrap. MICROWAVE 5 to 6 MINUTES on HIGH, or until fish flakes easily and appears opaque. Garnish with toasted almonds.

WHITE FISH POACHED IN WINE

2 servings
8 x 10 or 9 x 9-inch baking dish

2 tablespoons butter or margarine
½ small onion, chopped
½ teaspoon parsley
¼ teaspoon basil
½ teaspoon lemon juice
Salt
Pepper
8 to 10-ounces white fish (2 medium fillets)
¼ cup white wine

Place butter, onion, parsley, basil and lemon juice in (8 x 8-inch) baking dish. MICROWAVE 40 SECONDS on HIGH.

Salt and pepper fish fillets. Arrange fillets in dish, turning to coat with butter. Sprinkle with white wine. Cover with plastic wrap. MICROWAVE 3 MINUTES on HIGH, or until fish flakes easily with a fork.

Fabulous Baked Fish

FABULOUS BAKED FISH

3 to 4 servings
2-cup measure
12 x 8-inch baking dish

1 *pound whole fish (trout, pike, perch, haddock or*
  flounder)
4 *tablespoons butter or margarine*
2 *tablespoons finely chopped onion*
1 *cup dry bread crumbs*
1 *teaspoon salt*

Dry fish thoroughly. Rub inside with two tablespoons butter. Set aside.

Combine 2 tablespoons butter and onion in 2-cup measure. MICROWAVE on HIGH until butter is melted. Add bread crumbs and salt. Mix well.

Stuff fish with bread crumb mixture. Secure with string, wooden picks or poultry skewers. Place in (12 x 8-inch) baking dish. Spread any remaining stuffing over fish. Cover with plastic wrap. MICROWAVE 8 MINUTES on '7'. Garnish with lemon slices and parsley, if desired.

For ovens without solid state heat control, MICROWAVE 5 MINUTES, 30 SECONDS, or until fish flakes easily, turning once. Let stand 2 minutes, covered.

NOTE: If fish is too large for dish, wrap gently in plastic wrap and place on floor of oven.

BAKED FISH

3 to 4 servings
10 x 6 or 8 x 8-inch baking dish

1 *pound fresh or frozen fish fillets, defrosted*
1 *package (2-ounces) seasoned coating mix for fish*

Wash fillets and shake off excess water. Place coating mix in bag provided with mix. Add 1 or 2 fillets at a time and shake to coat with crumbs.

Place fillets in (10 x 6 or 8 x 8-inch) baking dish with thinner parts toward inside of dish. MICROWAVE 7 MINUTES on HIGH, or until fish flakes easily.

BAKED TORSK

4 to 6 servings
12 x 8-inch baking dish

1½ *pounds torsk, cut in serving pieces*
Salt and pepper
¼ *cup butter or margarine, melted*
¼ *cup green pepper, chopped*
1 *can (4-ounces) mushroom stems and pieces, drained*

Place torsk in (12 x 8-inch) baking dish. Sprinkle with salt and pepper. Combine butter, green pepper and mushrooms. Pour over fish. Cover. MICROWAVE 4 to 5 MINUTES on HIGH, or until fish flakes easily with a fork.

Garnish with lemon and lime wedges, if desired.

Salmon Steaks Limone.

SALMON PIQUANTE

4 to 6 servings
8 x 8 or 12 x 8-inch baking dish

1 *medium onion, thinly sliced*
1 *lemon, thinly sliced*
1 *clove garlic, thinly sliced*
1 *teaspoon mixed pickling spice*
1 *teaspoon salt*
1½ *pounds salmon or steaks*
½ *cup mayonnaise*
½ *cucumber, peeled and finely chopped*

Spread onion, lemon, garlic and spices on bottom of baking dish. Arrange salmon on top, thickest portions toward outside of dish. Cover tightly with plastic wrap. MICROWAVE 14 to 16 MINUTES on '8', or until salmon flakes easily.

Mix mayonnaise and cucumber. Serve as sauce for steaks. Garnish with lemon twists and parsley sprigs.

For ovens without solid state heat control, MICROWAVE 12 MINUTES on HIGH for steaks.

SALMON STEAKS LIMONE

4 servings
Custard cup
12 x 8-inch baking dish

1 *tablespoon butter or margarine*
1 *teaspoon lemon juice*
4 *salmon steaks, cut 1-inch thick (about 2-pounds) fresh, or frozen and defrosted*

Combine butter and lemon juice in custard cup. MICRO-WAVE on HIGH until butter melts.

Arrange salmon steaks in (12 x 8-inch) baking dish with meatiest portions to outside of dish. Brush with lemon butter. Cover with plastic wrap. MICROWAVE 14 to 16 MINUTES on '8', or until fish flakes easily. Let stand 5 minutes, covered. Garnish with lemon twists and parsley sprigs, if desired.

For ovens without solid state heat control, MICROWAVE 5 MINUTES, 30 SECONDS to 6 MINUTES, 30 SECONDS on HIGH.

SALMON LOAF SCANDINAVIAN

4 to 6 servings
9 x 5-inch loaf dish

1 *can (15½-ounces) salmon*
Milk
2 *eggs*
1 *cup coarsely crushed cracker crumbs*
3 *tablespoons chopped onion*
2 *tablespoons lemon juice*
¼ *teaspoon salt*
¼ *teaspoon pepper*
Cucumber sauce, below

Drain salmon into 2-cup measure. Add milk to make 1½-cups liquid. Set aside. Remove bones and skin from salmon and flake meat thoroughly.

In 2-quart bowl, beat eggs. Add salmon liquid. Stir in cracker crumbs, onion, lemon juice, salt and pepper. Add salmon and stir lightly until just moistened.
Handling gently, spread mixture in (9 x 5-inch) glass loaf dish. MICROWAVE 15 MINUTES on '7', or until center is set. Serve with cucumber sauce.

CUCUMBER SAUCE

½ *cup dairy sour cream*
½ *cup chopped cucumber*
2 *green onions, finely chopped*
2 *tablespoons light cream*

Combine all ingredients. Mix until blended. Serve over salmon loaf. MICROWAVE 1 MINUTE on '5' to warm.

For ovens without solid state heat control, MICROWAVE 8 to 10 MINUTES on HIGH, or until center begins to set, rotating dish ½ turn after 4 minutes. Let stand 3 to 5 minutes.

BAKED SALMON WITH MUSHROOMS

4 to 5 servings
8 x 8-inch or,
12 x 8-inch baking dish

2 pounds fresh or frozen salmon steaks, defrosted
¼ cup butter or margarine, melted
1 can (4-ounces) mushroom stems and pieces, drained
2 tablespoons lemon juice
1 teaspoon onion, grated
Salt and pepper to taste

Arrange salmon in baking dish with thin ends toward center. Combine butter, mushrooms, lemon juice and onion. Spoon over salmon. Cover with plastic wrap. MICROWAVE 12 MINUTES on HIGH, or until fish flakes easily. Let stand 5 minutes, covered. Season with salt and pepper.

FILLET OF SOLE CASSEROLE

4 to 6 servings
12 x 8-inch baking dish

1½ to 2 pounds fillet of sole, or other white fish, cut in serving pieces, fresh, or frozen and defrosted
1 can (10¾-ounces) condensed cream of shrimp soup, undiluted
½ cup toasted bread crumbs

Arrange fillets in (12 x 8-inch) baking dish, meatiest portions to outside of dish. Spread soup on fish. Sprinkle with crumbs. MICROWAVE 6 to 8 MINUTES on HIGH, or until fish flakes easily with a fork.

SAVORY FISH FILLETS

4 to 5 servings
10 x 8-inch baking dish

1 pound white fish fillets, fresh or defrosted
½ cup French dressing

Place fillets in (10 x 8-inch) baking dish. Pour dressing over, and turn to coat fillets. Cover and marinate at least 2 hours in refrigerator.

Drain. Arrange fish with thickest portions to outside of dish. Cover tightly with plastic wrap. MICROWAVE 5 MINUTES on HIGH, or until fish flakes. Let stand 2 minutes, covered.

HALIBUT HAWAIIAN

4 to 6 servings
8 x 8-inch baking dish

2 packages (12-ounces each) frozen Halibut steaks, defrosted
1 cup Sweet-Sour sauce, below
1 can (8-ounces) crushed pineapple, drained (reserve juice)
1 cup fine dry bread crumbs
3 tablespoons lemon juice
½ teaspoon curry powder
1 can (8-ounces) pineapple rings, drained (reserve juice)
Tomato wedges
Parsley sprigs

Cut Halibut in serving pieces. Arrange in (8 x 8-inch) baking dish. Set aside.

Prepare Sweet-Sour Sauce, using juice from crushed pineapple and pineapple rings. Reserve ½ cup sauce.

Combine remaining ½ cup Sweet-Sour Sauce, crushed pineapple, bread crumbs, lemon juice and curry powder. Spread mixture on Halibut. Pour reserved sauce evenly over top. Cover with plastic wrap. MICROWAVE 15 to 18 MINUTES on '8', or until fish flakes easily.

Garnish each serving with 1 pineapple ring. Place tomato wedge and parsley sprig in center of ring.

For ovens without solid state heat control, MICROWAVE 12 to 15 MINUTES on HIGH.

SWEET-SOUR SAUCE

1 cup
1-quart measure

½ cup pineapple juice
¼ cup distilled white vinegar
¼ cup firmly packed brown sugar
2 tablespoons salad oil
2 teaspoons soy sauce
½ teaspoon pepper

Combine all ingredients in 1-quart measure. MICROWAVE 2 MINUTES on HIGH, or until sauce boils.

Serve with eggs, fish, poultry or vegetables.

Beef

Juicy roast beef with a minimum of time and attention, flavor-blended, tender pot roasts and stews, quick meat loaves and ground beef dishes are all possible with heat control microwave ovens. You can even cook a frozen pot roast, from freezer to table, without defrosting.

If some of your guests or family prefer rare beef and others well done, the microwave oven solves that problem easily. After roast is carved, a few seconds in the microwave oven will bring rare meat to medium or well done.

ROAST BEEF

12 x 8-inch utility dish,
with microwave roasting rack

Beef rib roast

Place roast fat side down on microwave roasting rack in (12 x 8-inch) utility dish. MICROWAVE 5 MINUTES on HIGH.

Reduce setting. MICROWAVE on '6' or '5' for half the roasting time, (see chart, page 74). Turn roast fat side up. MICROWAVE on '6' or '5' until internal temperature of thickest part of meat registers 120° to 150°, depending on desired doneness. Let stand 10 minutes, tented with aluminum foil, shiny side in. Roast will continue to cook while standing.

NOTE: If thickness of rolled roast is greater than 5-inches, turn roast over 4 times, top to bottom and end to end.

When cooking a standing rib roast, turn meat over 3 times, side to side and fat side up.

Do not use a meat thermometer in the microwave oven unless you have a special microwave meat thermometer.

Inverted saucers may be substituted for roasting rack.

1 Peel white onions. Arrange in baking dish. Cover with plastic wrap. MICROWAVE 4 to 5 MINUTES on HIGH, or until onions have softened, but are not cooked. Set aside to cool.

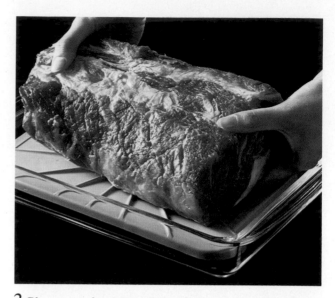

2 Place roast fat side down on microwave roasting rack in 12 x 8-inch utility dish. MICROWAVE 5 MINUTES on HIGH. *Reduce setting.* MICROWAVE on '6' or '5' for half the estimated roasting time. The initial 5 minutes on high is counted as part of the total time. (See chart on page 74.)

5 When meat has reached the proper temperature, tent with aluminum foil, shiny side in. Leave the ends open; if meat is tightly sealed it will acquire a slight steamed taste. Let roast stand 10 minutes.

6 While meat is standing, defrost, but do not cook peas. Set them aside. Melt 2 tablespoons of butter or margarine and 1 tablespoon of honey in measuring cup. Pour over frozen carrots. Cover. MICROWAVE 4 to 6 MINUTES on HIGH, or until carrots are tender.

3 While meat is roasting, prepare mushrooms. Wash mushrooms, dry with paper towel, trim the base of the stems. Using a sharp paring knife, flute mushrooms by making a V-shaped cut and lifting out wedge. Rotate mushroom against the knife for a spiraled cut.

4 Before the end of the estimated cooking time, check internal temperature of roast by inserting a meat thermometer into the thickest part. Refer to chart for temperature meat should be on removal from the oven, in order to reach your desired doneness after standing. If meat needs more cooking, remove thermometer (unless you have a special microwave thermometer) and return roast to oven.

7 While carrots are cooking, remove centers from softened onions. Fill hollows with peas. Set aside cooked carrots, covered. Place onions and peas in oven. MICROWAVE 3 to 4 MINUTES on HIGH, or until peas are hot.

8 Mushrooms in the picture were not cooked. If you wish to serve them hot, brush with butter or margarine and MICROWAVE 1 MINUTE, 30 SECONDS to 2 MINUTES on '6', or until hot. Mushrooms will lose their shape and design if overcooked. When cooking on '5', add 20 seconds more time.

73

BEEF BASICS

Recipes are provided for three types of beef: tender cuts, less tender cuts and ground beef.

Tender cuts, such as roast or steak, cook very rapidly. Because of its size and length of cooking time, a roast has time to brown in the microwave oven, but smaller cuts, such as steak, do not. If browning is desired, use the browning dish, or conventional fry pan to sear meat before finishing in the microwave oven.

Test roast beef for doneness with a meat thermometer. Unless you use a special microwave thermometer, do not use meat thermometer in the oven while cooking. During the last third of estimated cooking time, remove meat from the oven and test by inserting a meat thermometer in the thickest part, without touching bone. Remember that meat is easier to carve after standing, and will continue to cook. Remove meat from the oven when internal temperature registers 15 degrees lower than desired doneness.

The suggested times in our chart may be a little short for some tastes. Since power levels and personal preferences differ, we have given shorter times to prevent overcooking. It's easy to cook meat a little longer, but nothing can bring back an over done roast.

With lower heat control settings, less tender cuts, such as round steak, chuck roast or stew meat simmer to fork tenderness. With small tender cuts, meat is medium rare when beads of juice begin to appear on surface; medium when surface is moist with juice; well done when juice begins to retreat. Less tender cuts should be cooked until fork tender.

Most of these recipes call for lean ground beef. If you prefer to use regular ground beef, drain fat before adding sauce ingredients. Ground beef cooks quickly. When trying out ground beef for a casserole, microwave only until meat is set. It will finish cooking with the sauce.

SUGGESTED COOKING TIMES FOR TENDER CUTS OF BEEF

CUT	SET ON	RARE Remove at 120°	MED. Remove at 135°	WELL Remove at 150°	MICROWAVE INSTRUCTIONS Use 8 x 12-inch utility dish and microwave roasting rack.	STANDING TIME
Whole Beef Tenderloin	6	4 - 6	6 - 8	8 - 10	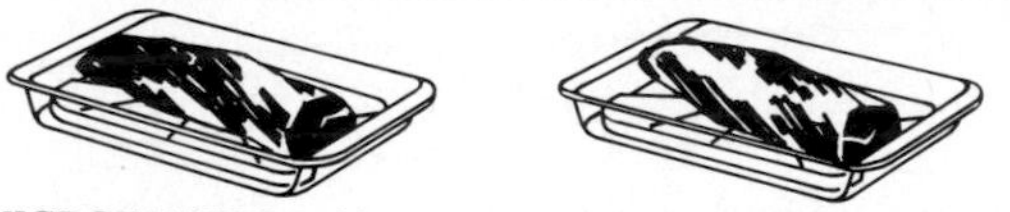	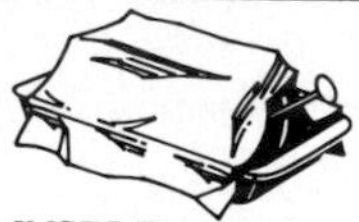
	5	5 - 7	7 - 9	9 - 11	MICROWAVE fat side down for ½ of total cooking time. (Begin with 5 min. on HIGH then reduce to '6' or '5'). TURN fat side up and MICROWAVE on '6' or '5' until done. Remove from oven.	INSERT meat thermometer. TENT with foil (shiny side in). LET STAND 10 min.
Small Rolled Rib Roast (less than 5-inches in diameter)	6	8 - 10	10 - 12	12 - 14	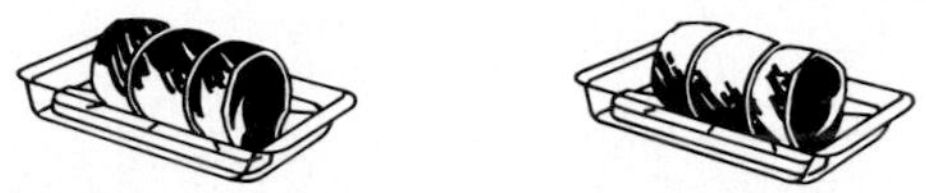	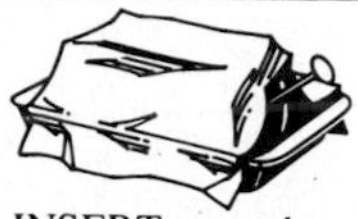
	5	9½ - 11½	11½ - 13½	13½ - 15½	MICROWAVE fat side down for ½ of total cooking time. (Begin with 5 min. on HIGH then reduce to '6' or '5'). TURN fat side up and MICROWAVE on '6' or '5' until done. Remove from oven.	INSERT meat thermometer. TENT with foil (shiny side in). LET STAND 10 min.
Large Rolled Rib Roast (more than 5-inches in diameter)	6	6 - 8	8 - 10	10 - 12		
	5	7 - 9	9½ - 11½	11½ - 13½	MICROWAVE fat side down for ¼ of total time (Begin with 5 min. on HIGH then reduce to '6' or '5'). TURN fat side up and MICROWAVE on '6' or '5' for ¼ of total time. TURN one end up and MICROWAVE on '6' or '5' for ¼ of total time. TURN other end up and MICROWAVE on '6' or '5' until done. Remove from oven.	INSERT meat thermometer. TENT with foil (shiny side in). LET STAND 15 - 20 min.
Standing Rib Roast	6	7 - 9	9 - 11	11 - 13		
	5	8½ - 10½	10½ - 12½	12½ - 14½	MICROWAVE cut side up for ⅓ of total cooking time. (Begin with 5 min. on HIGH then reduce to '6' or '5'). TURN roast top to bottom and MICROWAVE on '6' or '5' for ⅓ of total time. TURN fat side up (as shown) and MICROWAVE on '6' or '5' until done. Remove from oven.	INSERT meat thermometer. TENT with foil (shiny side in). LET STAND 10 min.

74

SIRLOIN STEAK

3 servings
Browning dish

1 pound sirloin steak, cut in three pieces

Place empty browner in oven. MICROWAVE 5 MIN-UTES on HIGH. Without removing browner from oven, drop steak pieces into dish. MICROWAVE 5 to 7 MINUTES on HIGH, or until desired doneness, turning meat over after 3 to 4 minutes.

NOTE: This recipe is a pattern for doing small steaks in the browning dish. If not using browning dish, pre-sear conventionally and cook on microwave roasting rack.

Cooking Beef At Other Settings

You may roast tender cuts of beef on the high setting, if you need to cook them quickly. Watch carefully. You may want to rotate the dish as well as turn the meat, to assure even cooking.

With variable heat control ovens, meats may also be roasted at lower settings such as '4'. This is a good choice when you have time to cook the roast, but are too busy to attend to it at short intervals. Less tender cuts should always be cooked on '6' or lower, since they need time to become tender.

Since power levels and personal preferences differ, recipes are for a minimum cooking time. You may find some of the timings short. If necessary, cook a little longer to bring meat to the doneness you prefer.

FRONTIER POT ROAST

1-quart measure
12 x 8-inch utility dish with microwave roasting rack

3 tablespoons butter or margarine
½ cup soy sauce
½ cup Worcestershire sauce
½ cup water
1 large onion, chopped
4 to 5 pound beef rump roast or 2-inch thick chuck pot roast

Place butter in 1-quart measure. MICROWAVE on HIGH until melted. Add soy sauce, Worcestershire sauce, water and onion. Place roast in plastic storage bag. Pour in marinade. Seal bag tightly with twist tie. Let stand overnight at room temperature.

To cook, place roast on microwave roasting rack in (12 x 8-inch) utility dish. (If roast has layer of fat, place fat side down.) MICROWAVE 60 to 65 MINUTES on '6', or until fork tender, turning roast over after 30 minutes.

Let stand 15 minutes, covered with tent of aluminum foil.

NOTE: Inverted saucers may be substituted for roasting rack.

For ovens without solid state heat control, during second cooking period, MICROWAVE 70 to 80 MINUTES on '5', turning after 35 minutes.

Solid State Heat Control Ovens

Variable and Defrost Heat Control Ovens

SUGGESTED COOKING TIMES FOR LESS TENDER CUTS OF BEEF

CUT	CONTAINER	SPECIAL INSTRUCTIONS	SETTING	MINUTES PER POUND	STANDING TIME
Rump roast	12 x 8 utility dish	Microwave on rack, fat side down, turn halfway through	6	12 - 16	15 min. under foil tent (foil shiny side in)
			5	14 - 17	
Round bone chuck pot roast	2-quart covered casserole	Microwave covered, turn halfway through	6	15 - 20	5 min. covered
			5	18 - 24	

A meat thermometer is not a satisfactory test for doneness when cooking less tender cuts of beef. The internal temperature of a less tender cut will reach ''well done'' in the same time as a tender one, but the meat will still need simmering in liquid before it will be tenderized.

EVERY DAY POT ROAST

6 to 8 servings
Shallow 2-quart casserole

3 to 4 pound beef chuck pot roast, trimmed of fat
1 envelope (¾-ounce) gravy mix
1 onion, thinly sliced
2 teaspoons instant beef bouillon, dissolved in 1 cup hot water
4 boiling potatoes, peeled and cut in ½-inch slices
4 carrots, quartered

Place pot roast in 2-quart casserole. Sprinkle gravy mix over roast. Spread onion slices on top. Add bouillon, potatoes and carrots. Cover.

MICROWAVE 50 to 60 MINUTES on '6', or until meat is fork tender, turning meat over after 30 minutes. Let stand 5 minutes, covered.

For ovens without solid state heat control, MICROWAVE 60 to 70 MINUTES on '5'.

FLANK STEAK ROLL-UP

4 to 6 servings
1-quart measure
8 x 8-inch baking dish

2 pounds beef flank steak
¼ cup butter or margarine
1 medium onion, finely chopped
½ cup celery, finely chopped
2 cups dried bread cubes, lightly crushed
1 teaspoon salt
½ teaspoon poultry seasoning
1 cup beef bouillon or 1 teaspoon instant bouillon dissolved in 1 cup hot water
2 teaspoons Worcestershire sauce

Cut flank steak in half crosswise. Score on both sides by slashing lightly in criss-cross pattern. Set aside.

Combine butter, onion and celery in 1-quart measure. MICROWAVE 4 to 5 MINUTES on HIGH, or until onions are transparent. Add crushed bread cubes, salt and poultry seasoning, toss lightly.

Spread half of stuffing across center of each flank steak. Fold short sides over stuffing. Secure with string or wooden picks.

Place rolls in (8 x 8-inch) baking dish, seam side down. Mix together bouillon and Worcestershire sauce. Pour over flank steak. Cover with plastic wrap. MICROWAVE 30 to 35 MINUTES on '6', or until fork tender, turning rolls over after 15 minutes.

Let stand 10 minutes, covered.

For ovens without solid state heat control, MICROWAVE 35 to 42 MINUTES on '5'.

SWISS STEAK

6 servings
Browning dish
12 x 8-inch baking dish

2 pounds beef round steak, cut ½-inch thick
Flour
2 tablespoons salad oil
1 onion, sliced
1 can (16-ounces) stewed tomatoes
1 tablespoon parsley flakes
Salt and pepper to taste

Sprinkle one side of meat with flour. Pound in. Turn meat, sprinkle with flour and pound in. Cut meat into serving pieces.

Place browning dish in oven. MICROWAVE 5 MINUTES on HIGH. Add oil and enough meat pieces to fit bottom without overlapping.

MICROWAVE 2 to 3 MINUTES on HIGH, or until browned, turning meat after 1 minute.

Remove meat to (12 x 8-inch) baking dish. Brown any remaining meat. (Preheat micro-browner 2 to 3 minutes, if necessary.)

Spread sliced onions on top of meat. Pour canned tomatoes over top. Sprinkle with parsley flakes. Cover with plastic wrap. MICROWAVE 50 MINUTES on '6', or until meat is fork tender. Season with salt and pepper before serving.

For ovens without solid state heat control, MICROWAVE 60 MINUTES on '5'.

COUNTRY STYLE SHORT RIBS

4 servings
3-quart casserole

¼ cup all-purpose flour
1 teaspoon salt
¼ teaspoon pepper
3½ pounds beef short ribs
1 large onion, sliced
1 medium green pepper, chopped
1 can (8-ounces) tomato sauce
1 teaspoon instant beef bouillon dissolved in 1 cup hot water
2 tablespoons dried parsley
½ teaspoon dry mustard
3 tablespoons vinegar
2 teaspoons Worcestershire sauce

Combine flour, salt and pepper. Coat short ribs with mixture. Place ribs in 3-quart casserole. Add onion, green pepper, tomato sauce, bouillon, parsley, mustard, vinegar and Worcestershire sauce. Mix gently. Cover. MICROWAVE 10 MINUTES on HIGH.

Reduce setting. MICROWAVE 20 to 30 MINUTES on '6', or until meat and vegetables are tender. Let stand 10 minutes, covered. Thicken gravy before serving, if desired.

For ovens without solid state heat control, during second cooking period, MICROWAVE 24 to 36 MINUTES on '5'.

76

PEPPER STEAK

4 servings
Browning dish

1 tablespoon salad oil
1 to 1½ pounds beef top round steak sliced and cut into strips ½-inch wide by 1½-inches long
1 clove garlic, pressed or finely chopped
½ teaspoon sliced candied ginger, or ¼ teaspoon ginger
½ cup water
1 teaspoon instant beef bouillon
2 cups 1-inch chunks green pepper
1 medium onion, thinly sliced
2 large stems celery, sliced diagonally
1 jar (2-ounces) chopped pimiento
1 teaspoon salt
¼ teaspoon pepper
2 teaspoons corn starch dissolved in 2 tablespoons soy sauce

Place browning dish in oven. MICROWAVE 5 MINUTES on HIGH. Add oil and beef strips. MICROWAVE 2 to 3 MINUTES on HIGH, or until meat is brown, stirring after 1 minute.

Add garlic and ginger. Cover. MICROWAVE 7 MINUTES on '6'.

Stir in remaining ingredients. Cover. MICROWAVE 7 to 10 MINUTES on '6', or until vegetables are tender-crisp.

NOTE: Meat may be browned on conventional range in 2-quart glass-ceramic casserole.

For ovens without solid state heat control, MICROWAVE 8 MINUTES and 9 to 12 MINUTES on '5'.

BEEF BOURGUIGNONNE

6 servings
2-quart casserole

4 slices bacon, quartered
2 pounds lean beef sirloin or top round steak, cut in ¾-inch cubes
¼ cup all-purpose flour
1 package (8-ounces) fresh mushrooms, sliced, or 2 cans (4-ounces each) sliced mushrooms, drained
1 medium onion, cut in eighths
1 clove garlic, pressed or finely chopped
1 bay leaf
1 tablespoon snipped parsley
½ teaspoon thyme
1¼ cups burgundy wine
2 teaspoons instant beef bouillon
1 teaspoon salt
¼ teaspoon pepper

Place bacon in 2-quart casserole. MICROWAVE 2 MINUTES on HIGH. Do not drain. Coat beef cubes with flour. Add to bacon and drippings. Toss to coat with fat. Sprinkle any remaining flour over meat.

Add mushrooms, onion, garlic, bay leaf, parsley and thyme. Stir in wine and bouillon. Cover. MICROWAVE 5 MINUTES on HIGH.

Reduce setting. MICROWAVE 30 MINUTES on '6', or until beef is fork tender, stirring once. Season with salt and pepper. Let stand 10 minutes, covered. Remove bay leaf. Serve over noodles.

For ovens without solid state heat control, MICROWAVE 36 MINUTES on '5'.

77

STROGANOFF SPECTACULAR

4 servings
Browning dish

3 *tablespoons butter or margarine*
1 *pound sirloin beef steak sliced and cut into strips
    ½-inch wide by 1½-inches long*
1 *can (3 to 4-ounces) sliced mushrooms or stems and
    pieces, drained*
½ *cup chopped onion*
½ *teaspoon dry mustard*
Pepper to taste
⅔ *cup milk*
1 *package (8-ounces) cream cheese, softened to room
    temperature*
Hot cooked noodles with snipped parsley

Place browning dish in oven. MICROWAVE 5 MINUTES on HIGH.

Add butter and beef strips. MICROWAVE 2 to 3 MINUTES on HIGH, or until meat is brown, stirring after 1 minute.

Add mushrooms, onion, mustard and pepper. MICROWAVE 3 MINUTES on HIGH, or until onion is transparent.

Stir in milk and cream cheese. MICROWAVE 6 MINUTES on HIGH, or until mixture comes to a boil. Stir. Cover.

Reduce setting. MICROWAVE 5 MINUTES on '6', or until cheese is creamy and hot. Stir to distribute heat. Serve over noodles garnished with parsley.

NOTE: Meat may be browned on conventional range in 2-quart glass-ceramic casserole.

For ovens without solid state heat control, during final cooking period, MICROWAVE 7 MINUTES on '5'.

CASSEROLE BEEFSTEAK

4 to 6 servings
3-quart casserole

1½ *pounds boneless beef round steak*
⅓ *cup flour*
2 *cups peeled and thinly sliced potatoes*
3 *tablespoons finely chopped onion*
6 *small cabbage leaves, cut in strips*
1 *cup sliced carrots*
6 *peppercorns*
⅔ *cup beef bouillon*
3 *tomatoes, sliced*

Dredge beef in flour and pound in. Cut into 2 x ½-inch strips. Place in 3-quart casserole.

Layer potatoes, onion, cabbage and carrots over beef. Scatter peppercorns on top. Pour in bouillon. Cover. MICROWAVE 5 MINUTES on HIGH.

Reduce setting. MICROWAVE 20 MINUTES on '6', or until meat and potatoes are tender. Arrange tomatoes over top. Let stand 5 minutes, covered.

For ovens without solid state heat control, MICROWAVE 25 MINUTES on '5'.

BEEF WITH ONIONS

6 servings

2 *tablespoons butter or margarine*
2 *tablespoons olive oil*
2 *pounds bottom round beef steak, cut in ¾-inch cubes*
3 *small onions, quartered*
4 *firm, ripe tomatoes, quartered, or 1 can (16-ounces)
    tomatoes*
2 *cloves garlic, pressed or finely chopped*
3 *tablespoons wine vinegar*
2 *bay leaves*
Salt and pepper to taste

Place browning dish in oven. MICROWAVE 5 MINUTES on HIGH. Add butter, olive oil and beef cubes. MICROWAVE 3 to 4 MINUTES on HIGH, or until brown, stirring twice.

Add onions, tomatoes, garlic, vinegar and bay leaves. Cover. MICROWAVE 50 MINUTES on '6', or until fork tender, stirring 3 times. Season with salt and pepper to taste. Remove bay leaf before serving.

For ovens without solid state heat control, MICROWAVE 60 MINUTES on '5'.

BEEF BIRDS

6 to 8 servings
1-quart measure
12 x 8-inch baking dish

2 *pounds beef round steak, cut ½-inch thick and
    pounded*
2 *tablespoons butter or margarine*
½ *cup chopped celery with leaves*
3 *tablespoons chopped onion*
1 *cup soft bread crumbs*
¼ *teaspoon rosemary*
¼ *teaspoon thyme*
⅛ *teaspoon pepper*
1 *can (10¾-ounces) condensed cream of mushroom
    soup, undiluted*

Cut round steak in 3 x 4-inch rectangles. Set aside.

Combine butter, celery and onion in 1-quart measure. MICROWAVE 2 to 3 MINUTES on HIGH, or until onion is transparent. Stir in bread crumbs, rosemary, thyme and pepper.

Spoon stuffing on end of beef strips. Roll up and secure with wooden pick. Arrange rolls in baking dish.

Spoon soup over rolls. Cover. MICROWAVE 20 MINUTES on '6', or until meat is fork tender. Let stand 5 minutes, covered.

For ovens without solid state heat control, MICROWAVE 25 MINUTES on '5'.

BASIC BEEF CASSEROLE

4 to 6 servings
3-quart casserole

3 tablespoons flour
1½ pounds beef round steak, cut in ¾-inch cubes
½ cup finely chopped onion
1 cup thinly sliced carrots
2½ cups water
1 teaspoon instant beef bouillon
1 teaspoon salt
1 teaspoon pepper

Measure flour into paper bag. Add beef cubes and toss to coat evenly.

Combine all ingredients in 3-quart casserole. Cover. MICROWAVE 5 MINUTES on HIGH.

Reduce setting. MICROWAVE 30 MINUTES on '6', or until meat and vegetables are tender.

For ovens without solid state heat control, during second cooking period MICROWAVE 36 MINUTES on '5'.

Variations:

CHINESE BEEF

Add:
½ pound fresh or frozen green beans, defrosted, cut in ½-inch lengths
1 green or sweet red pepper, cut in julienne strips
2½ tablespoons soy sauce
Serve with boiled rice.

AUSTRALIAN BEEF

Add:
¼ cup firmly packed brown sugar
1½ tablespoons Worcestershire sauce
1½ tablespoons catsup
1½ tablespoons vinegar
½ teaspoon nutmeg

Serve with a green vegetable and mashed or baked potatoes.

BELGIAN BEEF

Substitute 2½ cups beer for water
Add 1 clove garlic, finely chopped
Serve with boiled potatoes.

ENGLISH BEEF

Add:
1 small turnip, peeled and finely chopped
2 stems celery, finely chopped
1 cup fresh shelled peas
2 tomatoes, peeled and coarsely chopped
Garnish with snipped parsley

Serve with boiled or baked potatoes.

Basic Beef Ingredients.

NOTE: 1 cup frozen peas may be substituted for fresh. Add during last 5 minutes of cooking.

HUNGARIAN BEEF

Add:
4 medium carrots, thinly sliced
4 medium boiling potatoes, sliced
1 tablespoon paprika
1 clove garlic, pressed or finely chopped
Stir in 3 tablespoons dairy sour cream just before serving

Serve with macaroni, noodles or rice. Top each serving with additional sour cream, if desired.

INDIAN BEEF

1 to 1½ tablespoons curry powder (add with flour)
2 tomatoes, peeled and chopped
1 apple, peeled, cored and chopped
Stir in 1 tablespoon lemon juice and 2 tablespoons fruit chutney just before serving

Serve with rice, sliced bananas in lemon juice and fruit chutney.

Ground Beef

SALISBURY STEAK

4 to 5 servings
Browning dish

1½ pounds lean ground beef
1 package (¾-ounce) brown gravy mix
1 cup water
1 small onion, thinly sliced
1 teaspoon salt
¼ teaspoon pepper

Form ground beef into 4 to 5 ½-inch thick patties.

To preheat browning dish, MICROWAVE 4 MINUTES on HIGH. Add patties. MICROWAVE 4 MINUTES on HIGH, turning patties over after 2 minutes.

Add gravy mix, water and onion. Cover. MICROWAVE 6 to 8 MINUTES on HIGH, or until meat reaches desired doneness. Season with salt and pepper.

Variations:

SOUR CREAM SALISBURY STEAK

½ cup dairy sour cream
1 jar (2-ounces) mushroom stems and pieces, drained

Add sour cream and mushrooms during last 2 minutes of cooking. Heat until bubbly.

TASTY HERBED SALISBURY STEAK

Add 1 to 2 teaspoons of either parsley, basil or thyme with gravy mix.

SAUCY SALISBURY STEAK

¼ cup catsup
2 teaspoons Worcestershire sauce

Add catsup and Worcestershire sauce with gravy mix.

SPEEDY SHEPHERD'S PIE

4 to 5 servings
9-inch pie plate

1 pound lean ground beef
2 slices soft white bread, torn into coarse crumbs
⅔ cup milk
1 egg, slightly beaten
¼ cup onion, finely chopped
1 tablespoon Worcestershire sauce
1 teaspoon salt
3 cups hot mashed potatoes
1 cup finely diced American process cheese

Combine beef, bread, milk, egg, onion, Worcestershire sauce and salt in medium bowl. Spread evenly in 9-inch pie plate. MICROWAVE 7 MINUTES on '8'.

Mask meat with mashed potatoes. Sprinkle with cheese. MICROWAVE 5 MINUTES on '8', or until cheese is melted. Let stand 3 minutes.

For ovens without solid state heat control MICROWAVE 5 MINUTES, 30 SECONDS on HIGH, stirring twice. Add potatoes and cheese. MICROWAVE 4 MINUTES on HIGH.

SARA'S MEAT BALLS ❄

2 to 2½ dozen meat balls
12 x 8-inch baking dish

1 pound lean ground beef
½ pound lean ground pork
½ cup finely chopped onion
½ cup uncooked rice
½ cup bread or cracker crumbs
1 egg
½ teaspoon salt
⅛ teaspoon pepper
1 can (10¾-ounces) condensed tomato soup, diluted

Combine ground meats, onion, rice, bread crumbs, egg, salt and pepper in medium bowl. Mix well. Form into 2-inch balls. Place in (12 x 8-inch) baking dish. Pour diluted soup over meat balls. Cover. MICROWAVE 14 to 16 MINUTES on '8', or until rice is tender, rearranging meat balls carefully after 8 minutes.

NOTE: Can be made ahead and refrigerated. To reheat from refrigerated state, MICROWAVE 3 to 5 MINUTES on '8'.

For ovens without solid state heat control, MICROWAVE 11 to 12 MINUTES on HIGH. Reheat 2 to 4 MINUTES on HIGH.

SWEDISH MEATBALLS

4 servings
Browning dish

1 cup milk
½ cup crushed dry bread crumbs
½ pound lean ground beef
½ pound lean ground pork
1 egg, slightly beaten
1 small onion, chopped
1 tablespoon Worcestershire sauce
½ teaspoon salt
¼ teaspoon pepper
⅛ teaspoon cloves
2 tablespoons cooking oil
¼ cup all-purpose flour
½ cup cream
½ teaspoon instant beef bouillon dissolved in ½ cup
   hot water

Pour milk over bread crumbs in medium mixing bowl. Let stand 10 minutes. Add ground meats, egg, onion, Worcestershire sauce, salt, pepper and cloves. Blend well with fork. Form into 1-inch balls.

To preheat browning dish, MICROWAVE 5 MINUTES on HIGH. Add oil and meatballs. MICROWAVE 4 MINUTES on HIGH, turning meatballs over once. Remove meatballs. Set aside.

Stir flour into drippings until smooth and well blended. Gradually stir in cream and bouillon. Return meatballs to browner. Cover. MICROWAVE 6 to 8 MINUTES on '6', or until sauce is thickened and meatballs are cooked through. Let stand 5 minutes, covered.

For ovens without solid state heat control, when cooking meatballs in sauce, MICROWAVE 7 to 9 MINUTES, 30 SECONDS on '5'.

MEAT LOAF

4 to 5 servings
9 x 5-inch loaf dish

1 *egg, slightly beaten*
2 *tablespoons Worcestershire sauce*
1½ *pounds lean ground beef*
1 *cup crushed cracker crumbs*
½ *cup chopped onion*
1 *teaspoon salt*
¼ *teaspoon pepper*

Mix all ingredients thoroughly in (9 x 5-inch) loaf dish. Spread mixture evenly in dish. MICROWAVE 16 to 20 MINUTES on '6', or until set in center. Let stand 5 minutes. Garnish with slices of cherry tomato and parsley sprigs, if desired.
For ovens without solid state heat control, MICROWAVE 19 to 24 MINUTES on '5'.
Variations:

SAUCED LOAF

Before baking, spread ½ cup barbecue sauce, chili sauce or catsup over top of loaf.

MUSTARD LOAF

Reduce Worcestershire sauce to 1 tablespoon. Add 1 tablespoon prepared mustard, ½ teaspoon horseradish and ¼ teaspoon garlic salt.

SEASONED LOAF

Add ¼ cup chopped celery, 2 tablespoons catsup and 2 teaspoons dried parsley flakes. Serve with dairy sour cream and crumbled bacon.

CURRIED MEAT LOAF

Omit Worcestershire sauce. Add ¼ cup finely chopped green pepper and 2 tablespoons chili sauce. Top with 1 can (8¾-ounces) crushed pineapple, drained, mixed with ¼ teaspoon curry powder.

TOMATO SAUCED MEAT LOAF

6 to 8 servings
9 x 5-inch loaf dish

1 *pound lean ground beef*
¼ *pound lean ground pork*
¼ *pound lean ground veal*
1 *can (8-ounces) tomato sauce*
½ *cup finely chopped onion*
1 *egg, beaten*
½ *cup bread crumbs or quick rolled oats*
1 *teaspoon salt*
⅛ *teaspoon pepper*

Combine ground meats, ½ cup tomato sauce, onion, egg, bread crumbs, salt and pepper in large bowl. Mix thoroughly. Spread mixture in loaf pan.

Pour remaining tomato sauce over loaf. MICROWAVE 20 to 25 MINUTES on '6', or until set in center. Let stand 5 minutes.

For ovens without solid state heat control, MICROWAVE 25 to 30 MINUTES on '5'.

STUFFED CABBAGE ROLLS

8 servings
12 x 8-inch baking dish

8 *large cabbage leaves*
1 *pound lean ground beef*
1 *cup cooked rice*
1 *egg*
1 *teaspoon instant minced onion*
½ *teaspoon sage*
1 *can (8-ounces) tomato sauce*
2 *tablespoons brown sugar*
2 *tablespoons lemon juice or vinegar*
2 *tablespoons water*

To remove leaves from cabbage, place whole cabbage in microwave oven. MICROWAVE 2 to 3 MINUTES on HIGH, or until outer leaves peel off easily. Save remaining cabbage for soups or salads. With a sharp knife, cut hard cores from softened leaves.

Combine ground beef, rice, egg, onion and sage in medium mixing bowl. Mix thoroughly. Form into 8 small loaves. Overlap cut edges of cabbage leaf. Place loaf in center. Fold sides of leaf over stuffing and roll up ends to form neat package. Arrange cabbage rolls, seam side down, in (12 x 8-inch) baking dish.

Mix tomato sauce, brown sugar, lemon juice and water in 2-cup measure. Pour sauce over cabbage rolls. Cover with plastic wrap. MICROWAVE 3 MINUTES on HIGH.

Stuffed Pepper Pots.

Reduce setting. MICROWAVE 10 MINUTES on '6', until cabbage is tender and stuffing is cooked through.

NOTE: If large cabbage leaves are not available, stuffing may be divided between smaller leaves.

For ovens without solid state heat control, during second cooking period MICROWAVE 12 MINUTES on '5'.

HAMBURGER CREOLE

4 servings
2-quart casserole

3 *slices bacon, chopped*
½ *cup chopped onion*
1 *pound lean ground beef*
½ *cup chopped celery*
¼ *cup chopped green pepper*
2 *tablespoons flour*
1 *can (8-ounces) stewed tomatoes*
1 *teaspoon salt*

Combine bacon and onion in 2-quart casserole. MICROWAVE 2 to 3 MINUTES on HIGH, or until onion is transparent. Crumble ground beef into casserole. Mix well. MICROWAVE 3 MINUTES on HIGH, or until meat is set, stirring once.

Add remaining ingredients. Mix well. Cover. MICROWAVE 5 to 8 MINUTES on HIGH, stirring once. Serve over rice.

STUFFED PEPPER POTS

4 servings
Micro-browner or 1½-quart casserole
4 squares plastic wrap or 8 x 8-inch baking dish

4 *large green peppers*
1 *pound lean ground beef, crumbled*
1 *small onion, chopped*
2 *cups cooked rice*
1 *can (8-ounces) tomato sauce*
2 *tablespoons chopped celery*
Seasoned salt to taste

Cut thin slice from stem end of each pepper. Remove seeds and membrane. Rinse and drain.

(Preheat browning dish 4 MINUTES on HIGH, if used.) Combine beef and onion in browning dish or 1½-quart casserole. MICROWAVE 2 to 3 MINUTES on HIGH, or until onion is transparent, stirring after 1 minute.

Add rice, tomato sauce, celery and salt. Mix well. Stuff peppers with mixture. Garnish with ½ cherry tomato, if desired. Place each pepper on square of plastic wrap. Bring up corners and twist to seal tightly, or place peppers in (8 x 8-inch) baking dish and cover with plastic wrap. MICROWAVE 12 MINUTES on '8'.

NOTE: 1 cup diced, cooked beef may be substituted for ground beef. Omit browning dish and add beef with rice. Peppers and stuffing may be assembled for later cooking.

For ovens without solid state heat control, MICROWAVE 11 MINUTES on HIGH, rearranging individual peppers or rotating dish ½ turn after 5 minutes.

FREEZER TO TABLE BEEF

With this new method of variable heat cooking, you can not only microwave a less tender cut of beef, but you can take it from freezer to oven to table without separate defrosting. Cooking time is at least an hour less than by conventional methods, and meat needs only a minimum of attention.

Select a casserole just large enough to hold meat comfortably. A tight cover is essential. If your casserole lid is loose, cover the casserole with plastic wrap and place the lid over it firmly.

Standing time after cooking is also important. It helps make the meat tender and flavorful.

FREEZER TO TABLE RUMP ROAST

6 servings
Shallow 2½-quart casserole with tightly fitting cover

3 *pound beef boneless rump roast, frozen*
1 *envelope (⅞-ounce) onion gravy mix*
6 *medium carrots, halved crosswise and lengthwise*
6 *small onions*
6 *stems celery, coarsely sliced*

Place frozen roast in 2½-quart casserole. Cover tightly. MICROWAVE 30 MINUTES on '5'.

Turn roast over. Cover tightly. MICROWAVE 30 MINUTES on '5'.

Drain liquid. Turn meat over. Sprinkle with gravy mix. Spread vegetables over meat. Cover tightly. MICROWAVE 25 to 30 MINUTES on '5', or until meat is fork tender. Let stand 10 minutes, tightly covered.

NOTE: If potatoes are desired, cook them while beef stands. Cooking potatoes with meat increases cooking time.

FREEZER TO TABLE SWISS STEAK

4 to 6 servings
Shallow 1½-quart casserole with tightly fitting cover

2 *pound beef round steak, frozen*
1 *can (8-ounces) tomato sauce*
1 *can (4-ounces) mushroom stems and pieces, drained*
Salt and pepper

Place frozen round steak in 1½-quart casserole. Cover tightly. MICROWAVE 15 MINUTES on '5'.

Drain liquid. Turn meat over. Add tomato sauce and mushrooms. Spread over meat. Cover tightly. MICROWAVE 20 to 25 MINUTES on '5', or until fork tender. Season with salt and pepper. Let stand 5 minutes, tightly covered.

Freezer to Table Pot Roast.

FREEZER TO TABLE POT ROAST

4 to 6 servings
Shallow 2½-quart casserole with tightly fitting cover

3 *pound beef round-bone chuck roast, frozen*
1 *envelope (1¼-ounces) dried onion soup mix*
1 *onion, sliced and separated into rings*

Place frozen meat in 2½-quart casserole. Cover tightly. MICROWAVE 40 MINUTES on '5'.

Drain liquid. Turn meat over. Sprinkle with soup mix and spread evenly to edges. Cover tightly. MICROWAVE 30 to 40 MINUTES on '5', or until meat is fork tender.

Sprinkle onion rings over meat. Let stand 10 minutes, tightly covered.

NOTE: Heat from the meat will cook onion rings during standing time.

Veal

Veal Scalloppine.

VEAL CHOPS PARMIGIANA

4 servings
12 x 8-inch baking dish

1 *egg, beaten*
¼ *cup flour*
½ *cup zwieback or fine cracker crumbs*
1 *teaspoon salt*
¼ *teaspoon pepper*
½ *teaspoon paprika*
4 *veal loin chops, ¾-inch thick*
4 *slices mozzarella cheese*
3 *cans (4-ounces each) tomato sauce (1½ cups)*
¼ *cup grated parmesan cheese*

Beat egg in pie plate. Combine flour, crumbs, salt, pepper and paprika in shallow dish. Dip chops in beaten egg, then in flour mixture, coating well. Place in (12 x 8-inch) baking dish. Cover loosely. MICROWAVE 10 MINUTES on '8'.

Place slice of cheese on each chop. Cover with tomato sauce. Sprinkle with parmesan cheese. MICROWAVE 8 to 10 MINUTES on '6', or until cheese is melted and chops are fork tender.

For ovens without solid state heat control, MICROWAVE 8 MINUTES on HIGH and 9 MINUTES, 30 SECONDS to 12 MINUTES on '5'.

VEAL SCALLOPPINE

4 servings
Shallow 2-quart casserole
Platter

1½ *pounds veal cutlets, pounded until ¼-inch thick*
Salt and pepper
¼ *cup all-purpose flour*
3 *tablespoons butter or margarine*
1 *can (4-ounces) sliced mushrooms, drained*
1 *cup beef bouillon, or 1 teaspoon instant beef bouillon dissolved in 1 cup hot water*
1 *can (6-ounces) tomato paste*
1 *teaspoon lemon juice*
1 *tomato, sliced*

Season cutlets with salt and pepper. Coat with flour and shake off excess. Place butter in 2-quart casserole. MICROWAVE on HIGH until butter melts.

Place veal in casserole and turn to coat with butter. Cover. MICROWAVE 4 MINUTES on HIGH, turning cutlets over after 2 minutes. Add mushrooms. Stir bouillon, tomato paste and lemon juice together in 1-quart measure. Pour over cutlets. MICROWAVE 12 to 15 MINUTES on '6', or until veal is fork tender.

Arrange cutlets and sauce on platter. Garnish with tomato slices. MICROWAVE 2 MINUTES on '6', or until heated through.

For ovens without solid state heat control, MICROWAVE 2 MINUTES, 30 SECONDS on '5'.

VEAL VALENCIA

4 servings
Browning dish

¼ cup flour
1½ pounds veal, cut in ¾-inch chunks
2 tablespoons butter or margarine
1 can (16-ounces) tomatoes
½ cup finely chopped onion
1 jar (2½-ounces) button mushrooms
1½ cups beef stock or bouillon
1 bay leaf, crumbled

Place flour in paper bag. Add veal and shake to coat. Place browning dish in oven. MICROWAVE 5 MINUTES on HIGH.

Add butter and veal. MICROWAVE 2 to 4 MINUTES on HIGH, or until veal is brown, stirring twice.

Add remaining ingredients. Cover. MICROWAVE 5 MINUTES on HIGH. Stir and cover.

Reduce setting. MICROWAVE 12 MINUTES on '6', or until veal is fork tender. Serve over hot fluffy rice or buttered noodles.

NOTE: Veal may be browned on conventional range in 2-quart glass-ceramic casserole.

For ovens without solid state heat control, during final cooking period, MICROWAVE 14 to 15 MINUTES on '5'.

VEAL STEAKS IN ONION SAUCE

4 servings
Browning dish

½ cup flour
2 teaspoons dry mustard
½ teaspoon garlic salt
⅛ teaspoon pepper
4 veal arm steaks, ½-inch thick
2 tablespoons salad oil
1 package (1½-ounces) dry onion soup mix
½ cup water
½ cup chili sauce
2 tablespoons Worcestershire sauce
½ teaspoon salt

Mix flour, mustard, garlic salt and pepper together. Coat steaks on both sides in seasoned flour mixture.

To preheat browning dish, MICROWAVE 4 MINUTES on HIGH. Add oil and 2 steaks. MICROWAVE 4 to 6 MINUTES on HIGH, turning steaks over after 2 to 3 minutes. Set aside. Preheat browner again, if necessary. Brown remaining steaks. Return first two steaks to browner.

Combine soup mix, water, chili sauce, Worcestershire sauce and salt in small bowl. Pour over steaks. Cover. MICROWAVE 12 to 15 MINUTES on '6', or until steaks are fork tender.

For ovens without solid state heat control, after adding sauce MICROWAVE 14 to 18 MINUTES on '5'.

VEAL IN SOUR CREAM

6 servings
2-quart casserole

6 slices bacon, cut in quarters
2 large onions, thinly sliced
2 pounds veal, cut in ¾-inch cubes
¼ cup all-purpose flour
1 package (8-ounces) fresh mushrooms, thickly sliced
1 cup white wine
2 cups dairy sour cream
Paprika

Place bacon in 2-quart casserole. MICROWAVE 4 to 5 MINUTES on HIGH, or until crisp. Remove bacon with slotted spoon. Crumble. Set aside.

Add onions to bacon drippings. MICROWAVE 3 MINUTES on HIGH, or until onions are transparent.

Coat veal with flour. Add to onions and toss to coat. Sprinkle any remaining flour over meat. Add mushrooms. Pour in wine. Cover. MICROWAVE 12 to 14 MINUTES on '8', or until veal is fork tender.

Stir in sour cream. Sprinkle with crumbled bacon and paprika. MICROWAVE 2 to 3 MINUTES on '6', or until heated through.

For ovens without solid state heat control, to cook veal, MICROWAVE 13 to 17 MINUTES on '5'. Add sour cream, MICROWAVE 2 MINUTES, 30 SECONDS to 3 MINUTES, 30 SECONDS on '5'.

CREAMY VELVET VEAL

6 servings
Browning dish

1 can (10¾-ounces) condensed cream of mushroom soup, undiluted
¼ cup water
2 tablespoons red wine
2 teaspoons lemon juice
Dash pepper
2 tablespoons butter or margarine
1 medium onion, sliced
1 clove garlic, finely chopped
1½ pounds thinly sliced veal, cut in serving pieces
½ teaspoon paprika

Combine soup, water, wine, lemon juice and pepper in 1-quart measure. Set aside.

To preheat browning dish, MICROWAVE 4 MINUTES on HIGH. Add butter, onions and garlic. Stir. Add veal. MICROWAVE 4 MINUTES on HIGH, turning veal over after 2 minutes.

Pour sauce over veal. Cover. MICROWAVE 10 to 12 MINUTES on '6', or until sauce is hot and veal is fork tender. Sprinkle with paprika. Serve over buttered noodles, if desired.

For ovens without solid state heat control, after adding sauce, MICROWAVE 12 to 15 MINUTES on '5'.

Pork

ROAST PORK

12 x 8-inch utility dish with
microwave roasting rack

Pork loin roast
Salt and pepper

Rub seasonings into meat. Place roast fat side down on microwave roasting rack in (12 x 8-inch) utility dish. MICROWAVE 5 MINUTES on HIGH.

Reduce setting. MICROWAVE on '6' or '5' for half the roasting time.

Turn roast fat side up. MICROWAVE on '6' or '5' until internal temperature of thickest part of meat registers 165°. Let stand 15 minutes, tented with aluminum foil, shiny side in. Roast will continue to cook while standing.

NOTE: Do not use meat thermometer in microwave oven. Inverted saucers may be substituted for roasting rack.

Variations:

GARLIC STUDDED PORK

Make incisions in pork with sharp knife. Press 2 or 3 cloves garlic, peeled and quartered, into incisions.

HERBED PORK

Rub 1 clove garlic, halved, thyme and basil or sage, into meat.

SMOTHERED PORK TENDERLOINS

4 to 6 servings
12 x 8-inch baking dish
Medium mixing bowl

2 pork tenderloins, about 1 to 1¼-pounds each
Salt and pepper
3 tablespoons butter or margarine
1 medium onion, chopped
1 can (8-ounces) crushed pineapple with juice
2 teaspoons soy sauce
½ teaspoon ginger
2 cups dried bread crumbs

Place pork tenderloins in (12 x 8-inch) baking dish. Season with salt and pepper. Set aside.

Place butter in mixing bowl. MICROWAVE on HIGH until butter melts. Mix in onion, pineapple and juice, soy sauce, ginger and bread crumbs. Spread mixture over tenderloins. MICROWAVE 35 to 40 MINUTES on '6', or until meat is fork tender, or internal temperature registers 185°.

For ovens without solid state heat control, MICROWAVE 42 to 48 MINUTES on '5'.

Solid State Heat Control Ovens

Variable and Defrost Heat Control Ovens

SUGGESTED COOKING TIMES FOR PORK

CUT	COOKING CONTAINER	SPECIAL INSTRUCTIONS	SETTING	MINUTES PER POUND	STANDING TIME
Loin Roast, boneless	8 x 12 x 2 utility dish	Microwave fat side down on rack, 5 min. on High. Reduce setting and proceed as per chart, turning halfway through.	6	10 - 13	10 min. under foil tent. Foil shiny side in.
			5	11 - 14	
Loin Roast, bone in	8 x 12 x 2 utility dish		6	9 - 12	
			5	10 - 13	

Meat thermometer reads 165° to 175° on removal and 185° after standing.

BASIC PORK CASSEROLE

4 to 6 servings
3-quart casserole

1 tablespoon butter or margarine
1 onion, sliced
1½ pounds lean boneless pork, cut in ¾-inch cubes
¼ cup flour
2½ cups water
1 teaspoon instant chicken bouillon
1 teaspoon salt
¼ teaspoon pepper

Combine butter and onion in 3-quart casserole. MICRO-WAVE 3 MINUTES on HIGH, or until onion is transparent. Add pork. Sprinkle flour over pork. Toss to coat well. Add water, bouillon, salt and pepper. Cover. MICROWAVE 5 MINUTES on HIGH.

Reduce setting. MICROWAVE 30 MINUTES on '6', or until meat is fork tender.

For ovens without solid state heat control, during second cooking period, MICROWAVE 36 MINUTES on '5'.

Variations:

AMERICAN PORK

Add:
1 can (16-ounces) baked beans or red kidney beans, drained and rinsed
4 slices bacon, cut in 1-inch pieces
Serve with boiled potatoes

BELGIAN PORK

Substitute 1¼ cups wine for half the water
Add:
½ pound pitted prunes

Just before serving, stir in 1 tablespoon currant jelly. Sprinkle with snipped parsley.

CHINESE PORK

Substitute salad oil for butter
Add:
2 tablespoons firmly packed brown sugar
2 tablespoons catsup
2 tablespoons vinegar
2 tablespoons soy sauce
1 carrot cut in julienne strips
1 green pepper, cut in julienne strips

During last 15 minutes, add:
1 cup unsweetened pineapple cubes

Serve with boiled rice

FRENCH PORK

Add:
1 can (4-ounces) sliced mushrooms, drained
1 clove garlic, finely chopped

Just before serving, add:
2 tablespoons brandy
2 tablespoons cream

MICROWAVE 2 MINUTES on HIGH, or until hot but not boiling. Garnish with snipped parsley. Serve with new potatoes or egg noodles. Follow with tossed green salad.

ENGLISH PORK

Substitute cider for half the water. During last 15 minutes add:
1 teaspoon sage
2 apples, peeled, cored and sliced

Serve with a green vegetable and mashed potatoes.

GERMAN PORK

During last 15 minutes, add:
½ pound frankfurters, cut in 1-inch pieces
1 cup drained sauerkraut
½ teaspoon caraway seeds
1 teaspoon German mustard

Serve with boiled or sauteed potatoes.

HUNGARIAN PORK

Add:
4 carrots, sliced
4 medium boiling potatoes, peeled and sliced
2 tomatoes, peeled and quartered
1 tablespoon paprika

Just before serving, stir in:
3 tablespoons dairy sour cream

SCANDINAVIAN PORK

During last 15 minutes add:
2 apples, peeled, cored and chopped
½ pound cooked ham, diced

Just before serving add:
⅓ cup cream

MICROWAVE 2 MINUTES on HIGH, or until hot but not boiling. Serve with braised red cabbage and sauteed potatoes.

BARBECUED PORK CHOPS

4 servings
8 x 8-inch baking dish

4 *pork chops, cut ½-inch thick*
⅓ cup chopped celery
2 tablespoons firmly packed brown sugar
2 teaspoons lemon juice
½ teaspoon mustard
½ teaspoon salt
⅛ teaspoon pepper
1 can (12-ounces) tomato sauce
½ cup water

Arrange pork chops in (8 x 8-inch) baking dish. Sprinkle with celery, brown sugar, lemon juice, mustard, salt and pepper. Pour tomato sauce and water over chops. Cover with plastic wrap. MICROWAVE 5 MINUTES on HIGH. Reduce setting. MICROWAVE 15 to 18 MINUTES on '6', or until pork chops are fork tender.

For ovens without solid state heat control, during second cooking period, MICROWAVE 18 to 22 MINUTES on '5'.

STUFFED PORK CHOPS IN WINE

4 servings
Small mixing bowl
12 x 8-inch baking dish

2 tablespoons butter or margarine
1 medium onion, finely chopped
¼ cup finely chopped celery
1 cup dried bread crumbs
2 tablespoons snipped parsley
⅛ teaspoon sage
⅛ teaspoon celery seed
4 pork chops, 1½-inches thick, with pocket
2 tablespoons flour
1 cup chicken stock, or 2 teaspoons instant chicken
    bouillon dissolved in 1 cup boiling water
½ cup dry white wine

Combine butter, onion and celery in small mixing bowl. MICROWAVE 3 to 5 MINUTES on HIGH, or until onion is transparent.

Stir in bread crumbs, parsley, sage and celery seed. Fill pockets of pork chops with stuffing. Secure openings with wooden picks.

Arrange chops in (12 x 8-inch) baking dish, meatiest portions to outside. Sprinkle with flour. Pour chicken broth and wine over chops. Cover. MICROWAVE 35 to 40 MINUTES on '6', or until chops are fork tender.

For ovens without solid state heat control, MICROWAVE 42 to 48 MINUTES on '5'.

PORK AND APPLE PIE

4 to 6 servings
9 x 5-inch loaf dish

1 large onion, chopped
1 teaspoon sage
½ teaspoon salt
⅛ teaspoon pepper
2 pounds lean pork, cut in ¼ to ½-inch cubes
3 apples, peeled, cored and thinly sliced
2 cups mashed potatoes

Mix onion, sage, salt and pepper together in small bowl. In (9 x 5-inch) loaf dish, alternate layers of pork and layers of apple, sprinkling each layer with onion mixture. Use half the pork, half the apples and half the onions for each layer. Cover with plastic wrap. MICROWAVE 10 MINUTES on HIGH.

Spread mashed potatoes over top of loaf. Do not cover. MICROWAVE 10 MINUTES on '6', or until potatoes are heated through and meat is tender.

For ovens without solid state heat control, after spreading with potatoes, MICROWAVE 12 MINUTES on '5'.

ORIENTAL RIBS

4 servings
12 x 8-inch baking dish
1-quart measure

2 pounds pork spareribs, cut into 2 to 2½-inch pieces
1 cup dried apricots, chopped
1 clove garlic, pressed or finely chopped
2 tablespoons sugar
½ cup water
1 teaspoon salt
¼ teaspoon pepper
1 teaspoon ginger
¼ teaspoon cloves
1 tablespoon vinegar
½ teaspoon lemon juice

Place ribs in (12 x 8-inch) baking dish. Cover with waxed paper. MICROWAVE 5 MINUTES on HIGH. Drain excess juices. Rearrange ribs. In 1-quart measure, combine apricots, garlic, sugar, water, salt, pepper, ginger, cloves, vinegar and lemon juice. MICROWAVE 4 to 6 MINUTES on HIGH, or until mixture comes to a full boil. Stir. Pour over ribs. Cover with waxed paper. MICROWAVE 30 to 35 MINUTES on '8', or until tender. Rearrange once during cooking period.

For ovens without solid state heat control, after adding sauce to ribs, MICROWAVE 36 to 42 MINUTES on '5'.

PORK CHOPS CREOLE

4 servings
12 x 8-inch baking dish

4 *lean pork chops*
1 *medium onion, chopped*
1 *small green pepper, chopped*
¼ *cup chopped celery*
2 *teaspoons parsley flakes*
1 *teaspoon salt*
½ *teaspoon pepper*
1 *can (8-ounces) tomato sauce*
Dash hot pepper sauce

Arrange chops in (12 x 8-inch) baking dish with meatiest portions to outside of dish. Top with onion, green pepper and celery. Sprinkle with parsley, salt and pepper. Pour in tomato sauce. Add pepper sauce. Cover. MICROWAVE 5 MINUTES on HIGH.

Reduce setting. MICROWAVE 15 to 18 MINUTES on '6', or until chops are fork tender. Serve with rice.

For ovens without solid state heat control, during second cooking period, MICROWAVE 18 to 21 MINUTES on '5'.

BARBECUED SPARERIBS

4 servings
2-quart utility dish or,
8 x 8-inch baking dish

2 *pounds spareribs*
2½ *cups catsup*
½ *cup firmly packed brown sugar*
½ *cup cider vinegar*
1 *tablespoon horseradish*
1 *tablespoon Worcestershire sauce*
1 *teaspoon garlic salt*

Place spareribs bone side down in 2-quart dish. Mix remaining ingredients in 1-quart measure. Pour over ribs. Cover. MICROWAVE 5 MINUTES on HIGH.

Reduce setting. MICROWAVE 35 MINUTES on '6', or until meat is tender, turning ribs over after 15 minutes. Let stand 3 minutes.

For ovens without solid state heat control, MICROWAVE 42 MINUTES on '5' during second cooking period.

Variation:
Use country style spareribs. Add 5 to 10 minutes to final cooking time.
NOTE: If you have a favorite sauce recipe, substitute for the above.

Barbecued Spareribs.

Ham

SPICY HAM SLICE

4 to 6 servings
12 x 8-inch utility dish with
microwave roasting rack

1 *fully-cooked center-cut smoked ham slice, 1½-inches thick*
1 *cup catsup*
2 *tablespoons prepared mustard*
3 *tablespoons finely chopped green onion and tops*
Parmesan cheese

Slash edges of ham to prevent curling. Combine catsup, mustard and onions in 1-cup measure. Set aside. Place ham on microwave roasting rack in (12 x 8-inch) utility dish. MICROWAVE 10 MINUTES on '6'.

Turn ham over. Spread with sauce. Sprinkle with parmesan cheese. MICROWAVE 5 to 6 MINUTES on '6', or until ham is hot or internal temperature registers 150°. Let stand 3 minutes before serving.

NOTE: Do not use meat thermometer in microwave oven.

For ovens without solid state heat control, MICROWAVE 12 MINUTES on '5'. Turn ham. Spread with sauce. MICROWAVE 6 to 7 MINUTES on '5'.

Variations:
Substitute the following for catsup sauce:

1 *cup apricot or peach preserves, or*
½ *cup whole cranberry sauce mixed with ½ cup applesauce*

Solid State Heat Control Ovens		Variable and Defrost Heat Control Ovens	

FULLY-COOKED-HAM CHART

WEIGHT	TIME	
	SETTING '6'	SETTING '5'
2 - 4 Pounds	10-12 Min. per Pound	12 - 14 Min. per Pound
5 - 8 Pounds	8 - 10 Min. per Pound	10 - 12 Min. per Pound

BROWN SUGAR HAM

6 to 8 servings
Shallow baking dish

5 *pound canned ham*
1 *tablespoon whole cloves*
½ *cup firmly packed brown sugar*
2 *tablespoons bread crumbs*
1 *teaspoon prepared mustard*

Place ham in baking dish. Stud with cloves. Combine sugar, bread crumbs and mustard in a small bowl. Spread mixture on top of ham and press firmly. Cover with waxed paper. MICROWAVE 10 MINUTES on HIGH.
Rotate dish ½ turn. MICROWAVE 25 MINUTES on '6'. Let stand 10 minutes, covered with aluminum foil.

For ovens without solid state heat control, after rotating dish, MICROWAVE 30 MINUTES on '5'.

Variation:

1 *package (10-ounces) frozen raspberries, defrosted*
½ *cup sugar*
1 *teaspoon cinnamon*
¼ *teaspoon cloves*

Mix raspberries and sugar together in 1-quart measure. MICROWAVE 4 to 5 MINUTES on HIGH, or until mixture is syrupy. Stir in cinnamon and cloves. MICROWAVE 1 MINUTE on HIGH, or until hot. Glaze ham after turning.

LUAU KABOBS

4 servings
12 x 8-inch baking dish,
with microwave roasting rack
1-quart measure

¼ *cup butter or margarine*
1 *can (13-ounces) pineapple chunks, drained and juice reserved*
¼ *cup juice from pineapple chunks*
2 *tablespoons lemon juice*
¼ *cup firmly packed brown sugar*
⅛ *teaspoon ground cloves*
⅛ *teaspoon dry mustard*
1 *pound cooked ham, cut in 1-inch cubes*
1 *large orange, peeled and cut into sections*

Place butter in 1-quart measure. MICROWAVE on HIGH until butter melts. Stir in pineapple and lemon juices, brown sugar, cloves and mustard. MICROWAVE 1 to 2 MINUTES on HIGH, or until hot.

On each of 8 wooden skewers, alternate ham, pineapple chunks and orange sections. Place on microwave roasting rack in (12 x 8-inch) baking dish. Brush with sauce. MICROWAVE 2 MINUTES on HIGH. Turn. Brush with remaining sauce. MICROWAVE 2 MINUTES on HIGH, or until sizzling hot. Serve on rice with remaining sauce.

Baked Ham with Orange Potato Shells (page 142).

BAKED HAM

12 x 8-inch utility dish with
microwave roasting rack

Fully cooked ham
One of the following glazes, if desired

Score ham, if desired.

Place ham fat side down on microwave roasting rack in (12 x 8-inch) utility dish. Do not cover. MICROWAVE on '6' or '5' for half the roasting time (see chart).

Turn ham fat side up. Brush with glaze and stud with cloves, if desired. MICROWAVE on '6' or '5' for remaining time, or until internal temperature registers 140° to 150°. Let stand 15 minutes, tented with aluminum foil, shiny side in. (Temperature will rise 10 degrees during standing.)

NOTE: Inverted saucers may be substituted for roasting rack. Do not use meat thermometer in microwave oven.

HAM GLAZES

¼ *cup honey*
½ *cup firmly packed brown sugar*

Measure honey in 1-cup measure. MICROWAVE 1 to 2 MINUTES on HIGH, or until hot. Stir in brown sugar. Glaze ham after turning.

½ *cup firmly packed brown sugar*
2 *teaspoons prepared mustard*
1 *can (8-ounces) pineapple rings*

Blend sugar and mustard together. Add enough pineapple juice to make smooth paste.

After turning ham, arrange pineapple rings on top. Spoon on glaze. Garnish with maraschino cherries, if desired.

Lamb

SHISH KABOB

4 servings
1-quart measure
2-quart utility dish with microwave roasting rack

¼ cup olive or salad oil
2 tablespoons light corn syrup
2 teaspoons lemon juice
½ teaspoon savory
½ teaspoon thyme
1 pound lamb cut in 1-inch cubes
1 green pepper cut in 1-inch squares
4 small onions
4 large fresh mushrooms
4 cherry tomatoes

Combine olive oil, corn syrup, lemon juice, savory and thyme in 1-quart measure. MICROWAVE 3 MINUTES on HIGH. Stir. Cool slightly. Stir in lamb cubes. Marinate at least four hours or overnight.

Alternate lamb cubes and vegetables on each of 4 skewers. Lay carefully on roasting rack. MICROWAVE 8 to 10 MINUTES on '6', or until lamb is desired degree of doneness. Serve on bed of rice or barley.

NOTE: Two inverted saucers may be substituted for roasting rack.

For ovens without solid state heat control, MICROWAVE 10 to 12 MINUTES on '5'.

LAMB CURRY

6 to 8 servings
2-quart casserole

1 tablespoon butter or margarine
2 teaspoons curry powder
¼ cup chopped onion
1 clove garlic, pressed or finely chopped
1½ pounds lamb, cut in ¾-inch cubes
2 cups chopped celery
2 tablespoons flour
1 can (14-ounces) unsweetened pineapple tidbits
1 teaspoon salt
1 teaspoon garlic salt

Combine butter, curry powder, onion and garlic in 2-quart casserole. MICROWAVE 3 MINUTES on HIGH, or until onion is transparent. Add lamb cubes and celery. Sprinkle with flour. Toss to mix well.

Drain pineapple syrup into 1-quart measure. Add water to make 2 cups. Stir pineapple tidbits and liquid into lamb mixture. Cover. MICROWAVE 40 MINUTES on '6'. Add salts. Serve over rice.

For ovens without solid state heat control, MICROWAVE 45 to 50 MINUTES on '5'.

Solid State Heat Control Ovens

Variable and Defrost Heat Control Ovens

SUGGESTED COOKING TIMES FOR LAMB

CUT	COOKING CONTAINER	SPECIAL INSTRUCTIONS	MINUTES PER POUND	SETTING	TURN	STANDING TIME
Leg of Lamb	12 x 8 utility dish	Microwave fat side down on rack 5 min. on High Reduce setting and finish	9 - 11	6	Fat side up halfway through	10 min. under foil tent (foil shiny side in)
			10 - 12	5		
Lamb Chops	12 x 8 utility dish	Microwave on rack for 5 min. on High. Reduce setting to finish	7 - 9	6	Once	
			8 - 10	5		

These are approximate times for medium lamb. Adjust them if you prefer medium-rare or well-done lamb.

ROAST LEG OF LAMB

12 x 8-inch utility dish with
microwave roasting rack

Leg of lamb
1 clove garlic, halved

Rub lamb with garlic. Place fat side down on microwave roasting rack in (12 x 8-inch) utility dish. MICROWAVE 5 MINUTES on HIGH.

Reduce setting. MICROWAVE on '6' or '5' for half the roasting time.

Turn roast fat side up. MICROWAVE on '6' or '5' until internal temperature of thickest part of meat registers 150° to 160°, depending on desired doneness. Let stand 10 minutes, tented with aluminum foil, shiny side in. Roast will continue to cook while standing.

NOTE: Do not use meat thermometer in microwave oven. Inverted saucers may be substituted for roasting rack.

Variations:

GARLIC STUDDED LEG OF LAMB

Make incisions in lamb with sharp knife. Press 4 to 5 garlic cloves, peeled and quartered, into incisions.

HERBED LAMB

Rub 1 clove garlic, halved, and rosemary or thyme, into meat.

LEMON MARINATED LAMB CHOPS

4 servings
12 x 8-inch utility dish,
with microwave roasting rack
2-cup measure

4 lamb chops, ¾-inch thick
½ cup salad oil
½ cup sherry
⅓ cup cider vinegar
1 medium onion, chopped
2 tablespoons lemon pepper seasoning
1 teaspoon lemon juice
1 clove garlic, pressed or finely chopped
½ teaspoon rosemary
2 teaspoons Worcestershire sauce

Place lamb chops in (12 x 8-inch) utility dish.

Mix oil, sherry, vinegar, onion, lemon pepper seasoning, lemon juice, garlic, rosemary and Worcestershire sauce in 2-cup measure. MICROWAVE 1 MINUTE, 30 SECONDS on HIGH, or until hot. Pour over chops. Cover. Let stand 3 hours, or overnight, refrigerated.

Arrange marinated lamb chops on microwave roasting rack in (12 x 8-inch) utility dish. MICROWAVE 5 MINUTES on HIGH.

Turn chops over. MICROWAVE 10 to 15 MINUTES on '6', or until chops are of desired doneness.

For ovens without solid state heat control, MICROWAVE 12 to 18 MINUTES on '5'.

BASIC LAMB CASSEROLE

4 servings
2-quart casserole

1½ *pounds boneless lamb, cut in ¾-inch cubes*
2 *onions, cut in eighths*
¼ *cup flour*
2½ *cups water*
1 *teaspoon instant beef or chicken bouillon*
1 *teaspoon salt*
¼ *teaspoon pepper*

Combine lamb and onions in 2-quart casserole. Stir in flour to coat meat. Add water, bouillon, salt and pepper. Cover. MICROWAVE 5 MINUTES on HIGH. Stir.

Reduce setting. MICROWAVE 25 to 30 MINUTES on '6', or until meat is fork tender.

For ovens without solid state heat control, during second cooking period, MICROWAVE 30 to 36 MINUTES on '5'.

Variations:

FRENCH LAMB
Add:
8 *small whole onions*
1 *clove garlic, chopped*
⅓ *cup tomato paste*
½ *cup fresh shelled peas*
½ *teaspoon thyme or rosemary*
Bay leaf

Garnish with snipped parsley. Remove bay leaf. Serve with mashed or new potatoes.

NOTE: ½ cup frozen peas may be substituted for fresh. Add during last 5 minutes of cooking.

GREEK LAMB
Add:
½ *eggplant, peeled and diced*
4 *zucchini, sliced*
2 *tomatoes, peeled and chopped, or 2 tablespoons tomato paste*
Finely grated rind and juice of 1 *lemon*
Serve with boiled rice.

INDIAN LAMB
Add:
1 *tablespoon curry powder (add with flour)*
2 *stems celery, chopped*
1 *clove garlic, finely chopped*
2 *tablespoons raisins*
¼ *teaspoon ginger*
Stir in ⅓ *cup plain yogurt just before serving*
Serve with boiled rice and chutney.

ITALIAN LAMB
Add:
1 *can (16-ounces) Italian plum tomatoes*
1 *clove garlic, pressed or chopped*
½ *teaspoon basil*
½ *teaspoon oregano*
Garnish with grated Parmesan cheese

Serve with macaroni, noodles or rice.

IRISH LAMB
Add:
2 *(additional) onions, cut in eighths*
3 *slices bacon, chopped*
4 *medium boiling potatoes, thinly sliced*
Garnish with snipped parsley

NOTE: MICROWAVE 5 to 10 MINUTES longer, or until potatoes are tender.

AUSTRALIAN LAMB
Add:
1 *carrot, thinly sliced*
1 *small turnip, diced*
1 *cup diced pumpkin or winter squash*
1 *teaspoon rosemary*
Garnish with snipped parsley
Serve with a green vegetable and mashed potatoes.

LAMB RIBLETS IN TOMATO HONEY SAUCE

4 servings
2-quart casserole

2 *pounds lamb riblets*
1 *medium onion, sliced*
1 *can (10½-ounces) condensed golden mushroom soup, undiluted*
1 *can (8-ounces) tomato sauce*
2 *tablespoons honey*
½ *teaspoon salt*
⅛ *teaspoon pepper*
¼ *teaspoon thyme*

Place riblets in 2-quart casserole. Cover with onion slices. MICROWAVE 10 MINUTES on '6'. Drain fat.

Stir in soup, tomato sauce, honey, salt, pepper and thyme. Cover. MICROWAVE 40 to 50 MINUTES on '6', or until riblets are tender, stirring twice.

Serve over rice, noodles or biscuits.

For ovens without solid state heat control, MICROWAVE 12 MINUTES on '5', and 50 to 60 MINUTES on '5'.

LAMB PILAF

4 servings
1-quart measure
1½-quart casserole

2 cups chicken broth, or 3 teaspoons instant chicken
   bouillon dissolved in 2 cups boiling water
3 tablespoons butter or margarine
2 teaspoons lemon juice
1 teaspoon salt
1 bay leaf
1 cup uncooked white rice
1 medium onion, finely chopped
1 small green pepper, chopped
2 tablespoons butter or margarine
1 to 1½ cups cubed cooked lamb
¼ to ½ teaspoon thyme

Combine chicken broth, 3 tablespoons butter, lemon
juice, salt and bay leaf in medium sauce pan. Bring to boil
on conventional range. Add rice. Cover tightly. Lower
heat. Cook 18 to 20 minutes, or until rice is tender and all
liquid absorbed. (Or cook rice in broth according to
directions on page 155.) Remove bay leaf.

Combine onion, green pepper and 2 tablespoons butter in
1-quart measure. MICROWAVE 3 to 4 MINUTES on
HIGH, or until onion is transparent and green pepper is
tender-crisp.

Add lamb and thyme. Mix well. MICROWAVE 3
MINUTES on HIGH. Layer one third of cooked rice and
half of lamb mixture in 1½-quart casserole. Repeat
layers. Top with remaining one third rice. Cover.
MICROWAVE 5 MINUTES on '5', or until very hot.

LAMB CHOPS MARMALADE

4 servings
2-quart casserole

4 loin lamb chops, cut ¾ to 1-inch thick
Garlic salt
½ cup orange marmalade

Sprinkle lamb chops with garlic salt on both sides.
Arrange in 2-quart casserole, meatiest parts to outside of
dish. Spoon marmalade over chops. Cover. MICRO-
WAVE 5 MINUTES on HIGH.

Reduce setting. MICROWAVE 10 to 15 MINUTES on
'6', or until chops are desired doneness.

*For ovens without solid state heat control, during second
cooking period, MICROWAVE 9 to 12 MINUTES on
HIGH, rotating dish ½ turn after 5 minutes.*

LAMB STEW

4 to 6 servings
Shallow 2-quart casserole

2 pounds small boiling potatoes, peeled
2 large onions, sliced
Salt and pepper
2 pounds lamb shoulder, cut in ¾-inch cubes, excess
   fat removed
1 to 2 cups water, as needed
Snipped parsley

Set aside half the potatoes. Slice remaining potatoes
thinly. Spread sliced potatoes in bottom of 2-quart casserole. Layer half the onions over potatoes. Season lightly
with salt and pepper.

Spread meat over onions. Season lightly. Layer with
second half of onions. Arrange whole potatoes on top of
onions. Add just enough water to cover.

Cover tightly. MICROWAVE 30 to 40 MINUTES on '6',
or until meat is fork tender. Let stand 10 minutes,
covered. Sprinkle with parsley before serving in soup
plates.

NOTE: Use a casserole wide enough to take all the whole
potatoes in one layer. Lamb shoulder is high in fat
content. The whole potatoes absorb fat, enhancing their
flavor, while improving the character of the sauce.

*For ovens without solid state heat control, MICROWAVE
40 to 50 MINUTES on '5'.*

LAMB BURGER SPECIAL

4 servings
Browning dish

4 slices bacon, cooked crisp and crumbled (page 96)
1 pound ground lamb
1 teaspoon salt
¼ teaspoon pepper
½ teaspoon marjoram
2 teaspoons Worcestershire sauce
4 slices tomato
⅓ cup shredded cheddar cheese

Mix bacon, lamb, salt, pepper, marjoram and Worcestershire sauce together in medium bowl. Form into four
¾-inch thick patties. Set aside.

To preheat browning dish, MICROWAVE 4 MINUTES
on HIGH. Add meat patties, MICROWAVE 5 to 6
MINUTES on HIGH, or until desired doneness, turning
patties over once.

Top each with a tomato slice and shredded cheddar
cheese. MICROWAVE 1 MINUTE on HIGH, or until
cheese melts. Serve on roll or toast with tossed salad.

Corned Beef with Cabbage and Horseradish Sauce.

Bacon, Sausage & Specialty Meats

BACON BASICS

A few slices of bacon can be cooked on a bed of paper towels for easy clean-up. If you wish to save drippings, cook bacon in a baking dish. Very salty cures do not cook well on paper towels.

For larger quantities of bacon, use a microwave roasting rack in a 12 x 8-inch utility dish. Larger amounts can be cooked on paper towels, but they render more fat than the towels can absorb, so you'll need to wipe up the oven floor. When cooking bacon, cover with a paper towel to prevent spatters.

The chart is for medium-sliced bacon. Thinly sliced bacon should be microwaved for less time. Thickly sliced bacon will take a little longer. When microwaving special "home style" cures, reduce setting to '6' or '5' and experiment with times to suit your type of bacon.

SUGGESTED COOKING TIMES FOR BACON

NUMBER OF STRIPS	TIME	SETTING
2	2 min.	High
3	3½ min.	High
4	4 - 4½ min.	High
5	5 - 5½ min.	High
6	6 - 6½ min.	High

CORNED BEEF

6 to 8 servings
2-quart casserole

3 pound beef corned brisket with seasoning packet
2 cups water

Place beef in casserole. Sprinkle with seasonings. Pour water over meat. Cover. MICROWAVE 8 to 10 MINUTES on HIGH, or until water boils rapidly. Reduce setting. MICROWAVE 40 MINUTES on '6', or until fork tender, turning meat over after 20 minutes. Let stand 15 minutes in juices, covered. Serve with Horseradish Sauce.

NOTE: If cabbage is desired, cook during standing time, following directions on page 148.

For ovens without solid state heat control, during second cooking period, MICROWAVE 50 MINUTES on '5', turning meat over after 25 minutes.

HORSERADISH SAUCE

½ cup
1-cup measure

1 package (3-ounces) cream cheese
2 teaspoons horseradish
1 tablespoon cream

Place cream cheese in 1-cup measure. MICROWAVE 2 MINUTES on '6', or until softened. Stir in horseradish and cream. MICROWAVE 1 MINUTE on '6'. Serve warm.

For ovens without solid state heat control, to soften cheese, MICROWAVE 2 MINUTES, 30 SECONDS on '5'. To warm sauce, MICROWAVE 1 MINUTE, 15 SECONDS on '5'.

ORANGE-BERRY GLAZED LUNCHEON MEAT

4 servings Plate

1 can (12-ounces) luncheon meat
¾ cup cranberry-orange relish

Make slashes in luncheon meat ¾-inch apart, cutting to within ¾-inch of bottom. Fill slits with cranberry-orange relish. Place ham on plate. Cover loosely with waxed paper. MICROWAVE 4 to 5 MINUTES on '6', or until heated through.

For ovens without solid state heat control, MICROWAVE 6 MINUTES, 30 SECONDS to 7 MINUTES on '5'.

CORNED BEEF ROAST

8 to 12 servings
12 x 8-inch utility dish with microwave roasting rack

4½ pound corned beef brisket
Spice packet (optional)

Wash brisket. Place on microwave roasting rack in (12 x 8-inch) utility dish. Sprinkle with spices, if desired. Cover tightly with plastic wrap. MICROWAVE 2 MINUTES on HIGH.

Reduce setting. MICROWAVE 25 MINUTES on '5'.

Turn brisket over. Cover. MICROWAVE 25 to 30 MINUTES on '6', or until meat is fork tender or internal temperature registers 155°. Let stand 15 minutes, covered.

NOTE: Do not add water. Do not use meat thermometer in microwave oven. Inverted saucer may be substituted for roasting rack.

For ovens without solid state heat control, MICROWAVE 30 MINUTES on '5'. Turn brisket over. MICROWAVE 30 to 36 MINUTES on '5'.

SMOKED BRATWURST

4 to 5 servings
8 x 8-inch baking dish

1 pound smoked bratwurst

Place bratwurst in (8 x 8-inch) baking dish. MICROWAVE 5 MINUTES, 30 SECONDS to 6 MINUTES on '6', or until sausages are hot. Serve with pickle relish or sauerkraut on bun, or with German potato salad.

Variation:
Pour ½ cup beer over bratwurst. Cover. MICROWAVE 5 MINUTES, 30 SECONDS to 6 MINUTES on '6'.

FRIED LIVER AND ONION

4 to 6 servings
Browning dish

¼ cup all-purpose flour
1 teaspoon salt
⅛ teaspoon pepper
1 pound beef liver, cut in serving pieces
2 tablespoons salad oil
2 medium onions, sliced

Combine flour, salt and pepper. Coat liver pieces with flour.

To preheat browning dish, MICROWAVE 4 MINUTES on HIGH. Add oil. Place half the liver and half the onion in browner. MICROWAVE 2 MINUTES on HIGH, depending on doneness desired, turning liver over once. Repeat with remaining liver and onions. Return all liver to browner. Spoon onions on top of liver. MICROWAVE 10 to 12 MINUTES on '6', or until liver is tender.

For ovens without solid state heat control, MICROWAVE 12 to 14 MINUTES on '5'.

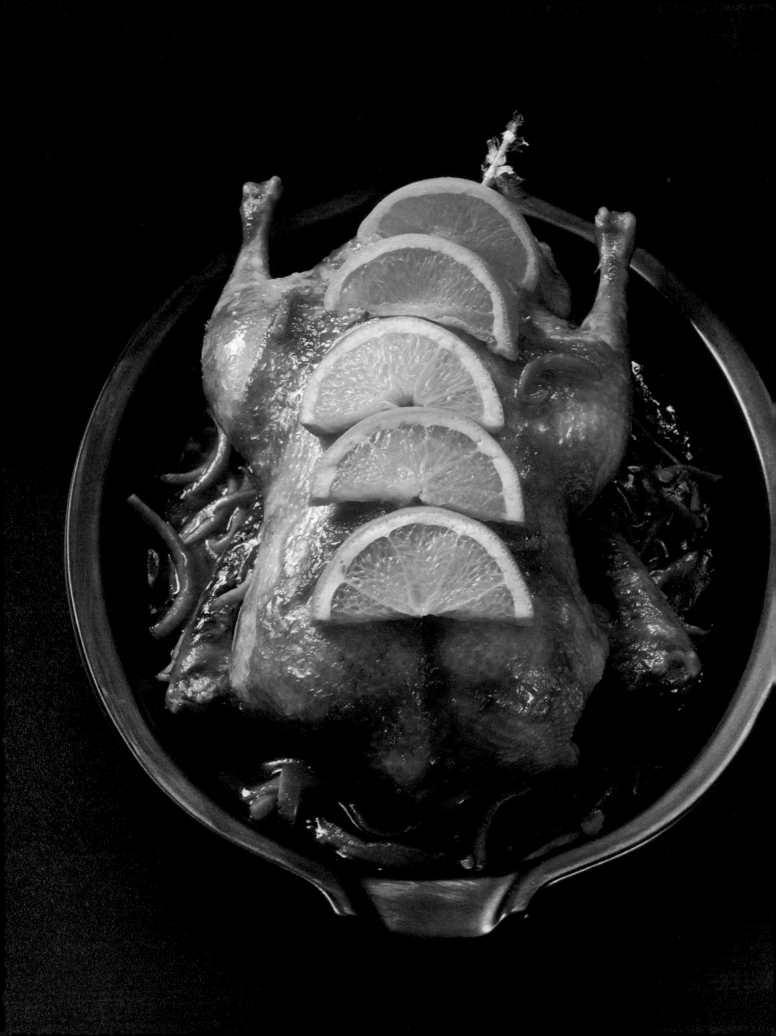

Poultry

Sautéed or braised chicken parts cook juicy and tender when microwaved on high for about half the time it takes to cook them conventionally. With heat control microwave ovens, whole birds, from Cornish hens up to a 10 pound turkey, are cooked on a low setting to minimize shielding and turning. When buying turkey over 10 pounds, ask your butcher to saw it into halves or quarters, and try the recipes for roasted turkey parts.

DUCKLING A L'ORANGE 🔲

3 to 4 servings
2-quart utility dish with
microwave roasting rack

4 to 5 pound fresh or frozen duckling, defrosted
1 orange, quartered
1 small onion, quartered
2 stems celery, cut in thirds
Orange sauce, below

Remove giblets and wash cavity. If duckling is defrosted, keep in original wrappings. Prick plastic bag with a fork near backbone.

Place duckling on rack in (2-quart) utility dish, breast side up. MICROWAVE 7 to 9 MINUTES on HIGH, or until duckling begins to exude fat. Let stand 5 minutes to allow fat to run out. Prepare orange sauce, below.

Remove duckling from bag. Drain fat from utility dish. Secure neck skin of duckling to back with wooden picks. Lift wing tips up and over back. Fill cavity with orange and onion quarters and celery pieces.

Place duckling breast side down on rack. MICROWAVE 12 to 17 MINUTES on '6'. Turn breast side up. Brush with orange sauce. MICROWAVE 20 to 25 MINUTES on '6'. Let stand 5 minutes, tented with aluminum foil,

shiny side in. Serve with remaining orange sauce and garnish with orange segments if desired.

Orange Sauce

2-cup measure

1 orange
1 cup orange juice
2 tablespoons corn starch
2 tablespoons soy sauce
¼ cup orange liqueur or sherry
3 tablespoons honey

Pare orange thinly, being careful not to take white membrane. Cut peel in julienne strips. Set aside.

Combine orange juice, corn starch and soy sauce in 2-cup measure. Mix well. MICROWAVE 2 to 3 MINUTES on HIGH. Stir. Mix in orange peel, liqueur and honey. MICROWAVE 2 MINUTES on HIGH, or until sauce is thick and glossy.

For ovens without solid state heat control, to roast duckling, MICROWAVE 60 to 70 minutes on '5', turning and glazing after 25 minutes.

POULTRY BASICS

To prepare whole birds for cooking, remove giblets, wash thoroughly and pat dry with paper towels. Do not stuff poultry until just before cooking.

You can try microwaving turkeys over 10 pounds, but large turkeys require less attention when roasted in a conventional oven. Roasting large birds conventionally frees the microwave oven for cooking side dishes, thus reducing over-all preparation time.

Poultry parts should be washed, cut into serving pieces if necessary, and dried with paper towels unless they are to be coated with crumbs. Arrange them in the dish with meatiest portions to the outside.

Fried chicken is best cooked conventionally. The amount of fat necessary to fry chicken becomes dangerously hot in the microwave oven.

The most reliable test for poultry doneness is a meat thermometer. Unless you have a special microwave thermometer, do not use a meat thermometer in the microwave oven while cooking. To test internal temperature of whole birds, insert thermometer in fleshy part of the inside thigh muscle without touching the bone. Remove bird from the oven when temperature registers 175°. Tent with foil and let stand to complete cooking.

Other tests for poultry doneness are:

Pierce inside thigh muscle deeply with fork. If juices run clear without a tinge of pink, poultry is done.

Press thickest part of drumstick meat between fingers, it should be very soft. With whole birds, move drumstick up and down. Joint should move freely or break when bird is done.

DUCKLING A L'ORANGE continued

Variations:

ORIENTAL DUCKLING

Substitute Pineapple Sauce for Orange Sauce.

2-cup measure

1 *can (13¼-ounces) pineapple tidbits*
½ *cup juice from pineapple*
½ *cup chicken broth*
2 *tablespoons corn starch*
2 *tablespoons soy sauce*
½ *green pepper, finely chopped*

Drain ½ cup juice from pineapple into 2-cup measure. Set pineapple tidbits aside. Add chicken broth, corn starch and soy sauce to juice. Beat well with wire whip. MICROWAVE 4 to 5 MINUTES on HIGH, or until thick and glossy, stirring once with wire whip. Use to glaze duckling.

Just before serving, stir pineapple tidbits and green pepper into remaining sauce. Serve with duckling.

ROAST DUCKLING WITH CHERRIES

Substitute Cherry Sauce for Orange Sauce

2-cup measure

1 *can (16-ounces) pitted black or red cherries*
½ *cup juice from cherries*
½ *cup red wine*
2 *tablespoons corn starch*

Drain ½ cup juice from cherries into 2-cup measure. Set cherries aside. Add wine and corn starch. Beat well with wire whip. MICROWAVE 4 to 5 MINUTES on HIGH, or until thick and glossy, stirring once with wire whip. Use to glaze duckling.

Just before serving, add fully drained cherries to remaining sauce. Serve with duckling.

PHEASANT IN WINE CREAM SAUCE

6 to 8 servings
Shallow 3-quart casserole
Serving dish or platter

3 *pheasants, skinned and cut in serving pieces*
2 *teaspoons salt*
¼ *teaspoon pepper*
½ *teaspoon rosemary*
1 *cup finely chopped onion*
1 *cup parsley*
½ *cup dry white wine*
1 *teaspoon instant chicken bouillon dissolved in 1 cup hot water*
¼ *cup corn starch*
1 *cup light cream*
Paprika

Place pheasants in 3-quart casserole. Season with salt, pepper and rosemary. Sprinkle with onion and parsley. Pour in wine and bouillon. Cover. MICROWAVE 60 to 70 MINUTES on HIGH, or until pheasants are fork tender, turning and rearranging pieces after 30 minutes.

Remove pheasants to serving dish. Set aside.

Blend corn starch with cream until smooth. Stir into hot broth. MICROWAVE 5 to 6 MINUTES on '8', or until thickened, stirring once. Pour over pheasants. Sprinkle with paprika. MICROWAVE 2 to 3 MINUTES on '8', or until heated through.

For ovens without solid state heat control, when making sauce, MICROWAVE 5 to 6 MINUTES on HIGH, stirring twice. To reheat pheasant, MICROWAVE 2 to 3 MINUTES on HIGH.

SUGGESTED COOKING TIMES FOR POULTRY

ITEM	COOKING METHOD	MINUTES PER POUND		SETTING	TURN	STANDING TIME
Cornish Game Hen	8 x 8-inch baking dish. Start breast side down	14 - 16		6	once	5 min.
		16 - 19		5		
Cornish Game Hens, 4 stuffed	12 x 8-inch baking dish or platter. Start breast side down.	6 - 8		High	once	7 min.
		6 - 8		High		
Duckling	2-quart utility dish on rack or inverted saucer	⅕ total cooking time on High, then . .	9 - 11	6	once	10 min. under foil tent
			10½ - 12½	5		
Roasting Hen	12 x 8-inch baking dish on rack or inverted saucer	⅕ total cooking time on High, then . .	9 - 11	6	once	15 min. under foil tent
			10½ - 12½	5		

NOTE: Meat thermometer reads 175° on removal and 195° after standing.

DELECTABLE DUCKLING

4 servings
12 x 8-inch utility dish

5 *pound duckling*
Stuffing if desired
1 *teaspoon Kitchen Bouquet dissolved in 1 teaspoon water*

Remove giblets and wash cavity. If duckling is defrosted, keep in original wrapping. Prick plastic bag with a fork near backbone.

Place duckling on rack in 2-quart utility dish breast side up. MICROWAVE 10 MINUTES on HIGH, or until duckling begins to exude fat. Let stand 5 minutes to allow fat to run out.

Remove duckling from bag. Drain fat from utility dish. Wash duckling and pat dry. If desired, stuff cavity, packing loosely. Secure cavity with string or wooden picks. Lift wing tips up and over back.

Place duckling breast side down on rack. Brush with Kitchen Bouquet mixture. MICROWAVE 14 MINUTES on '6'.

Turn duckling breast side up. Brush with Kitchen Bouquet mixture. MICROWAVE 22 MINUTES on '6', or until duckling is fork tender. Let stand 10 minutes tented with aluminum foil, shiny side in.

For ovens without solid state heat control, follow above procedure, reduce setting to '5'. Use cooking times of 16 to 20 MINUTES and 26 to 34 MINUTES.

WILD RICE STUFFING

4 cups
1½-quart bowl or casserole

2 *cups cooked wild rice, or wild and white (page 155)*
2 *tablespoons butter or margarine*
1 *small onion, finely chopped*
½ *cup finely chopped celery*
2 *cans (4-ounces each) mushroom stems and pieces, drained and finely chopped*
1 *can (8-ounces) water chestnuts, drained and finely chopped*

Combine butter, onion and celery in 1½-quart bowl. MICROWAVE 3 MINUTES on HIGH, or until onion is transparent. Lightly mix in wild rice, mushrooms and water chestnuts.

Use to stuff 1 roasting chicken or 4 Cornish hens.

NOTE: Recipe may be halved easily to stuff 2 Cornish hens.

101

Coq Au Vin

COQ AU VIN

4 to 6 servings
2-quart casserole

1 cup all-purpose flour
2 teaspoons salt
¼ teaspoon pepper
3 pound frying chicken, cut in serving pieces
3 slices bacon, cut in 1-inch pieces
1 large onion, cut in quarters
1 package (8-ounces) fresh mushrooms, sliced
1 clove garlic, pressed or finely chopped
1 cup red wine
2 tablespoons brandy
1 bay leaf
1 tablespoon snipped parsley

Combine flour, salt and pepper in a shallow dish. Dredge chicken in flour mixture. Set aside.

Place bacon in 2-quart casserole. MICROWAVE 2 MINUTES on HIGH, or until almost crisp.

Add chicken and remaining seasoned flour to bacon and drippings. Mix in onion, mushrooms, garlic, wine, brandy, bay leaf and parsley. Cover tightly. MICROWAVE 15 MINUTES on HIGH.

Stir. Do not cover. MICROWAVE 10 MINUTES on HIGH, or until chicken is fork tender. Let stand 5 to 10 minutes, covered. Remove bay leaf before serving.

CHICKEN CACCIATORI

4 to 6 servings
3-quart casserole

3 to 3½ pounds frying chicken, cut in serving pieces
¼ cup flour
1 can (16-ounces) Italian style tomatoes, drained
1 can (8-ounces) tomato paste
2 medium onions, sliced
1 clove garlic, pressed or finely chopped
1½ teaspoons oregano
¼ teaspoon thyme
2 teaspoons parsley flakes
¼ teaspoon pepper
½ cup red wine
1½ cups water
1 can (4-ounces) sliced mushrooms, drained
1 teaspoon salt

Dredge chicken in flour.

Combine tomatoes, tomato paste, onions, garlic, oregano, thyme, parsley, pepper, wine and water. Stir until well-blended. Add chicken pieces, turning to coat well with sauce. Cover. MICROWAVE 25 to 30 MINUTES on HIGH, or until chicken is fork tender, stirring after 15 minutes. Stir in mushroom slices and salt. Let stand 5 minutes. Serve over spaghetti.

CHICKEN MARENGO

4 to 6 servings
2-quart casserole

1 cup all-purpose flour
1 teaspoon salt
¼ teaspoon pepper
1 teaspoon paprika
2½ to 3 pounds frying chicken, cut in serving pieces
1 clove garlic pressed or finely chopped
1 teaspoon sugar
½ teaspoon basil
1 package (8-ounces) fresh mushrooms, sliced
1 can (8-ounces) tomato sauce
8 to 10 stuffed olives
½ cup sherry
1 tablespoon olive brine
¼ cup almonds, toasted
½ pound mozzarella cheese, grated

Combine flour, salt, pepper and paprika in a shallow dish. Coat chicken with flour mixture. Place in 2-quart casserole. Add garlic, sugar, basil and mushrooms. Mix in any remaining seasoned flour. Stir in tomato sauce, sherry and olives. Sprinkle with almonds and cheese. Cover. MICROWAVE 25 MINUTES on HIGH, or until chicken is fork tender, stirring once. Let stand 5 to 10 minutes, covered.

CHICKEN SALTIMBOCCA

4 servings
8 x 8-inch baking dish

4 *chicken breasts, skinned and boned*
3 *tablespoons butter or margarine*
Salt and pepper
4 *thin slices boiled ham, 4 x 3-inches*
4 *thin slices mozzarella cheese, 4 x 3-inches*
4 *teaspoons grated parmesan cheese*

Place chicken breasts between 2 pieces of waxed paper. Pound to flatten slightly.

Place 3 tablespoons butter in (8 x 8-inch) baking dish. MICROWAVE on HIGH until butter melts. Add chicken breasts, turning to coat with butter. Cover. MICROWAVE 20 to 25 MINUTES on HIGH, or until chicken is fork tender.

Drain and reserve broth from baking dish. Season chicken with salt and pepper. Top each breast with slice of ham and slice of cheese. Sprinkle each with 1 teaspoon reserved broth and 1 teaspoon parmesan cheese. MICROWAVE 3 MINUTES on HIGH or until cheese melts.

CHICKEN BRAISED IN WINE

4 to 6 servings
3-quart casserole

2½ *to 3 pounds frying chicken, cut in serving pieces*
¼ *cup flour*
2 *tablespoons butter or margarine*
1 *medium onion, sliced*
4 *green onions with tops, sliced*
1 *clove garlic, pressed or finely chopped*
3 *large carrots, thinly sliced*
1 *tablespoon parsley*
¼ *teaspoon thyme*
¼ *teaspoon oregano*
1 *bay leaf*
1 *cup white or red wine*
1 *can (4-ounces) mushroom stems and pieces, drained*
1 *teaspoon salt*

Coat chicken pieces thoroughly with flour. Set aside.

Combine butter, onion, green onion, garlic and carrots in 3-quart casserole. Place chicken on top. Sprinkle with parsley, thyme and oregano. Add bay leaf and wine. Cover. MICROWAVE 25 to 30 MINUTES on HIGH, stirring once.

Add mushrooms. Cover. MICROWAVE 3 to 5 MINUTES on HIGH, or until chicken and carrots are tender. Remove bay leaf and stir in salt before serving.

CHICKEN PARISIENNE

4 servings
12 x 8-inch baking dish

4 *large chicken breasts (2½-pounds)*
1 *can (10¾-ounces) condensed cream of mushroom soup, undiluted*
1 *can (4-ounces) mushroom stems and pieces, drained*
1 *cup dairy sour cream*
½ *cup sherry*
Paprika

Arrange chicken breasts skin side up in (12 x 8-inch) baking dish.

Stir together soup, mushrooms, sour cream and sherry in 1-quart bowl. Pour over chicken breasts. Sprinkle generously with paprika. Cover. MICROWAVE 35 to 40 MINUTES on '5', or until chicken is fork tender, rotating dish ½ turn after 15 minutes.

SHERRIED CHICKEN BREASTS

4 servings
10 x 8-inch utility dish

1 *package (8-ounces) fresh mushrooms, sliced*
3 *tablespoons butter or margarine*
1 *tablespoon flour*
1 *cup whipping cream*
2 *tablespoons sherry*
4 *chicken breasts (1½-pounds)*

Combine mushrooms and butter in 1½-quart bowl. MICROWAVE 1 to 2 MINUTES on HIGH, or until butter melts and mushrooms soften. Stir in flour, cream and sherry, mixing until smooth. MICROWAVE 4 to 5 MINUTES on '6', or until mixture boils, stirring once. Set aside.

Arrange chicken breasts, skin side down, in (10 x 8-inch) utility dish, with meatiest portions to outside. Cover. MICROWAVE 10 MINUTES on HIGH, turning chicken over after 5 minutes.

Pour sauce over chicken. Cover. MICROWAVE 10 to 15 MINUTES on HIGH, or until chicken is fork tender.

For ovens without solid state heat control, when making cream sauce MICROWAVE 5 to 6 MINUTES on '5'.

CHICKEN BARBECUE

4 servings
12 x 8-inch baking dish

2 *to 3-pound frying chicken, cut in serving pieces*
¼ *cup butter or margarine, melted*
1½ *cups Barbecue Sauce (page 157)*

Arrange chicken in (12 x 8-inch) baking dish, with meatiest portions toward outside of dish. Brush with melted butter. Pour barbecue sauce over chicken. Cover with plastic wrap. MICROWAVE 25 to 30 MINUTES on HIGH. Let stand 5 minutes, covered.

ROAST CHICKEN

4 to 6 servings
12 x 8-inch utility dish with
microwave roasting rack

5 *pound roasting chicken*
Stuffing, if desired
¼ *cup honey*
1 *teaspoon Worcestershire sauce*
1 *teaspoon soy sauce*

Remove giblets. Wash chicken well with cold water. Pat dry. Stuff cavity, packing loosely. Secure cavity with wooden picks or poultry skewers.

Place chicken breast side down on microwave roasting rack in (12 x 8-inch) utility dish. MICROWAVE 10 MINUTES on HIGH.

Reduce setting. MICROWAVE 14 MINUTES on '6'.

Combine honey, Worcestershire sauce and soy sauce in 1-cup measure. Baste chicken with glaze.

Turn breast side up. Brush with glaze. MICROWAVE 22 MINUTES on '6', or until thickest part of inside thigh muscle registers 175°, rotating dish ½ turn if necessary. Let stand 15 minutes, tented with aluminum foil.

NOTE: Do not use meat thermometer in microwave oven. Cooking times are the same for unstuffed chicken.

For ovens without solid state heat control, follow above procedure. Reduce setting to '5', use cooking times of 17 MINUTES and 26 MINUTES.

EASY-BAKE CHICKEN

4 servings
12 x 8-inch baking dish

1 *package (2⅜-ounces) seasoned coating mix for*
chicken
2 *to 3 pounds frying chicken, cut up*

Place coating mix in bag provided with mix. Add chicken pieces, two or three at a time, and shake until evenly coated. Arrange chicken in (12 x 8-inch) baking dish, with meaty pieces toward outside of dish. Cover with waxed paper. MICROWAVE 20 to 30 MINUTES on HIGH, or until thickest pieces are fork tender.

STUFFING SUPREME

5 cups
3-quart bowl

½ *cup butter or margarine*
½ *cup chopped onion*
1 *cup chopped celery*
5 *cups (about 7 or 8-ounces) seasoned dry bread*
cubes
1 *egg, beaten*
⅓ *cup water*

Combine butter, onion and celery in 3-quart bowl. MICROWAVE 3 MINUTES on HIGH, or until onion is transparent. Add bread cubes, egg and water. Mix well. Use to stuff poultry.

NOTE: Recipe may be doubled. Microwave vegetables 5 minutes.

CRANBERRY SAUCE

2 cups
1-quart casserole

1 *pound fresh cranberries*
1 *to 1½ cups sugar*
¼ *cup water*

Combine all ingredients in 1-quart casserole. MICROWAVE 4 to 5 MINUTES on HIGH, or until cranberries pop. Let stand covered for 5 minutes. Can be served hot or cold. Serve with poultry.

Variation:
Substitute orange or pineapple juice for water.

CHICKEN MAJORCA

6 servings
12 x 8-inch baking dish

6 *chicken breasts*
1 *bottle (8-ounces) Italian salad dressing*
1 *jar (12-ounces) apricot preserves*

Place chicken in deep bowl. Pour Italian dressing over chicken and turn pieces to coat well. Cover. Marinate at least 2 hours at room temperature, or overnight in refrigerator.

Drain chicken and add apricot preserves to dressing. Mix well. Place chicken skin side up in (12 x 8-inch) baking dish. Pour glaze over and turn chicken to coat well. Cover with plastic wrap. MICROWAVE 36 MINUTES on '5', or until chicken is tender, turning breasts over after 18 minutes. Let stand 3 minutes.

NOTE: If chicken has been refrigerated, add a few minutes to cooking time.

CHICKEN LIVERS CHABLIS

4 servings
2-quart casserole

2 *tablespoons butter or margarine*
2 *packages (8-ounces each) frozen chicken livers,*
  defrosted
3 *tablespoons flour*
¼ *cup finely chopped onion*
2 *tablespoons catsup*
¾ *cup chablis or white grape juice with 1 teaspoon*
  lemon juice

Place butter in 2-quart casserole. MICROWAVE on HIGH until melted.

Dredge livers in flour. Arrange in casserole in single layer. Cover loosely with waxed paper. MICROWAVE 7 MINUTES on '8', turning livers over after 4 minutes.

Gently stir in onion, catsup and wine. Cover with waxed paper. MICROWAVE 5 MINUTES on '8', or until livers are tender. Stir. Serve hot on bed of rice.

For ovens without solid state heat control, MICROWAVE 5 to 6 MINUTES on HIGH, turning livers over every 2 minutes. Add remaining ingredients. MICROWAVE 4 MINUTES on HIGH, stirring twice.

CHICKEN A LA KING

5 to 6 servings
1½-quart casserole

¼ *cup butter or margarine*
¼ *cup flour*
1 *cup chicken broth*
1 *cup milk*
1½ *cups diced cooked chicken or turkey*
1 *cup frozen peas, defrosted*
1 *jar (2-ounces) chopped pimiento*
½ *teaspoon celery seed (optional)*
⅛ *teaspoon pepper*
Seasoned salt
1 *tablespoon grated sharp cheese*

Place butter in 1½-quart casserole. MICROWAVE on HIGH, until butter is melted. Stir in flour to make a smooth paste. Add chicken broth and milk, beating with wire whip. MICROWAVE 6 to 7 MINUTES on '8', or until thick, stirring after 4 minutes and again when thick.

Add chicken, peas, pimiento, celery seed and pepper. Cover. MICROWAVE 4 MINUTES on HIGH, or until hot. Just before serving, stir in seasoned salt to taste and grated cheese. Serve on biscuits, buttered toast or patty shells.

For ovens without solid state heat control, MICROWAVE 5 to 6 MINUTES on HIGH, stirring every 1½ to 2 minutes.

TURKEY ROAST

4 to 6 servings
Glass loaf pan

1 *pound, 11-ounce frozen turkey roast*

Place frozen turkey roast in loaf pan upside down. Cover with waxed paper. MICROWAVE 5 MINUTES on HIGH.

Turn turkey roast over. Reduce setting. MICROWAVE 28 MINUTES on '6', or until roast reaches an internal temperature of 175°, rotating dish halfway through cooking time. Let stand 15 minutes, covered with aluminum foil.

NOTE: If package includes gravy mix, add water to drippings as package directs. MICROWAVE on HIGH until boiling. Stir in mix. Let stand 2 to 3 minutes, or until thick. Do not use meat thermometer in microwave oven.

For ovens without solid state heat control, during second cooking period MICROWAVE 33 to 34 MINUTES on '5', rotating dish halfway through cooking time.

ROASTED HALF TURKEY

4 servings
12 x 8-inch baking dish with
microwave roasting rack

½ *turkey (4½-pounds)*
½ *teaspoon Kitchen Bouquet diluted with ½ teaspoon*
  water

Wash turkey and pat dry. Brush skin evenly with Kitchen Bouquet mixture. Arrange turkey skin side up on rack in (12 x 8-inch) baking dish. MICROWAVE 25 MINUTES on '6'.

Turn turkey skin side down. MICROWAVE 35 MINUTES on '6'.

Turn turkey skin side up. MICROWAVE 10 MINUTES on '6', or until internal temperature of thickest part of inside thigh muscle reaches 175°. Cover with foil. Let stand 8 to 10 minutes to complete cooking.

NOTE: Do not use meat thermometer in the oven when cooking. Inverted saucers may be substituted for rack.

For ovens without solid state heat control MICROWAVE 84 MINUTES on '5', turning after 30 minutes and 40 minutes.

Variation:
Glazed Turkey. Omit Kitchen Bouquet. Brush with desired glaze when turning turkey.

105

ORANGE-GLAZED TURKEY QUARTER

2 servings
8 x 8-inch baking dish

1 *cup orange juice*
1 *cup firmly packed brown sugar*
¼ *turkey (about 2-pounds)*

Combine orange juice and sugar in 2-cup measure. Mix well. Place dry turkey, skin side up, in (8 x 8-inch) baking dish. Brush with orange glaze. MICROWAVE 15 MINUTES on '6', rotating dish ½ turn (so that front is toward back of oven) after 10 minutes.

Turn turkey flesh side up. Brush with glaze. MICROWAVE 15 MINUTES on '6', rotating dish ½ turn after 10 minutes.

Turn turkey skin side up. Brush with glaze. MICROWAVE 5 MINUTES on '6'. Let stand 5 minutes.

For ovens without solid state heat control, following above procedure, set oven on '5', use cooking times of 18 minutes and 6 minutes.

TURKEY DIVAN

4 servings
8 x 8-inch baking dish

1 *package (10-ounces) frozen chopped broccoli*
1 *can (11¾-ounces) cream of chicken soup, undiluted*
¼ *cup milk or light cream*
2 *tablespoons dry sherry*
6 *to 8 turkey slices*
⅓ *cup grated parmesan cheese*

Place broccoli in baking dish. Cover tightly with plastic wrap. MICROWAVE 3 to 4 MINUTES on HIGH, or until hot. Drain.

Blend soup, milk and sherry in 1-quart measure. Spoon half over broccoli. Top with turkey slices. Add half the grated cheese to remaining soup. Spoon over turkey. Top with remaining cheese. Cover lightly. MICROWAVE 5 MINUTES on HIGH, or until sauce bubbles and cheese browns lightly.

Roast Cornish Hens

HOT TURKEY SALAD

4 to 6 servings
1½-quart casserole

2 *cups diced cooked turkey*
2 *cups finely chopped celery*
½ *small onion, thinly sliced*
1 *can (6-ounces) water chestnuts, drained and sliced*
½ *small green pepper, cut in short, thin strips*
2 *tablespoons chopped pimiento or stuffed olives*
1 *cup mayonnaise*
2 *tablespoons lemon juice*
1 *cup crushed corn chips*
1 *cup shredded sharp cheddar cheese*

Combine turkey, celery, onion, water chestnuts, green pepper, pimiento, mayonnaise, and lemon juice in 1½-quart casserole. Cover. MICROWAVE 10 MINUTES on '8', stirring after 5 minutes. Sprinkle with corn chips and cheese. MICROWAVE 1 MINUTE on HIGH, or until cheese melts.

For ovens without solid state heat control, for first cooking period, MICROWAVE 8 MINUTES on HIGH, stirring every 2 minutes.

ROAST CORNISH HENS

4 servings
12 x 8-inch utility dish with
microwave roasting rack, if desired

4 1-*pound Cornish hens*
4 *cups stuffing*
½ *cup cranberry-orange relish*
1 *tablespoon honey*

Stuff Cornish hens. Secure cavity with wooden picks. Mix cranberry-orange relish and honey in small bowl.

Arrange hens breast side down and at least 1-inch apart, in (12 x 8-inch) utility dish. Brush hens with glaze. Cover with waxed paper. MICROWAVE 12 to 15 MINUTES on HIGH, rotating dish once if necessary.

Turn hens over so that breast sides are up and outside edges are reversed to inside of dish. Brush with glaze. Cover with waxed paper. MICROWAVE 15 MINUTES on HIGH, or until internal temperature of thickest part of inside thigh muscle registers 175°. Let stand 7 minutes, tented with aluminum foil.

If desired, serve on bed of wild rice, garnished with green beans and spiced peaches.

NOTE: Do not use meat thermometer in microwave oven.

SINGLE CORNISH HEN

1 serving
8 x 8-inch baking dish

1 *pound Cornish hen*
1 *cup stuffing*
½ *teaspoon Kitchen Bouquet mixed with ½ teaspoon water*

Stuff Cornish hen. Secure cavity with wooden picks. Place hen breast side down in (8 x 8-inch) baking dish. Brush with Kitchen Bouquet mixture. Cover with waxed paper. MICROWAVE 5 MINUTES on '6', rotating dish once, if necessary.

Turn hen breast side up. Brush with Kitchen Bouquet mixture. Cover with waxed paper. MICROWAVE 9 to 11 MINUTES on '6', or until legs can be moved easily. Let stand 5 minutes, tented with aluminum foil.

For ovens without solid state heat control, follow above procedure, reduce setting to '5'. Use cooking times of 6 MINUTES and 11 to 13 MINUTES.

CORNISH HENS FOR TWO

2 servings
1-cup measure
8 x 8-inch baking dish

2 1-*pound Cornish hens*
2 *cups stuffing*
½ *cup pineapple jelly*
1 *tablespoon dry sherry*

Stuff Cornish hens. Secure cavities with wooden picks.

Measure jelly in 1-cup measure. MICROWAVE 30 SECONDS to 1 MINUTE on HIGH, or until jelly softens. Stir in sherry.

Place hens breast side down in (8 x 8-inch) baking dish. Brush with glaze. Cover with waxed paper. MICROWAVE 13 MINUTES on '6'.

Turn hens over so that breast sides are up and outside edges are reversed to inside of dish. Brush with glaze. Cover with waxed paper. MICROWAVE 13 to 15 MINUTES on '6', or until thickest part of inside thigh muscle reaches 175°. Let stand 7 minutes, tented with aluminum foil.

NOTE: Do not use meat thermometer in microwave oven.

For ovens without solid state heat control, follow above procedure, reduce setting to '5'. Use cooking times of 16 MINUTES and 16 to 18 MINUTES.

Casserole Cookery

M icrowave cooking produces superior casseroles. Vegetables cook tender while retaining character, color and crispness. Precooked meats taste fresh cooked. Many casseroles can be made ahead and reheated, or divided into single portions for split-shift dining.

When a recipe makes more servings than you need, freeze single portions in boil-in-bags for a variety of homemade frozen entrees.

Oven Stew. Recipe on following page.

CASSEROLE BASICS

Casseroles may require occasional stirring to distribute heat. They cook more evenly when made with ingredients of similar size and shape. Because of their shorter cooking time, casseroles cooked in the microwave oven generally need less liquid. Casseroles with cream and cheese sauces, or meats which need slower cooking to tenderize, do best on lower heat control settings.

A number of these casserole recipes call for leftover meats, because leftovers remain flavorful and fresh tasting when reheated in the microwave oven. Any casserole leftovers can be frozen in individual servings.

When cooking a favorite casserole, make two and freeze the second for future use. Line a casserole or baking dish with plastic wrap. Transfer the cooked food to the lined container and freeze. As soon as the food is frozen in the shape of the dish, remove it and wrap with freezer paper. Later it can be unwrapped and returned to the container for defrosting and heating. See the chart for reheating frozen casseroles at the end of the Convenience Food Guide.

OVEN STEW

4 to 6 servings
3-quart casserole

2 *pounds beef bottom round steak cut in ¾-inch cubes*
½ *cup flour*
2 *cups carrots, cut in ½-inch slices*
6 *to 8 small onions*
2 *medium boiling potatoes, quartered*
2 *bay leaves*
½ *teaspoon marjoram*
1 *teaspoon salt*
¼ *teaspoon pepper*
1 *can (10½-ounces) condensed tomato soup, undiluted*
1 *can (10¼-ounces) consomme, undiluted*
1½ *cups water*
1 *package (10-ounces) frozen peas*

Coat beef cubes with flour. Combine beef, carrots, onions, potatoes, bay leaves, marjoram, salt and pepper in 3-quart casserole. Stir in soups and water until well mixed. Cover. MICROWAVE 5 MINUTES on HIGH. Stir.

Reduce setting. MICROWAVE 50 to 60 MINUTES ON '6', or until meat and vegetables are tender, stirring 2 or 3 times. Add peas during last 10 minutes of cooking.

Let stand 10 minutes, covered. Remove bay leaves. Serve over biscuits, if desired.

For ovens without solid state heat control, MICROWAVE 60 to 73 minutes on '5.'

GOULASH

8 servings
4-quart casserole

2 *tablespoons salad oil*
2 *chopped onions*
1 *clove garlic, pressed or finely chopped*
1 *teaspoon paprika*
2 *pounds beef stew meat, cut in ¾-inch cubes*
4 *medium boiling potatoes, peeled and cut in small cubes*
4 *medium tomatoes, peeled and chopped, or 1 can (14-ounces) stewed tomatoes*
1 *green pepper, chopped*
½ *teaspoon caraway seeds*
4 *cups beef broth, or ¼ cup instant beef bouillon dissolved in 4 cups hot water*
Salt and pepper
Dairy sour cream

Combine oil, onion and garlic in 4-quart casserole. MICROWAVE 2 to 3 MINUTES on HIGH, or until onion is transparent. Stir in paprika.

Add beef, potatoes, tomatoes, green pepper, caraway seeds and beef broth. Cover. MICROWAVE 5 MINUTES on HIGH.

Reduce setting. MICROWAVE 45 to 60 MINUTES on '6', or until meat is fork tender, stirring once. Season with salt and pepper. Let stand 5 minutes, covered.

Serve in bowls with sour cream spooned on top.

For ovens without solid state heat control, during second cooking period, MICROWAVE 55 to 75 MINUTES on '5'.

EASY BEEF STEW SUPREME

6 to 8 servings
4-quart casserole

2 *pounds beef round steak, cut in ½-inch cubes*
1 *bottle (8-ounces) Italian dressing*
2 *medium onions, quartered*
4 *potatoes, quartered*
4 *carrots, quartered*
2 *cans (10½-ounces each) condensed tomato soup, undiluted*
4 *bay leaves*
½ *teaspoon salt*
⅛ *teaspoon pepper*

Marinate beef overnight in Italian dressing. Drain meat. Combine with onions, potatoes and carrots in 4-quart casserole. Cover with soup. Add bay leaves, salt and pepper. Cover. MICROWAVE 60 MINUTES on '6', or until meat and vegetables are tender, stirring twice. Remove bay leaves before serving.

For ovens without solid state heat control, MICROWAVE 72 MINUTES on '5'.

FIJI BEEF CHUNKS

4 to 6 servings
2-quart casserole

2 pounds beef round steak, cut in ¾-inch cubes
1 clove garlic, finely chopped
¼ cup wine vinegar
1 can (10½-ounces) beef broth
½ cup sliced celery
1 small green pepper, chopped
1 large onion, sliced
2 large tomatoes, cut in wedges
1 can (13½-ounces) pineapple chunks, with juice
3 tablespoons firmly packed brown sugar
2 tablespoons cornstarch
1 tablespoon soy sauce
1 teaspoon paprika
¼ cup water

Sprinkle beef cubes with chopped garlic and 2 tablespoons of the vinegar. Pour beef broth over meat. Cover. MICROWAVE 8 MINUTES on HIGH, stirring after 5 minutes.

Add celery, green pepper and onion. Cover. MICROWAVE 20 MINUTES on '6'. Stir in tomatoes and pineapple chunks. Blend brown sugar, corn starch, soy sauce, paprika, water and remaining vinegar. Stir into sauce. MICROWAVE 4 to 6 MINUTES on '6', or until sauce has thickened and meat is fork tender.

For ovens without solid state heat control, MICROWAVE 24 MINUTES and 5 to 7 MINUTES on '5'.

LAZY BEEF CASSEROLE

3 to 4 servings
2-quart casserole

¼ cup flour
1 pound beef top round steak, cut in ½ to ¾-inch cubes
1 can (10½-ounces) condensed beef bouillon, diluted with water to make 2 cups
1 can (6-ounces) tomato paste
1 small onion, thinly sliced
¾ teaspoon salt
⅛ teaspoon pepper

Measure flour into paper bag. Add meat cubes and shake to coat thoroughly.

Combine meat, bouillon, tomato paste, onion, salt and pepper in 2-quart casserole. Stir until tomato paste is mixed with broth. Cover. MICROWAVE 5 MINUTES on HIGH.

Reduce setting. MICROWAVE 25 MINUTES on '6', or until meat is fork tender, stirring after 15 minutes.

For ovens without solid state heat control, during second cooking period, MICROWAVE 30 MINUTES on '5', stirring after 15 minutes.

ROAST BEEF STEW

4 to 5 servings
2-quart casserole

2 cups diced roast beef
1 cup chopped onion
1 cup thinly sliced carrots
1 cup diced potatoes
1 package (¾-ounce) brown gravy mix
½ teaspoon salt
½ teaspoon celery salt
2 teaspoons instant beef bouillon dissolved in 1½ cups hot water
1 bay leaf

Combine all ingredients in 2-quart casserole. Cover. MICROWAVE 20 MINUTES on HIGH, or until vegetables are tender crisp, stirring twice. Remove bay leaf.

SAUCY BEEF HASH

4 to 5 servings
1½-quart casserole

2 cups cooked rice
2 cups diced cooked beef
1 small onion, chopped
½ cup snipped parsley
1 can (10½-ounces) condensed cream of tomato soup, undiluted
2 teaspoons Worcestershire sauce
⅛ teaspoon pepper
4 to 5 thin slices cheddar cheese

Combine rice, beef, onion, parsley, soup, Worcestershire sauce and pepper in 1½-quart casserole. Cover. MICROWAVE 8 to 10 MINUTES on HIGH, or until hot and bubbly. Let stand 3 minutes, covered. When serving, top each serving with thin slice of cheese. Serve with dinner rolls and Whipped Herb Butter.

WHIPPED HERB BUTTER

1-cup measure

½ cup butter or margarine
1 teaspoon parsley flakes

Place butter in 1-cup measure. MICROWAVE 1 MINUTE to 1 MINUTE, 30 SECONDS on '2', or until soft. Whip in parsley flakes. Keeps well in refrigerator, covered.

For ovens without variable heat control, MICROWAVE 20 to 30 SECONDS on '5', watching carefully.

111

All In One Beef Dinner

COOKED-BEEF STROGANOFF

4 to 6 servings
2-quart casserole

3 tablespoons butter or margarine
1 clove garlic, pressed or chopped
1 onion, finely chopped
1 green pepper, cut in thin strips
4 ounces mushrooms, sliced
1 tablespoon tomato paste
2 tablespoons flour
1½ to 2 cups julienned cooked beef
½ cup beef stock, or 1 teaspoon beef bouillon
   dissolved in 1 to 2 cups boiling water
½ cup dry red wine (or 1 cup beef stock)
½ teaspoon paprika
Salt and pepper to taste
1 carton (8-ounces) dairy sour cream

Combine butter, garlic, onion, green pepper and mushrooms in 2-quart casserole dish. MICROWAVE 3 MINUTES on HIGH, or until onion is transparent.

Stir in tomato paste. Sprinkle flour over contents of dish. Blend until smooth. Add beef, toss. Add beef stock and wine gradually, stirring until mixture is smooth. MICROWAVE 3 MINUTES on HIGH, or until mixture thickens, stirring after 1 minute, 30 seconds.

Add paprika, salt and pepper. Stir in sour cream. MICROWAVE 1 MINUTE on HIGH. Serve with buttered noodles.

ALL IN ONE BEEF DINNER

4 servings
2-quart casserole

1½ to 2 cups cut up, cooked roast beef
1 large onion, thinly sliced
2 cups frozen cut green beans, defrosted
1 can (6-ounces) tomato paste
1 package (¾-ounce) brown gravy mix
1 cup hot water
2½ cups mashed potatoes
Paprika

Combine roast beef, onion, green beans, tomato paste, gravy mix and water in 2-quart casserole. Cover. MICROWAVE 6 to 8 MINUTES on HIGH, or until mixture is bubbly.

Spoon mounds of mashed potatoes on top of dish, or pipe with pastry tube. Sprinkle with paprika. MICROWAVE 4 to 6 MINUTES on '8', or until potatoes are heated through and well set.

For ovens without solid state heat control, when heating mashed potatoes, MICROWAVE 3 TO 5 MINUTES on HIGH.

NOTE: Any leftover vegetables or gravy can be added to this dish.

CHILI ✤

4 to 5 servings
2-quart casserole

1 *pound ground beef*
½ *cup chopped onion*
1 *can (16-ounces) stewed tomatoes*
1 *can (8-ounces) tomato sauce*
1 *can (15¼-ounces) kidney beans, drained*
1 *small green pepper, chopped*
1½ *teaspoons parsley flakes*
1 *teaspoon salt*
¼ *teaspoon dried oregano*
¼ *teaspoon chili powder*
⅛ *teaspoon pepper*

Crumble ground beef into 2-quart bowl. Add onion. MICROWAVE 4 to 5 MINUTES on HIGH, or until meat is no longer pink, stirring once. Drain fat.

Add remaining ingredients. Mix well. Cover with waxed paper or paper towel. MICROWAVE 10 MINUTES on '8', or until hot, stirring once.

NOTE: Recipe can be doubled easily, using a 4-quart bowl. First cooking period MICROWAVE 10 to 12 MINUTES on HIGH. Second cooking period MICROWAVE 15 MINUTES on HIGH, stirring twice.

For ovens without solid state heat control, during second cooking period MICROWAVE 8 MINUTES on HIGH, stirring twice.

NOODLES BOLOGNESE

6 to 8 servings
2-quart casserole
3-quart casserole

3 *cups noodles, cooked and drained*
1½ *pounds lean ground beef*
5 *green onions, including tops, chopped*
1 *can (8-ounces) tomato sauce*
1 *teaspoon salt*
¼ *teaspoon garlic salt*
Pepper to taste
1 *cup dairy sour cream*
1 *cup small curd cottage cheese*
1 *cup grated cheddar or finely diced American process cheese*

Crumble beef into 2-quart casserole. Mix in onion. MICROWAVE 5 MINUTES on HIGH.

Add tomato sauce, salts and pepper. MICROWAVE 2 MINUTES on HIGH.

Combine noodles, sour cream and cottage cheese. Layer one third noodle mixture and one third sauce in 3-quart casserole. Repeat layers. Cover. MICROWAVE 12 MINUTES on '8'.

Sprinkle with cheese. Let stand 3 minutes, or until cheese melts. Garnish with parsley sprigs.

For ovens without solid state heat control, after layering noodles and sauce, MICROWAVE 9 to 10 MINUTES on HIGH, rotating dish ½ turn after 5 minutes.

LASAGNE FOR 4 ✤

4 servings
2-quart bowl
10 x 8-inch utility dish

½ *pound lean ground beef*
1 *can (16-ounces) tomatoes*
1 *can (8-ounces) tomato sauce*
¼ *cup chopped onion*
1 *tablespoon olive oil*
1 *clove garlic, pressed or finely chopped*
¾ *teaspoon salt*
⅛ *teaspoon pepper*
½ *teaspoon oregano*
2 *tablespoons snipped parsley*
¼ *pound lasagne noodles, cooked and drained*
8-*ounces thinly sliced mozzarella cheese*
8-*ounces ricotta or cottage cheese*
¼ *cup parmesan cheese*

Combine ground beef, tomatoes, tomato sauce, onion, oil, garlic, salt, pepper, oregano and parsley in 2-quart bowl. MICROWAVE 20 MINUTES on HIGH, or until sauce thickens, stirring after 10 minutes.

Layer ⅓ each of noodles, meat sauce, mozzarella and ricotta in (10 x 8-inch) utility dish. Sprinkle with parmesan cheese. MICROWAVE 8 to 10 MINUTES on HIGH, or until cheese melts and center is hot.

ONE DISH SPAGHETTI ✤

4 to 6 servings
2-quart casserole

1 *tablespoon butter or margarine*
1 *large onion, sliced*
1 *clove garlic, pressed or finely chopped*
1 *pound lean ground beef*
1 *teaspoon parsley flakes*
½ *teaspoon salt*
¼ *teaspoon pepper*
½ *teaspoon oregano*
2 *cans (8-ounces each) tomato sauce*
1½ *cups water*
¼ *pound uncooked spaghetti*
Grated parmesan cheese

Combine butter, onion and garlic in 2-quart casserole. MICROWAVE 2 to 3 MINUTES on HIGH, or until onion is transparent.

Crumble ground beef into casserole. MICROWAVE 3 MINUTES, 30 SECONDS to 4 MINUTES, 30 SECONDS on HIGH, or until beef loses its pink color.

Add parsley flakes, salt, pepper and oregano. Stir in tomato sauce and water. Cover. MICROWAVE 4 MINUTES on HIGH.

Break spaghetti in half. Mix into sauce. Cover. MICROWAVE 10 to 12 MINUTES on HIGH, or until spaghetti is tender, stirring twice. Let stand 5 to 10 minutes, covered. Serve with grated parmesan cheese.

JOHNNY MARZETTI

6 servings
3-quart casserole

1 *package (10-ounces) wide egg noodles, cooked and drained*
1 *pound lean ground beef*
½ *cup chopped onion*
¼ *cup chopped green pepper*
1 *jar (2½-ounces) mushroom stems and pieces, drained*
1 *clove garlic, pressed or chopped*
⅛ *teaspoon pepper*
1 *can (10¾-ounces) condensed cream of mushroom soup, undiluted*
1 *can (8-ounces) tomato sauce*
1 *cup finely diced American process cheese*

Crumble ground beef into 3-quart casserole. Add onion, green pepper, mushrooms, garlic and pepper. MICRO-WAVE 5 MINUTES on HIGH, or until meat is set and onion transparent.

Add cooked noodles and mushroom soup. Mix well. Pour tomato sauce over mixture. Sprinkle with cheese. Cover. MICROWAVE 5 MINUTES on HIGH, or until cheese is melted and bubbly. Let stand 3 minutes. Garnish with parsley, if desired.

SATURDAY SPECIAL

6 servings
2-quart casserole

1 *pound lean ground beef*
½ *cup chopped onion*
1 *cup dairy sour cream*
1 *can (10¾-ounces) condensed cream of mushroom soup, undiluted*
1 *can (16-ounces) whole kernel corn, drained*
1 *jar (2-ounces) chopped pimiento*
1 *teaspoon salt*
⅛ *teaspoon pepper*
1 *large tomato, thinly sliced*

Crumble ground beef into 2-quart casserole. Add onion. MICROWAVE 5 MINUTES on HIGH until beef is set and onion is transparent.

Add sour cream, soup, corn, pimiento, salt and pepper. Cover with waxed paper. MICROWAVE 5 MINUTES on HIGH.

Top with tomato slices. MICROWAVE 3 MINUTES on HIGH, or until tomatoes are slightly softened. Garnish with canned French fried onion rings, if desired. Let stand 3 minutes, uncovered.

TOP THE 'TATERS DINNER

4 servings
1½-quart casserole

1 *pound lean ground beef*
2 *tablespoons chopped onion*
1 *can (10¾-ounces) condensed tomato soup, undiluted*
1 *can (15½-ounces) French-cut green beans with juice*
Instant mashed potatoes, prepared for 4

Crumble ground beef into 1½-quart casserole. Mix in onions. MICROWAVE 3 to 4 MINUTES on HIGH, or until meat is no longer pink.

Stir in soup and beans. MICROWAVE 5 to 6 MINUTES on HIGH, or until hot and bubbly.

Serve over mashed potatoes.

GARBANZO CASSEROLE

6 to 8 servings
2½-quart casserole

1 *pound lean ground beef*
1 *large onion, chopped*
1 *can (15-ounces) garbanzo beans, drained*
1 *can (15-ounces) chili without beans*
1 *can (16-ounces) corn, drained*
½ *cup sharp cheddar cheese, cubed*

Crumble ground beef in 2½-quart casserole. Add onion. MICROWAVE 4 to 5 MINUTES on HIGH, or until meat is no longer pink. Drain excess fat.

Mix in beans, chili and corn. Carefully stir in cheese cubes. Cover. MICROWAVE 10 to 12 MINUTES on '8', or until mixture is heated through and cheese cubes have started to melt. Let stand 10 minutes, covered.

For ovens without solid state heat control, during second cooking period MICROWAVE 8 to 10 MINUTES on HIGH, rotating dish ½ turn after 4 minutes.

GROUND BEEF "ADD MEAT" DINNER

4 servings
Browning dish
3-quart casserole

1 *tablespoon salad oil*
1 *pound ground beef*
1 *package (7-ounces) "add meat" dinner mix for hamburger*

To preheat browning dish, MICROWAVE 4 MINUTES on HIGH. Add oil. Crumble beef into browner. MICRO-WAVE 3 to 5 MINUTES on HIGH, or until meat loses its pink color.

Remove meat from browner to 3-quart casserole. Add mix and hot tap water as directed on package. Cover. MICRO-WAVE 20 to 22 MINUTES on HIGH. Stir well. Let stand 5 minutes, covered.

QUICK BEEF CHIP CASSEROLE

3 to 4 servings
1-quart mixing bowl
2-quart casserole

1 *pound lean ground beef*
1 *large onion, chopped*
2 *cups corn chips*
1 *can (15-ounces) chili with beans*
1 *can (8-ounces) tomato sauce*
¼ *cup grated cheddar cheese*

Crumble meat into 1-quart mixing bowl. Add onion. MICROWAVE 4 MINUTES on HIGH, or until meat is set.

In 2-quart casserole, layer half the corn chips, half the meat, half the chili and half the tomato sauce. Repeat layers. Cover. MICROWAVE 6 MINUTES on HIGH. Sprinkle grated cheese on top. MICROWAVE 30 SECONDS on HIGH, or until cheese melts.

MOM'S TATER TOT HOT DISH 🔲

4 to 6 servings
10 x 8-inch utility dish

1 *pound lean ground beef*
1 *envelope dry onion soup mix*
1 *can (10½-ounces) condensed cream of chicken soup, undiluted*
1 *package (10-ounces) Tater Tots*

Lightly spread ground beef in bottom of (10 x 8-inch) utility dish. Sprinkle soup mix on top. Mask with soup. Top with Tater Tots. MICROWAVE 10 to 11 MINUTES on HIGH, or until soup is bubbly and ground beef firm. Let stand 3 to 5 minutes.

COUNTRY PIE

6 servings
10-inch pie plate

2 *cans (8-ounces each) tomato sauce*
½ *cup soft bread crumbs*
1 *small green pepper, chopped*
1 *medium onion, chopped*
1 *pound lean ground beef*
1⅓ *cups instant rice*
1 *cup water*
1 *cup grated cheddar cheese*
1 *teaspoon salt*
⅛ *teaspoon oregano*
⅛ *teaspoon pepper*

Combine ½ can tomato sauce, bread crumbs, green pepper, onion and ground beef in medium mixing bowl. Mix well. Pat mixture onto bottom and sides of 10-inch pie plate.

Combine rice, water, ¼ cup cheese, remaining tomato

sauce, salt, oregano and pepper. Spoon into pie plate. Cover with plastic wrap. MICROWAVE 20 to 25 MINUTES on '8', or until rice is fluffed and tender.

Sprinkle with remaining cheese. MICROWAVE 3 to 4 MINUTES on '8', or until cheese is melted. Cut into wedges to serve.

For ovens without solid state heat control, MICROWAVE 16 to 20 MINUTES on HIGH and 2 to 3 MINUTES on HIGH.

ITALIAN LIVER BAKE

6 servings
3-quart casserole

1 *package (7-ounces) macaroni, cooked and drained*
1 *pound liver, cut in ¾-inch pieces*
1 *onion, chopped*
1 *green pepper, chopped*
¾ *to 1 cup chopped fresh mushrooms*
1 *can (16-ounces) tomatoes*
1 *clove garlic, finely chopped*
1 *teaspoon salt*
⅛ *teaspoon pepper*
1 *cup grated cheddar cheese*

Combine all ingredients, except grated cheese, in 3-quart casserole. Cover. MICROWAVE 9 to 10 MINUTES on HIGH, or until mixture is hot and green pepper tender crisp.

Sprinkle with grated cheese. Cover. Let stand 3 to 5 minutes.

DRIED BEEF BAKE

6 to 8 servings
3-quart casserole

2 *cups macaroni, uncooked*
4 *cups hot water*
1 *teaspoon salad oil*
¼ *pound dried beef*
½ *pound colby cheese, cubed*
1 *small onion, chopped*
4 *hard cooked eggs, chopped*
1 *can (10¾-ounces) condensed cream of mushroom soup, undiluted*
1 *can (10½-ounces) condensed cream of chicken soup*
2 *cups milk*

Combine macaroni, water and oil in 3-quart casserole. MICROWAVE 10 to 12 MINUTES on HIGH, or until macaroni is beginning to soften. Drain.

Add dried beef, cheese, onion, eggs, soups and milk. Mix together carefully. Cover. MICROWAVE 10 MINUTES on HIGH, or until mixture is bubbly and noodles fully cooked, stirring twice.

SAUSAGE NOODLE CASSEROLE

4 servings
1½-quart casserole

1 pound pork sausage roll, cut into ½-inch chunks
1 large onion, sliced
1 small green pepper, diced
½ cup diced celery
1 package (1½-ounces) dry chicken noodle soup mix
1 can (10¾-ounces) condensed cream of mushroom
    soup, undiluted
1 cup cooked rice
½ cup water

Combine sausage and onions in 1½-quart casserole. Cover. MICROWAVE 4 to 5 MINUTES on HIGH, or until sausage is set. Drain fat.

Add green pepper, celery, soup mix, soup, rice and water. Cover. MICROWAVE 6 to 8 MINUTES on HIGH, or until bubbly.

WEENIE-MAC

4 to 6 servings
3-quart casserole

1 jar (8-ounces) process cheese spread
1 package (6-ounces) elbow macaroni, cooked and
    drained
1 pound wieners, cut in ½-inch pieces
½ cup chopped green onions, including green tops
1 tablespoon prepared mustard

Remove lid from jar of process cheese spread. MICRO-WAVE on HIGH, until cheese melts.

Combine all ingredients in 3-quart casserole. MICRO-WAVE 4 MINUTES on HIGH, or until bubbly.

NOTE: An excellent dish for children to cook as well as eat.

LEFTOVER HAM CASSEROLE ▣

6 servings
2-quart casserole

1 package (7-ounces) macaroni, cooked and drained
½ cup milk
1 can (10¾-ounces) condensed cream of mushroom
    soup, undiluted
1 cup dairy sour cream
2 teaspoons prepared mustard
1 green onion, including top, chopped
⅛ teaspoon pepper
2 cups diced, cooked ham
¼ cup slivered almonds

Combine all ingredients except almonds in 2-quart casserole. MICROWAVE 5 MINUTES on HIGH. Stir.

Top with almonds. MICROWAVE 4 to 5 MINUTES on HIGH, or until bubbly. Let stand 3 to 5 minutes.

HAWAIIAN SWEET SOUR HAM ▣

4 to 6 servings
1½-quart casserole

2 cups cubed, cooked ham
2 tablespoons firmly packed brown sugar
1½ tablespoons corn starch
1 cup pineapple tidbits
2 teaspoons prepared mustard
3 to 4 teaspoons vinegar
¾ cup water
½ teaspoon salt
2 cups hot, cooked rice

Place ham in 1½-quart casserole. Combine sugar and corn starch in 1-quart measure. Drain juice from pineapple tidbits into sugar mixture. Stir in mustard, vinegar and water. Pour over ham. MICROWAVE 4 to 6 MINUTES on HIGH, or until sauce is thickened.

Stir in pineapple. MICROWAVE 1 MINUTE on HIGH. Stir in salt. Serve over cooked rice.

HEAVENLY HAM LOAF

4 to 6 servings
9 x 5-inch glass loaf dish

2 eggs
¾ pound lean ground ham
½ pound lean ground veal
¼ pound lean ground pork
¾ cup bread crumbs
¾ cup milk
2 tablespoons finely chopped onion
¼ teaspoon pepper
¼ cup firmly packed brown sugar
1 tablespoon prepared mustard
⅓ cup pineapple juice

Break eggs into large mixing bowl. Beat lightly with fork. Add ham, veal and pork. Mix to combine meats. Add bread crumbs, milk, onion and pepper. Mix thoroughly. Spread in (9 x 5-inch) loaf dish.

Mix sugar and mustard together. Spread on top of loaf. Pour pineapple juice over all. Cover with waxed paper. MICROWAVE 5 MINUTES on HIGH.

Reduce setting. MICROWAVE 15 MINUTES on '6', until firm, or meat thermometer registers 160°. Let stand 5 minutes uncovered. Garnish with parsley, if desired.

NOTE: Do not use meat thermometer in oven while cooking.

For ovens without solid state heat control, during second cooking period, MICROWAVE 18 MINUTES on '5'.

ASPARAGUS HAM BIRDS

4 servings
1-quart measure
Shallow dish

12 *spears fresh or frozen asparagus, cooked and*
  drained, (page 146)
2 *tablespoons butter or margarine*
2 *tablespoons flour*
½ *teaspoon salt*
½ *teaspoon dry mustard*
1 *cup milk*
2 *egg yolks, slightly beaten*
4 *slices leftover or boiled ham*
½ *cup grated sharp cheddar cheese*

Place butter in 1-quart measure. MICROWAVE on HIGH
until butter melts. Stir in flour, salt and mustard to make a
smooth paste. Gradually stir in milk. MICROWAVE 2
MINUTES, 30 SECONDS to 3 MINUTES on HIGH, or
until thickened, stirring once with a wire whip.

Stir a little of the hot mixture into egg yolks. Blend
warmed yolks into hot sauce.

Wrap each slice of ham around three asparagus spears,
secure with wooden pick. Arrange roll ups in shallow
dish. Pour white sauce over them. MICROWAVE 4 to 5
MINUTES on '5', or until heated through. Sprinkle with
cheese. MICROWAVE 20 SECONDS on '5', or until
cheese melts.

Serve on buttered toast triangles, if desired.

Asparagus Ham Birds.

CONFETTI CASSEROLE

4 to 6 servings
12 x 8-inch baking dish

1 *tablespoon butter or margarine*
1 *large onion, chopped*
½ *green pepper, chopped*
1½ *cups cubed, cooked ham*
1 *can (10¾-ounces) condensed cream of mushroom*
  soup, undiluted
1 *can (4-ounces) sliced mushrooms, drained*
1 *can (2-ounces) chopped pimiento, drained*
8 *pitted black olives, quartered*
⅓ *cup broken cashews*
2 *cans (15-ounces each) macaroni and cheese*

Combine butter, onion and pepper in (12 x 8-inch) baking
dish. MICROWAVE 3 MINUTES on HIGH, or until
onion is transparent.

Mix in ham, soup, mushrooms, pimiento, olives, cashews
and macaroni and cheese. Cover with plastic wrap.
MICROWAVE 10 to 12 MINUTES on HIGH, or until hot
and bubbly.

HAM 'N OYSTER CASSEROLE

4 to 5 servings
1½-quart casserole

2 *tablespoons butter or margarine*
1 *medium onion, chopped*
2 *tablespoons flour*
¼ *cup milk*
1 *can (10¼-ounces) condensed oyster stew, undiluted*
Dash hot pepper sauce
1 *cup chopped, cooked ham*
2 *cups cooked noodles, drained*
1 *tomato, sliced*
Grated parmesan cheese

Combine butter and onion in 1½-quart casserole. MICRO-
WAVE 2 to 3 MINUTES on HIGH, or until onion is trans-
parent. Mix in flour to make a smooth paste. Stir in milk,
oyster stew and hot pepper sauce. Do not cover. MICRO-
WAVE 4 to 6 MINUTES on HIGH, or until thickened.
Stir well.

Carefully mix in ham and noodles. Cover. MICRO-
WAVE 8 to 10 MINUTES on HIGH, or until heated
through.

Arrange tomato slices on top of noodle mixture. Sprinkle
with cheese. Cover. MICROWAVE 1 to 2 MINUTES on
HIGH, or until tomato slices are warm. Let stand 3
minutes, covered.

BOLOGNA CHEESE BAKE

4 to 5 servings
1½-quart casserole

1 to 1½ cup diced raw potatoes
½ pound bologna, diced
3 tablespoons minced green pepper
1 tablespoon minced onion
1 can (10¾-ounces) condensed cream of celery soup,
   undiluted
1 cup grated sharp cheddar cheese

Combine potatoes, bologna, green pepper, onion and soup in 1½-quart casserole. Cover. MICROWAVE 15 MINUTES on HIGH, or until potatoes are tender. Top with grated cheese. Let stand, uncovered, until cheese is just melting.

SCALLOPED BOLOGNA BAKE

4 to 6 servings
2-quart casserole

1 package (5½-ounces) scalloped potato mix
1 ring (1-pound) coarse ground bologna, skinned and
   cut in ¾-inch slices

Use ¼ cup less water than amount recommended in mix. Pour water over potatoes in 2-quart casserole. Let stand 20 minutes.

Add bologna slices, sauce mix and milk, omit butter or margarine. Cover. MICROWAVE 10 to 15 MINUTES on '6', or until potatoes are tender.

For ovens without solid state heat control, MICROWAVE 12 to 17 MINUTES on '5'.

Scalloped Bologna Bake

PORK AND BEAN CASSEROLE

4 servings
2-quart casserole

1 *pound lean ground beef*
1 *small onion, chopped*
1 *can (16-ounces) pork and beans*
1 *can (8-ounces) tomato sauce*
2 *tablespoons prepared mustard*
2 *teaspoons Worcestershire sauce*
½ *teaspoon salt*
¼ *teaspoon pepper*

Crumble ground beef into 2-quart casserole. Add onion, MICROWAVE 4 to 5 MINUTES on HIGH, or until meat loses its pink color.

Stir in pork and beans, tomato sauce, mustard, Worcestershire sauce, salt and pepper. Cover. MICROWAVE 8 to 10 MINUTES on '8', or until hot.

For ovens without solid state heat control, during second cooking period MICROWAVE 6 to 8 MINUTES on HIGH, stirring once.

COOKED PORK AND SAUERKRAUT

6 servings
2-quart casserole or baking dish

2 *tablespoons butter or margarine or bacon drippings*
3 *cups sauerkraut, drained*
6 *slices cooked pork roast, cut ¼-inch thick*
¼ *teaspoon salt*
Pepper
½ *cup water*

Place butter or bacon drippings in 2-quart casserole. MICROWAVE on HIGH until melted. Stir in sauerkraut and spread evenly.

Arrange pork slices on sauerkraut. Season with salt and pepper. Pour water over all. MICROWAVE 8 MINUTES on HIGH, or until hot. Let stand 3 minutes covered.

ORIENTAL HASH

6 servings
Browning dish

2 *tablespoons salad oil*
1½ *cups cubed pork, cooked*
2 *cups rice, cooked*
3 *tablespoons soy sauce*
Dash garlic powder
2 *eggs, well beaten*
2 *cups shredded lettuce*

Place empty browning dish in oven. MICROWAVE 4 to 5 MINUTES on HIGH. Add oil and cooked pork. MICROWAVE 2 to 3 MINUTES on HIGH, or until lightly browned, stirring once.

Mix in rice, soy sauce and garlic powder. Cover. MICROWAVE 3 to 4 MINUTES on HIGH, or until steaming. Stir in beaten eggs. MICROWAVE 1 MINUTE on HIGH, or until eggs are set.

Add shredded lettuce and toss to combine. Serve immediately.

CHOW MEIN

4 servings
2-quart casserole

1 *pound chow mein meat (½ pork, ½ veal)*
2 *cups diagonally sliced celery (½-inch slices)*
1 *medium onion, sliced*
1 *can (4-ounces) mushroom stems and pieces, drained*
3 *tablespoons corn starch*
3 *tablespoons soy sauce*
1 *can (16-ounces) chow mein vegetables, rinsed and drained*
1 *can (8½-ounces) water chestnuts, drained and sliced*
1 *cup water*
½ *teaspoon ginger*

Combine chow mein meat, celery, onion and mushrooms in 2-quart casserole. Cover. MICROWAVE 4 to 6 MINUTES on HIGH, or until meat loses its pink color.

Dissolve corn starch in soy sauce. Stir into meat mixture. Mix in chow mein vegetables, water chestnuts, water and ginger. Cover. MICROWAVE 4 to 6 MINUTES on HIGH, or until vegetables are tender crisp.

ORIENTAL FRANKFURTERS

4 servings
1½-quart casserole

2 *tablespoons butter or margarine*
1 *pound wieners, sliced diagonally*
1 *small onion, chopped*
½ *green pepper, cut in strips*
¼ *cup raisins*
¼ *cup firmly packed brown sugar*
¾ *cup water*
2 *tablespoons corn starch dissolved in ¼ cup water*
¼ *cup cider vinegar*
1 *package (10-ounces) frozen green beans, cooked and drained (page 147)*
1 *can (13-ounces) chow mein noodles*

Combine butter, wieners, onion, green pepper, raisins, brown sugar and water. Stir in corn starch mixture. Cover. MICROWAVE 6 to 8 MINUTES on HIGH, or until mixture is bubbling and starting to thicken. Stir well.

Stir in vinegar. MICROWAVE 3 MINUTES on HIGH, or until sauce is thick and glossy. Stir in green beans. Let stand 5 minutes, covered. Serve over chow mein noodles.

SAUCY TURKEY AND RICE

4 servings
2-quart casserole
1½-quart casserole

Rice:
½ cup uncooked rice
¼ cup chopped onion
¼ cup chopped celery
¼ cup chopped green pepper
1½ cups chicken broth
¼ teaspoon seasoned salt

Turkey Sauce:
2 tablespoons butter or margarine
¼ cup flour
2 cups milk
½ teaspoon salt
Dash paprika
1 teaspoon instant chicken bouillon
2 cups cubed cooked turkey

Combine rice, onion, celery and green pepper in 2-quart casserole. Add chicken broth and salt. Cover. MICRO-WAVE 13 MINUTES on HIGH. Let stand, covered, while preparing sauce.

Place butter in 1½-quart casserole. MICROWAVE on HIGH, until melted. Stir in flour to make a smooth paste. Gradually add milk, stirring until blended. MICRO-WAVE 6 MINUTES on '8', or until thickened, stirring after 4 minutes.

Beat in salt, paprika and bouillon with a wire whip until bouillon is dissolved and sauce is smooth. Stir in turkey. Cover. MICROWAVE 5 MINUTES on '8', or until hot.

For ovens without solid state heat control, when cooking sauce, MICROWAVE 5 MINUTES on HIGH, stirring twice during second half of cooking period. Add turkey. MICROWAVE 3 to 4 MINUTES on HIGH.

BUSY DAY CASSEROLE

6 servings
2-quart casserole

1 can (10½-ounces) cream of onion soup, undiluted
1 can (10¾-ounces) chicken gumbo soup, undiluted
2½ to 3 cups large chunks cooked turkey or chicken
½ cup seasoned croutons

Combine soups in 2-quart casserole. Stir until well blended. Stir in turkey. Sprinkle with croutons. MICRO-WAVE 8 to 10 MINUTES on HIGH, or until hot.

TURKEY SPECIAL

4 to 6 servings
3-quart casserole

1 can (10¾-ounces) condensed cream of mushroom soup, undiluted
1 can (10½-ounces) condensed turkey vegetable soup, undiluted
1½ soup cans milk or water
1 cup chopped fresh spinach
1 cup chopped cooked turkey

Combine all ingredients in 3-quart casserole. Stir until well blended. Cover. MICROWAVE 7 to 8 MINUTES on HIGH, or until hot.

CHICKEN-TUNA BAKE

3 to 4 servings
2-quart casserole

2 cans (10¾-ounces) condensed cream of mushroom or chicken soup, undiluted
½ cup milk
3 cups cooked chopped chicken
1 can (6½-ounces) tuna, drained and flaked
1⅓ cups finely chopped celery
¼ cup finely chopped onion
1 can (3-ounces) chow mein noodles
⅓ cup slivered almonds, toasted if desired

Combine soup and milk in 2-quart casserole. Blend well. Stir in chicken, tuna, celery, onion and chow mein noodles. Cover. MICROWAVE 8 to 10 MINUTES on HIGH, or until hot in the center. Sprinkle with almonds. Let stand 3 minutes, covered.

CHICKEN AND WILD RICE CASSEROLE

6 to 8 servings
3-quart casserole

4 *cups diced, cooked chicken or turkey*
4 *cups cooked wild rice*
1 *medium onion, chopped*
½ *cup chopped celery*
¼ *cup chopped pimientos*
½ *cup slivered almonds*
2 *tablespoons butter or margarine*
2 *eggs, well beaten*
1 *cup chicken broth, or 1 teaspoon instant chicken*
   bouillon dissolved in 1 cup hot water
½ *cup milk*
½ *cup dry white wine*
1 *teaspoon salt*

Mix all ingredients in 3-quart casserole. Cover. MICRO-WAVE 8 to 10 MINUTES on HIGH, or until center is hot, stirring twice.

POTATO-CHEESE CASSEROLE

4 to 6 servings
8 x 8-inch baking dish
2-cup measure

4 *cups sliced cooked potatoes*
1 *tablespoon butter or margarine*
1 *small onion, finely chopped*
1 *tablespoon flour*
¼ *teaspoon salt*
Dash pepper
¼ *teaspoon dry mustard*
½ *teaspoon Worcestershire sauce*
½ *cup shredded American process cheese*
¾ *cup milk*
4 *slices American process cheese*

Arrange potato slices in (8 x 8-inch) baking dish. Set aside.

Combine butter and onion in 2-cup measure. MICRO-WAVE 3 MINUTES on HIGH, or until onion is transparent. Stir in flour, salt, pepper, mustard, Worcestershire sauce, shredded cheese and milk. MICROWAVE 3 to 4 MINUTES on HIGH, or until mixture is hot and cheese is melted. Stir.

Pour over potatoes. Top with cheese slices. MICRO-WAVE 6 to 8 MINUTES on '6', or until potatoes are heated through and cheese is melted.

For ovens without solid state heat control, MICROWAVE 7 to 9 MINUTES on '5'.

CRAB GUMBO

4 servings
2½-quart casserole

½ *cup onion, chopped*
½ *cup celery, chopped*
2 *tablespoons green pepper, finely chopped*
1 *clove garlic, pressed or minced*
2 *tablespoons butter or margarine*
1 *package (10-ounces) frozen okra, partially defrosted*
   and sliced
1 *can (14½-ounces) stewed tomatoes*
¼ *teaspoon sugar*
1 *bay leaf*
¼ *teaspoon thyme*
1 *teaspoon salt*
1 *can (6½-ounces) crab meat, drained and broken up*
   with fork
1½ *cups cooked rice*

Combine onion, celery, green pepper, garlic and butter in 2-quart casserole. MICROWAVE 3 to 4 MINUTES on HIGH, or until onion is transparent.

Add okra, tomatoes and seasonings. Cover tightly. MICROWAVE 12 MINUTES on HIGH, or until okra is tender and mixture is bubbly.

Remove bay leaf. Add crab meat. Cover and let stand 5 minutes. Serve over rice.

OYSTERS AND MACARONI AU GRATIN

6 servings
1-quart measure
1½-quart casserole

3 *tablespoons butter or margarine*
3 *tablespoons flour*
1½ *cups milk*
1 *cup macaroni, cooked and drained*
2 *cans (8-ounces) oysters, drained*
Salt and pepper
1 *cup grated cheddar cheese*

Place butter in 1-quart measure. MICROWAVE on HIGH until butter melts. Blend in flour to make a smooth paste. Gradually stir in milk. MICROWAVE 2 MINUTES, 30 SECONDS to 3 MINUTES, 30 SECONDS on HIGH, or until thickened, stirring once with wire whip.

Layer half the macaroni and half the oysters in 1½-quart casserole. Season with salt and pepper. Sprinkle with one-third of the cheese. Repeat layers. Pour sauce over and top with remaining cheese. MICROWAVE 10 MIN-UTES on '8', or until heated through. Garnish with parsley if desired.

For ovens without solid state heat control, MICROWAVE 8 MINUTES on HIGH, rotating dish ½ turn after 4 minutes.

TASTY TUNA BAKE

6 to 8 servings
2-quart casserole

1 can (3-ounces) French fried onion rings
1 package (7-ounces) macaroni, cooked and drained
2 cans (6½-ounces each) tuna, flaked and drained
1 can (13-ounces) evaporated milk
1 can (10¾-ounces) condensed cream of mushroom
   soup, undiluted
1 jar (2½-ounces) mushroom pieces and stems,
   drained
1 jar (4-ounces) chopped pimiento

Reserve ½ French fried onion rings. Combine remaining onion rings, macaroni, tuna, milk, soup, mushrooms and pimiento in 2-quart casserole. Mix well. MICROWAVE 10 MINUTES on HIGH, or until center is hot, stirring once.

Spread reserved onion rings over casserole. Let stand 3 to 5 minutes.

Variation:
Substitute 1 can (16-ounces) salmon for tuna.

TUNA CHOW MEIN

4 servings
1½-quart casserole

2 tablespoons butter or margarine
½ cup finely chopped onion
1 cup finely chopped celery
2 tablespoons finely chopped green pepper
1 can (10¾-ounces) condensed cream of mushroom
   soup, undiluted
1 can (3-ounces) chow mein noodles, ⅓ cup reserved
1 can (6½-ounces) tuna, drained and flaked
Salt and pepper to taste

Combine butter, onion, celery and green pepper in 1½-quart casserole. MICROWAVE 4 MINUTES on HIGH, or until onion is transparent.

Add soup, noodles, tuna, salt and pepper. Mix well. Cover. MICROWAVE 5 MINUTES on HIGH. Let stand 3 minutes, covered. Top with reserved chow mein noodles before serving.

ORIENTAL TUNA

6 servings
2-quart casserole

1 can (3-ounces) chow mein noodles
1 can (10¾-ounces) condensed cream of mushroom
   soup, undiluted
¼ cup water
1 can (6½-ounces) tuna, drained and flaked
1 package (4-ounces) salted cashews, chopped
½ cup finely chopped celery
¼ cup finely chopped onion
1 tablespoon soy sauce

Reserve ½ can chow mein noodles. Combine remaining noodles with soup, water, tuna, cashews, celery, onion and soy sauce. Mix well. MICROWAVE 8 to 10 MINUTES on HIGH, or until hot, stirring once. Top with reserved noodles and let stand 3 to 5 minutes.

TUNA "ADD MEAT" DINNER 🔲

4 servings
3-quart casserole

1 package (8¾-ounces) "add meat" dinner mix for
   tuna
1 can (6½-ounces) tuna

In 3-quart casserole, prepare dinner as directed on package. Cover. MICROWAVE 20 to 22 MINUTES on HIGH, stirring twice. Let stand 5 minutes, covered.

NOODLES ROMANO

4 servings
2-cup measure

1 package (8-ounces) medium noodles, cooked and
   drained (page 154)
¼ cup butter or margarine
½ cup whipping cream
1 egg yolk, slightly beaten
½ cup freshly grated romano or parmesan cheese
1 tablespoon snipped parsley

Place butter in 2-cup measure. MICROWAVE on HIGH until butter melts. Stir in cream. MICROWAVE 1 MINUTE on HIGH, or until cream is warm.

Stir a little of the cream mixture into egg yolk. Add warmed egg yolk to cream mixture, stirring with fork. Pour sauce over steaming hot noodles. Sprinkle with cheese. Toss gently to coat well. Garnish with parsley.

MUSHROOM-BARLEY CASSEROLE

6 to 8 servings
3-quart casserole

1 *can (4-ounces) mushrooms, drained*
¼ *cup butter or margarine*
1 *cup chopped onion*
1 *cup medium barley*
4 *cups chicken broth*
½ *teaspoon salt*
⅛ *teaspoon pepper*

Combine all ingredients in 3-quart casserole. Cover with waxed paper. MICROWAVE 35 MINUTES on HIGH, or until barley is tender, stirring after 15 minutes.

Let stand 3 minutes, covered with waxed paper.

Serve with chicken, duck or Cornish hens.

NOODLES ALMONDINE

6 to 8 servings
1-quart casserole
1-cup measure

1 *package (7-ounces) egg noodles, cooked and drained (page 154)*
3 *tablespoons butter or margarine*
¼ *cup slivered almonds*

Place noodles in 1-quart casserole.

Combine butter with almonds in 1-cup measure. MICROWAVE 5 MINUTES on HIGH, or until almonds are golden, stirring once.

Pour over noodles. MICROWAVE 3 MINUTES on HIGH, or until butter is bubbly and noodles are hot.

MACARONI AND CHEESE DINNER MIX

3 to 4 servings
3-quart casserole

2 *cups water*
1 *teaspoon salt*
1 *tablespoon oil*
1 *package (7½-ounces) macaroni and cheese mix*

Combine water, salt, oil and macaroni in 3-quart casserole. Cover. MICROWAVE 18 to 20 MINUTES on HIGH, or until tender, stirring twice.

Stir in cheese mixture thoroughly. Let stand 5 minutes, covered.

SPEEDY MACARONI AND CHEESE

4 servings
1½-quart casserole

1 *cup finely diced American process cheese*
1 *cup white sauce, (page 157)*
1 *cup macaroni, cooked*

Stir cheese into hot white sauce until melted. Combine cheese sauce and cooked macaroni in 1½-quart casserole. Toss lightly to mix. Cover. MICROWAVE 5 MINUTES on '8', until bubbly, stirring after 3 minutes. Let stand 3 minutes, covered. Garnish with parsley, if desired.

For ovens without solid state heat control, MICROWAVE 4 MINUTES on HIGH, stirring after 2 minutes.

Variation:
Substitute 1 jar (16-ounces) process cheese spread for cheese sauce.

Add one of the following:
½ *cup ham cubes*
½ *cup tuna, drained*
1 *cup wieners, cut into ¼-inch slices*
¼ *cup onion*

Speedy Macaroni and Cheese

Eggs & Cheese

High and handsome cheese souffles, creamy quiches, puffy omelets are just a few of the egg and cheese dishes you can prepare in heat control microwave ovens. Eggs scrambled by microwave are not only faster and easier, they're better. You get greater volume, fluffier eggs and no crusty pan to clean. Cheese melts rapidly, making it an attractive finish for casseroles and sandwiches.

CHEESE SOUFFLE

6 servings
1½-quart casserole
2-quart souffle dish

¼ cup all-purpose flour
¾ teaspoon salt
½ teaspoon dry mustard
⅛ teaspoon paprika
1⅔ cup evaporated milk, undiluted

¼ teaspoon hot pepper sauce
5 ounces sharp cheddar cheese, grated
6 eggs, separated
1 teaspoon cream of tartar

Blend flour, salt, mustard and paprika in 1½-quart casserole. Add evaporated milk and pepper sauce. Stir. MICROWAVE 3 to 4 MINUTES on HIGH, or until thickened, stirring after 2 minutes, then every 30 seconds.

Add cheese. Stir until melted. If necessary, MICROWAVE 1 to 2 MINUTES on HIGH until cheese melts, stirring every minute.

Beat egg whites with cream of tartar until stiff but not dry. Set aside. Beat egg yolks until thick and lemon colored. Slowly pour cheese mixture over beaten egg yolks, beating constantly until well combined. Spoon mixture over egg whites. Fold in gently until just blended. Turn into ungreased 2-quart souffle dish. MICROWAVE 20 to 30 MINUTES on '3', or until top is dry, rotating dish every 10 minutes. Serve immediately.

NOTE: This recipe is not suitable for ovens without variable heat control.

EGG BASICS

Eggs cook differently by microwave. The high fat content of egg yolks absorbs energy, so yolks cook faster than whites. It's easy to poach eggs in a microwave oven, but if you want soft yolks, remove eggs from the oven before whites are completely cooked. A brief standing time allows whites to set without overcooking yolks. Check eggs for doneness early, they toughen when overcooked.

When eggs and yolks are mixed together for omelets, scrambled eggs or custards, they cook evenly and need less stirring than with conventional cooking methods.

Do not try to cook eggs in the shell. Steam can build up inside the shells, causing them to burst.

POACHED EGGS

4 servings
1-quart casserole

2 *teaspoons vinegar*
1½ *cups boiling water*
4 *eggs*

Add vinegar to boiling water in 1-quart casserole. Carefully break eggs into water. Cover with waxed paper. MICROWAVE 1 MINUTE, 30 SECONDS to 2 MINUTES on '5', depending on doneness desired.

Let stand 1 to 2 minutes, or until whites coagulate, covered.

EGGS BENEDICT

4 servings
8 x 8-inch baking dish

2 *English muffins, split, toasted and buttered*
4 *slices ham, approximately 3-inches square*
4 *eggs, poached*
Mock Hollandaise Sauce, below, or Fluffy Hollandaise (page 157)

Arrange muffin halves in (8 x 8-inch) baking dish. Place ham slice on buttered side of each muffin. Top with poached egg. Spoon Hollandaise sauce over eggs. Sprinkle with paprika, if desired. MICROWAVE 1 MINUTE, 30 SECONDS to 2 MINUTES on '5', or until heated through.

MOCK HOLLANDAISE SAUCE

About 1 cup
2-cup measure

2 *tablespoons butter or margarine*
1 *cup mayonnaise or salad dressing*
2 *to 4 tablespoons lemon juice*

Place butter in 2-cup measure. MICROWAVE on HIGH until butter melts. Stir in mayonnaise and lemon juice. MICROWAVE 2 MINUTES on '6', or just until hot.

For ovens without solid state heat control, during second cooking period, MICROWAVE 2 MINUTES, 25 SECONDS on '5'.

SCRAMBLED EGGS

2 servings
1-quart casserole

1 *tablespoon butter or margarine*
4 *eggs*
¼ *cup milk*
¼ *teaspoon salt*
⅛ *teaspoon pepper*

Place butter in 1-quart casserole. MICROWAVE on HIGH until butter is melted. Add eggs, milk, salt and pepper. Beat with fork to scramble. MICROWAVE 2 MINUTES, 30 SECONDS to 3 MINUTES, or until eggs are almost set, stirring after 2 minutes.

Stir and let stand to complete cooking.

NOTE: For 6 to 8 eggs, use 2 tablespoons butter, ⅓ to ½ cup milk. Cover casserole. MICROWAVE 3 MINUTES, 30 SECONDS to 4 MINUTES, 30 SECONDS, stirring after 2 minutes, 45 seconds.

Variations:
Add one or two of the following:
½ *cup grated cheese*
1 *can (4-ounces) mushroom stems and pieces, drained*
1 *can (6½-ounces) minced clams, drained*
¼ *cup finely chopped onion or green pepper*
1 *tablespoon parsley flakes*

PREPARATION INSTRUCTIONS FOR SCRAMBLED EGGS

EGGS	MILK	BUTTER	SETTING	TIME
2	2 Tbsp.	1 Tbsp.	High	1-2 Min.
4	¼ Cup	1 Tbsp.	High	2-3 Min.
6	⅓ Cup	2 Tbsp.	High	3-4½ Min.
8	½ Cup	2 Tbsp.	High	4-5½ Min.

Salt and pepper to taste.

Stir half-way through cooking time.

OMELET DELUXE

2 to 4 servings
9-inch pie plate

4 *eggs, separated*
¼ *cup milk*
½ *teaspoon salt*
Dash pepper
¼ *teaspoon baking powder*
1 *tablespoon butter or margarine*

In 1-quart bowl, beat egg whites until stiff peaks form. In small bowl, beat egg yolks with milk, salt, pepper and baking powder until lemon colored. Gently fold into beaten egg whites.

Place butter in 9-inch pie plate. MICROWAVE on '6' until butter melts. Pour egg mixture into hot butter and spread evenly in pie plate. MICROWAVE 6 to 8 MINUTES on '6', or until center is almost set. Fold in half and serve.

NOTE: Omelet should be removed from oven before it is completely set, since it will continue to cook.

For ovens without solid state heat control, MICROWAVE 7 MINUTES to 9 MINUTES, 30 SECONDS on '5'.

Variations:
FILLED OMELETS
Before folding omelet, fill with one of the following combinations:

Crumbled cooked bacon
Finely chopped green onion
Grated cheddar cheese
Chopped ham
Finely chopped green pepper
Finely chopped onion
Chopped tomato

SAUCED OMELETS
Top omelet with one of the following sauces:

Spanish sauce (page 65)
Fluffy hollandaise (page 157)
Mornay sauce (page 157)
Newburg sauce (page 157)

WESTERN OMELET
Fold into omelet before cooking:

¼ *cup finely chopped ham*
1 *tablespoon chopped onion*
1 *tablespoon finely chopped green pepper*

EGGS A LA GOLDENROD

4 servings
1-quart casserole

6 *eggs, hard cooked*
2 *cups white sauce, (page 157)*
Toast

Cook eggs on conventional range. Reserve two yolks, and cut whites and remaining yolks in ½-inch dice.

Prepare white sauce and pour into 1-quart casserole. Stir in diced eggs. MICROWAVE 2 MINUTES on HIGH.

Serve on toast with reserved egg yolks sieved over the top.

Variation:
Substitute cheese sauce (page 157) for white sauce. Dice 6 hard cooked eggs and stir into sauce.

CURRIED EGGS

2 to 3 servings
1-quart casserole

1 *can (10¾-ounces) condensed cream of celery soup, undiluted*
1 *tablespoon milk*
1 *teaspoon curry powder*
4 *eggs, hard cooked and sliced*

Combine soup, milk and curry powder in 1-quart casserole. Mix well. Cover. MICROWAVE 3 MINUTES on '8', or until hot.

Add eggs. Cover. MICROWAVE 3 MINUTES on '8', or until hot.

Serve as a side dish over green beans, broccoli or cooked noodles.

For ovens without solid state heat control, follow above directions, using HIGH, and stirring after every 1 minute, 30 seconds.

CHEESE SCRAMBLED EGGS

4 servings
Shallow 2-quart casserole

2 *tablespoons butter or margarine*
8 *eggs*
½ *cup milk*
Salt and pepper
4 *thin slices Swiss or cheddar cheese*

Place butter in shallow 2-quart casserole. MICROWAVE on HIGH until butter is melted.

Add eggs, milk, salt and pepper. Beat with fork to scramble. MICROWAVE 4 to 5 MINUTES on HIGH, or until eggs are almost set but very soft, stirring once.

Top with cheese. MICROWAVE 30 SECONDS to 1 MINUTE on HIGH, or until cheese is softened.

CURRIED EGGS AND SHRIMP

6 to 8 servings
8 x 8-inch baking dish
1-quart measure
2-cup measure

8 hard cooked eggs
⅓ cup mayonnaise or salad dressing
1 teaspoon paprika
½ teaspoon salt
½ teaspoon curry powder
¼ teaspoon dry mustard
2 tablespoons butter or margarine
2 tablespoons flour
1 can (10½-ounces) condensed cream of shrimp soup,
   undiluted
1¼ cups milk
½ cup shredded, sharp American process cheese
2 tablespoons butter or margarine
1 cup dry bread crumbs

Cut eggs in half lengthwise, remove yolks and mash in a small bowl. Blend in paprika, salt, curry powder and dry mustard. Fill egg whites. Arrange in (8 x 8-inch) baking dish.

Place butter in 1-quart measure. MICROWAVE on HIGH until butter melts. Blend in flour to make a smooth paste. Stir in soup, milk and shredded cheese. MICROWAVE 3 to 4 MINUTES on '8', or until mixture is hot and cheese melted. Stir well. Cover eggs with sauce.

Place 2 tablespoons butter in 2-cup measure. MICRO-WAVE on HIGH until butter melts. Stir in bread crumbs. Sprinkle crumb mixture around edge of dish. MICRO-WAVE 3 to 4 MINUTES on '8', or until sauce begins to bubble.

For ovens without solid state heat control, to heat sauce MICROWAVE 2 MINUTES, 30 SECONDS to 3 MIN-UTES, 30 SECONDS on HIGH, stirring once. To heat casserole, MICROWAVE 2 MINUTES, 30 SECONDS to 3 MINUTES, 30 SECONDS on HIGH, rotating dish once.

EGG FOO YUNG

4 servings
2-quart casserole

6 eggs
1 medium onion, chopped
1 small green pepper, diced
1 can (10½-ounces) bean sprouts, drained
½ teaspoon salt

Beat eggs until thick and lemon colored, in 2-quart casserole. Fold in remaining ingredients. MICROWAVE 7 to 9 MINUTES on '6', or until eggs are nearly set. Let stand 1 to 2 minutes, covered.

For ovens without solid state heat control, MICROWAVE 8 MINUTES, 30 SECONDS to 11 MINUTES on '5'.

EGG FOO YUNG GRAVY

1-quart measure

1½ cups chicken broth
2 teaspoons corn starch
½ teaspoon sugar
½ teaspoon salt
Dash pepper
1½ to 2 teaspoons soy sauce

Blend chicken broth and corn starch in 1-quart measure. Stir in remaining ingredients. MICROWAVE 4 to 5 MINUTES on HIGH, or until mixture thickens. Stir once with wire whip. Pour over Egg Foo Yung before serving.

Variation:

SEAFOOD EGG FOO YUNG

Add 1 cup diced, cooked shrimp or flaked crabmeat to egg mixture.

QUICHE

4 to 6 servings
9-inch quiche or pie dish

1 recipe plain pastry, (page 172)
Filling, below

On a lightly floured cloth or board, roll out pastry ⅛-inch thick. Lift pastry over rolling pin and unroll into 9-inch quiche or pie dish. Press pastry into dish from center to edges, using the back of the fingers. Prick pastry lightly but thoroughly with fork. MICROWAVE 4 MINUTES on '8'.

Fill quiche shell according to one of the variations below. MICROWAVE 5 to 6 MINUTES on '6', or until a metal knife inserted in center comes out clean.

For ovens without solid state heat control, to bake pastry, MICROWAVE 4 MINUTES on HIGH, rotating dish ½ turn after 2 minutes. To bake filled quiche, MICROWAVE 6 to 7 MINUTES on '5'.

QUICHE LORRAINE

4 to 6 servings
9-inch quiche or pie dish

Baked quiche shell
6 slices bacon cooked crisp and crumbled
2 eggs, beaten
¾ cup evaporated milk or light cream
6 shallots, thinly sliced or 1 small onion, thinly sliced
¼ cup grated Swiss cheese
Pinch pepper

Sprinkle cooked bacon over bottom of baked shell. Beat eggs with wire whip. Stir in evaporated milk, shallots, cheese and pepper. Pour into shell. Microwave as directed above.

CHEESE AND ONION QUICHE

5 to 6 servings
2-cup measure

Baked quiche shell
2 onions, finely chopped
2 tablespoons butter or margarine
2 eggs
¾ cup evaporated milk or light cream
1 cup shredded cheddar or gruyere cheese
¼ teaspoon dry mustard
¼ teaspoon salt
Pinch white pepper

Combine onions and butter in 2-cup measure. MICRO-WAVE 2 MINUTES on HIGH, or until onions are transparent. Spread in bottom of baked quiche shell.

Beat eggs lightly with wire whip. Stir in evaporated milk, cheese, mustard, salt and pepper. Pour over onions. Microwave as directed above.

SHRIMP AND ASPARAGUS QUICHE

5 to 6 servings
Baked quiche shell

Baked quiche shell
½ cup cooked shrimp or 1 can (6½-ounces) shrimp drained
1 can (8-ounces) asparagus, drained and cut in 1-inch lengths
1 egg
¾ cup evaporated milk or light cream
¼ teaspoon salt
Pinch white pepper
1½ tablespoons grated Parmesan cheese

Flake shrimp and mix with asparagus. Spread over bottom of baked quiche shell. Beat egg lightly with wire whip. Stir in evaporated milk, salt and pepper. Sprinkle with Parmesan cheese. MICROWAVE 6 to 7 MINUTES on '6', or 7 to 8 MINUTES 30 SECONDS on '5'.

SPINACH QUICHE

5 to 6 servings
1-quart bowl

Baked quiche shell
1 cup cooked and well drained spinach
2 eggs, beaten
½ cup evaporated milk or light cream
½ teaspoon nutmeg
¼ teaspoon salt
Pinch pepper
1½ tablespoons grated Parmesan cheese

Combine spinach, eggs, evaporated milk, nutmeg, salt and pepper. Pour into baked quiche shell. Sprinkle with Parmesan cheese. Microwave as directed above.

MUSHROOM QUICHE

5 to 6 servings
2-cup measure

Baked quiche shell
1 onion, sliced
1 cup sliced mushrooms
2 tablespoons butter or margarine
3 tablespoons flour
¾ cup milk
1 egg, beaten
¼ cup evaporated milk or cream
¼ teaspoon salt
Pinch pepper

Combine onion, mushrooms and butter in 2-cup measure. MICROWAVE 2 to 3 MINUTES on HIGH.

Add flour and mix well. Stir in milk. MICROWAVE 1 to 2 MINUTES on '8', or until mixture boils.

Stir a little of the hot liquid into beaten egg. Stir egg mixture, evaporated milk, salt and pepper into hot mushroom sauce. Pour into baked quiche shell. Microwave as directed above.

For ovens without solid state heat control, when boiling milk, MICROWAVE 1 to 2 MINUTES on HIGH, stirring once.

AFTER CHRISTMAS QUICHE

5 to 6 servings
1-quart bowl

Baked quiche shell
1 cup diced cooked turkey or chicken and ham, mixed
2 eggs
¾ cup evaporated milk or light cream
1 teaspoon chopped chives (optional)
¼ teaspoon salt
Pinch white pepper

Spread diced meats in bottom of baked quiche shell. Beat eggs lightly with wire whip. Stir in evaporated milk, chives, salt and pepper. Pour over meat. Microwave as directed above.

CHEESE BASICS

Because of its high fat content, cheese melts rapidly and can become tough or stringy when overcooked. When cheese is combined with eggs, cream or milk, use a lower heat control setting to produce a smooth and creamy dish without excessive stirring.

SWISS LUNCHEON BAKE

6 servings
8 x 8-inch baking dish
2-cup measure

2 *tablespoons butter or margarine*
2 *cups sliced onions*
6 *hard cooked eggs, sliced*
2 *cups shredded Swiss cheese*
1 *can (10½-ounces) condensed cream of chicken or*
   cream of celery soup, undiluted
¾ *cup milk*
Dash pepper
6 *½-inch thick slices French bread, buttered*

Combine butter and onion in (8 x 8-inch) baking dish. MICROWAVE 4 to 5 MINUTES on HIGH, or until onion is transparent. Reserve 6 egg slices for garnish. Top onion with remaining eggs, then cheese. Mix soup, milk and pepper together in 2-cup measure. MICROWAVE 3 to 4 MINUTES on HIGH, or until hot.

Pour over eggs and cheese. Top with bread slices, MICROWAVE 4 to 6 MINUTES on HIGH, or until heated through.

WELSH RAREBIT

4 servings
1-quart casserole

½ *cup beer*
1 *teaspoon dry mustard*
½ *teaspoon paprika*
Dash cayenne
1 *teaspoon Worcestershire sauce*
1 *pound cheddar cheese, shredded*
1 *egg, slightly beaten*
4 *slices toast, cut in triangles*

Combine beer, mustard, paprika, cayenne and Worcestershire sauce in 1-quart casserole. MICROWAVE 2 MINUTES on HIGH, or until mixture is warm.

Stir in cheese. MICROWAVE 4 MINUTES on '6', or until cheese melts, stirring twice. Stir a little of the hot mixture into egg. Add warmed egg to cheese mixture. Stir until smooth. MICROWAVE 2 MINUTES on '6'. Stir and serve over toast triangles.

For ovens without solid state heat control, MICROWAVE 5 MINUTES on '5', and 2 MINUTES, 10 SECONDS on '5'.

HAM AND EGGS AU GRATIN

4 to 6 servings
1½-quart casserole

4 *tablespoons butter or margarine*
¼ *cup flour*
2 *cups milk*
1½ *teaspoons prepared mustard*
2 *teaspoons Worcestershire sauce*
1 *cup shredded sharp cheddar cheese*
1 *cup cubed, cooked ham (½-inch cubes)*
6 *hard cooked eggs, halved*

Place butter in 1½-quart casserole. MICROWAVE on HIGH until butter melts. Blend in flour. Stir in milk. MICROWAVE 4 to 6 MINUTES on HIGH, or until thickened. Beat with wire whip.

Add mustard, Worcestershire sauce and cheese. MICROWAVE 1 MINUTE on HIGH, or until cheese melts.

Mix in ham and eggs. MICROWAVE 1 MINUTE, 30 SECONDS to 2 MINUTES on HIGH, or until bubbly. Serve over toast.

CLASSIC CHEESE STRATA

6 servings
8 x 8-inch baking dish

8 *slices day old bread*
8 *slices sharp American process cheese*
4 *eggs*
2½ *cups milk*
1 *small onion, chopped*
½ *teaspoon prepared mustard*
1 *teaspoon salt*
⅛ *teaspoon pepper*

Trim crusts from 5 slices of bread, cut in half diagonally, making triangles. Use trimmings and remaining 3 slices untrimmed bread to cover the bottom of (8 x 8-inch) baking dish. Top with cheese. Arrange the trimmed triangles on top of the cheese so that points of triangles overlap bases of preceding triangles.

Beat eggs in medium bowl. Stir in milk, onion, mustard, salt and pepper. Pour over bread and cheese. Cover with waxed paper. Let stand 1 hour at room temperature. MICROWAVE 26 to 28 MINUTES on '6', or until knife inserted in center comes out clean. Let stand 5 minutes before serving to firm.

For ovens without solid state heat control, MICROWAVE 31 to 36 MINUTES on '5'.

CHEESE FONDUE

6 cups

2-quart casserole or ceramic fondue dish

3 *cups shredded natural Swiss cheese*
1 *cup finely diced gruyere cheese*
1½ *tablespoons flour*
¼ *teaspoon nutmeg*
¼ *teaspoon pepper*
1 *clove garlic, pressed or finely chopped*
2 *cups dry white wine*
3 *tablespoons dry sherry*

Lightly toss cheese, flour, nutmeg, pepper and garlic together in 2-quart bowl. Set aside.

Pour wine into 2-quart casserole or fondue dish. MICROWAVE 5 to 6 MINUTES on '6', or until wine is hot. Stir in cheese mixture. MICROWAVE 2 to 4 MINUTES on '6', or until cheese melts. Stir well.

Stir in sherry, serve immediately. Can be kept hot or reheated as needed.

For ovens without solid state heat control, to heat wine, MICROWAVE 6 to 7 MINUTES on '5'. Stir in cheese mixture. MICROWAVE 3 MINUTES, 30 SECONDS to 5 MINUTES on '5'.

NOTE: Serve with crusty French bread cut into 1 to 1½-inch squares. For variety experiment with other breads, such as rye, whole wheat or herb breads, bread sticks or pretzels.

MUSHROOM CHEESE FONDUE DIP

2 cups

1-quart casserole or ceramic fondue pot

1 *roll (5½-ounces) garlic cold pack club cheese, softened*
1 *can (10¾-ounces) condensed cream of mushroom soup, undiluted*
½ *cup water*
½ *teaspoon instant beef bouillon*
1 *teaspoon sherry*
Crisp raw vegetables, such as cauliflowerets, green pepper strips, celery sticks, zucchini sticks

Combine cheese, soup, water, bouillon and sherry in casserole or fondue pot. Mix well. MICROWAVE 4 MINUTES on HIGH, or until creamy, stirring after 2 minutes.

Keep warm over warming candle. Serve with assorted raw vegetables or crisp crackers.

NOTE: Can be reheated if necessary.

Cheese Fondue.

CHEESE TOPPERS

To add variety to casseroles or vegetables, top with one of the following combinations. Add topping and MICROWAVE 20 SECONDS to 1 MINUTE on HIGH, or until cheese melts.

¼ *cup parmesan cheese*
½ *cup fine bread crumbs*
½ *teaspoon favorite herbs*

¼ *cup process cheese spread, softened*
1 *teaspoon seasoned salt*

Grated cheddar or Swiss cheese
Snipped parsley or chives

Slices or triangles of Swiss, cheddar, Monterey jack, mozzarella or colby

Cubes of seasoned cheese, such as onion, salami, garlic, pepper or spice

Vegetables

If you've never tasted vegetables cooked in a microwave oven, you don't really know how delicious vegetables can be. Some vegetables, such as corn, onions or peas cook in their own natural moisture. Others need only a few tablespoons of butter, margarine or water to cook tender crisp. All will have their flavors enhanced by microwave cooking and retain their color and nutrients.

CORN ON THE COB cooked in the microwave oven comes to the table tender, sweet and piping hot. You can prepare it in several ways. With fresh corn, strip back the husk, remove silk, bring the husk back up over the corn and microwave. Husked corn may be arranged in a baking dish with a small amount of water and covered with plastic wrap. Individual ears may be wrapped in waxed paper and arranged on the oven floor. For cooking times, see the Vegetable Chart.

ASPARANUTS

6 to 8 servings
1½-quart casserole

2 packages (10-ounces each) frozen asparagus
2 tablespoons butter or margarine
¼ cup finely chopped or slivered almonds
1 teaspoon tarragon vinegar

Place asparagus in 1½-quart casserole. Cover tightly. MICROWAVE 10 to 12 MINUTES on HIGH, or until asparagus is tender-crisp. Rearrange asparagus after 6 minutes.

Combine butter, almonds and vinegar in small mixing bowl. MICROWAVE 30 to 45 SECONDS on HIGH, or until butter is melted.

Pour almond butter sauce over asparagus. Serve immediately.

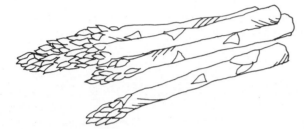

MUSHROOM CREAMED BEANS

4 servings
1-quart casserole

1 can (15-ounces) green beans, drained
¾ cup condensed cream of mushroom soup, undiluted
¾ cup canned French fried onion rings

Combine beans and soup in 1-quart casserole. Cover. MICROWAVE 3 MINUTES on HIGH. Stir in onion rings. MICROWAVE 2 MINUTES on HIGH or until bubbly. Garnish with additional onion rings.

CREAM-CURRY BEANS

4 servings
1-quart casserole

1 package (9-ounces) frozen green or wax beans
2 tablespoons butter or margarine
½ teaspoon salt
Dash of pepper
¼ to ½ teaspoon curry powder
½ cup dairy sour cream

Combine beans, butter, salt and pepper in 1-quart casserole. Cover. MICROWAVE 4 to 6 MINUTES on HIGH, or until beans are tender crisp.

Stir curry powder into sour cream. Fold into beans. MICROWAVE 1 MINUTE on '6', or until heated through.

For ovens without solid state heat control, to heat sauce MICROWAVE 1 MINUTE, 20 SECONDS on '5'.

FOOD FOR THE GODS WITH GREEN BEANS

4 to 6 servings
1½-quart casserole

2 cups green beans, cooked and drained (page 147)
3 tablespoons vinegar
2 tablespoons butter or margarine
1 tablespoon sugar
1 tablespoon chicken broth, or 1 tablespoon hot water
   and ⅛ teaspoon instant chicken bouillon
Dash dill seed
Dash pepper
1 tablespoon corn starch
1 tablespoon water
2 packed cups chopped cabbage

Combine vinegar, butter, sugar, chicken broth, dill seed and pepper in 1½-quart casserole. MICROWAVE 1 to 2 MINUTES on HIGH, or until mixture begins to boil.

Mix corn starch and water together. Stir into boiling liquid. MICROWAVE 2 MINUTES on HIGH, or until mixture thickens.

Stir in cabbage. Cover. MICROWAVE 3 to 4 MINUTES on HIGH, or until cabbage is tender. Stir in cooked green beans. Let stand 3 minutes, covered.

GREEN BEAN AND BACON CASSEROLE

4 servings
1-quart casserole

4 slices bacon
¼ cup bread cubes
1 package (9 to 10-ounces) frozen green beans,
   cooked and drained (page 147)
⅓ cup condensed cream of mushroom soup, undiluted

Place bacon in 1-quart casserole. MICROWAVE 2 to 3 MINUTES on HIGH. Remove bacon, crumble and set aside.

Add bread cubes to bacon drippings. Stir. MICROWAVE 2 MINUTES on HIGH, stirring once. Drain and set aside.

Combine beans, bacon and soup in 1-quart casserole. Mix well. Top with bread cubes. MICROWAVE 4 to 5 MINUTES on HIGH, or until hot.

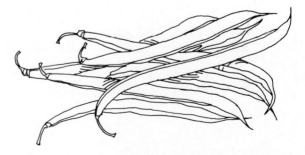

CHEESY TOMATO BEANS

4 servings
1-quart casserole

1 *package (4-ounces) green beans, cooked and*
  drained (page 147)
1 *tablespoon butter or margarine, melted*
½ *teaspoon salt*
Dash pepper
2 *tomatoes, peeled and quartered*
⅛ *teaspoon oregano*
½ *cup shredded cheddar cheese*

Place hot cooked beans in 1-quart casserole. Drizzle with butter. Season with salt and pepper. Spread tomato quarters on top. Sprinkle with oregano and cheese. MICROWAVE 2 to 4 MINUTES on '6', or until tomatoes are hot and cheese has melted.

For ovens without solid state heat control, MICROWAVE
2 MINUTES, 30 SECONDS to 5 MINUTES on '5'.

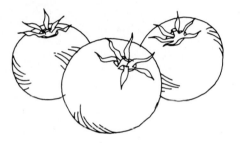

COLOSSAL BAKED LIMAS

8 servings
2 to 3-quart casserole or bowl

1 *pound dried lima beans*
1 *teaspoon salt*
½ *cup butter, cut in chunks*
½ *cup firmly packed brown sugar*
2 *tablespoons molasses*
1 *tablespoon prepared mustard*
1 *teaspoon salt*
1 *cup dairy sour cream*

In 2 to 3-quart casserole, soak lima beans overnight in water to cover.

Drain beans. Cover with fresh water. Add salt. Cover. MICROWAVE 30 to 35 MINUTES on '8', or until beans are tender. Drain.

Add butter chunks to hot beans. Stir in sugar, molasses, mustard and salt. Gently fold in sour cream. MICRO-WAVE 5 MINUTES on '6', or until hot.

For ovens without solid state heat control, after adding
sour cream MICROWAVE 6 MINUTES on '5'.

MAPLE GLAZED LIMA BEANS

4 to 6 servings
1-quart casserole

1 *package (10-ounces) frozen lima beans*
2 *tablespoons hot water*
¼ *cup maple syrup*
¼ *cup firmly packed brown sugar*
1 *tablespoon catsup*
1 *teaspoon prepared mustard*
2 *tablespoons butter or margarine, cut in bits*

Place frozen beans in 1-quart casserole. Add 2 tablespoons hot water. Cover. MICROWAVE 4 MINUTES on HIGH. Stirring with fork after 2 minutes.

Drain beans. Add maple syrup, sugar, catsup and mustard. Mix well. Cover. MICROWAVE 3 MINUTES on HIGH. Stir.

Dot with butter. Cover. MICROWAVE 2 to 3 MINUTES on HIGH, or until beans are tender-crisp. Let stand 3 to 5 minutes, covered.

JAZZY BAKED BEANS

4 servings
1-quart casserole

4 *slices bacon, cooked crisp (page 96) and crumbled*
1 *can (15-ounces) baked beans in tomato sauce*
½ *cup finely chopped onion*
½ *cup catsup*
⅓ *cup firmly packed brown sugar*
1 *teaspoon dry mustard*

Prepare bacon and set aside.

Combine remaining ingredients in 1-quart casserole. Mix well. Cover. MICROWAVE 6 MINUTES on HIGH, or until hot.

Sprinkle with bacon before serving.

NOTE: For variety, add 1 cup cubed cooked ham.

BEANS AND BURGUNDY

4 to 5 servings
1-quart casserole

1 *can (15-ounces) kidney beans, drained*
¼ *cup finely chopped onion*
2½ *tablespoons dry red wine*
½ *teaspoon salt*
1 *tablespoon butter or margarine, cut in small bits*

Combine beans, onion, wine and salt in 1-quart casserole. Mix well. Dot with butter. Cover. MICROWAVE 5 to 6 MINUTES on HIGH, or until hot.

TANGY CREAMED BEETS

4 servings
1-quart casserole

1 can (16-ounces) sliced or diced beets, drained
4 tablespoons dairy sour cream
1 tablespoon vinegar
1 teaspoon sugar
½ teaspoon salt
⅛ teaspoon garlic powder
⅛ teaspoon onion powder
2 teaspoons snipped fresh chives

Combine beets, sour cream, vinegar, sugar, salt, garlic and onion powders in 1-quart casserole. Mix well. MICROWAVE 3 MINUTES on HIGH, or until hot. Sprinkle with chives before serving.

HARVARD BEETS

4 servings
1-quart casserole

¼ cup sugar
1 tablespoon corn starch
½ teaspoon salt
Dash white pepper
1 can (16-ounces) sliced beets
Liquid drained from beets
¼ cup vinegar
¼ cup orange juice
1 teaspoon grated orange rind

Combine sugar, corn starch, salt and pepper in 1-quart casserole.

Drain beet liquid into 1-cup measure. If necessary, add water to make ¾ cup. Set beets aside.

Stir beet liquid, vinegar and orange juice into sugar mixture. Cover. MICROWAVE 5 to 7 MINUTES on HIGH, or until mixture is glossy and slightly thickened, stirring twice. Sprinkle with orange rind before serving.

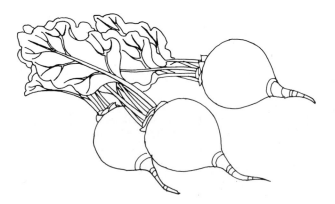

BROCCOLI ITALIAN STYLE

4 servings
2-cup measure

1 pound fresh broccoli, or 1 package (10-ounces) frozen broccoli spears, cooked and drained (page 148)
2 tablespoons butter or margarine
¼ cup sliced green onions, including tops
1 jar (4-ounces) chopped pimiento
2 teaspoons lemon juice
½ teaspoon salt
⅛ teaspoon pepper
¼ teaspoon oregano

Combine butter and onions in 2-cup measure. MICROWAVE 2 MINUTES on HIGH, or until onions are transparent. Stir in pimiento, lemon juice, salt, pepper and oregano. Pour over cooked and drained broccoli. Reheat if necessary.

BROCCOLI & MUSHROOMS IN SOUR CREAM

6 to 8 servings
2-quart casserole
2-cup measure

2 packages (10-ounces each) frozen whole broccoli spears, cooked and drained (page 148)
1½ tablespoons butter or margarine
1 package (8-ounces) fresh mushrooms, stems removed, or 2 jars (4-ounces each) mushroom caps drained
½ teaspoon onion salt
Dash pepper
1 tablespoon white wine
1 tablespoon dry sherry
½ cup dairy sour cream
1 teaspoon snipped chives
3 tablespoons chopped cucumber (optional)

Place hot, cooked broccoli in 2-quart casserole. Cover. Set aside.

Combine butter and mushroom caps in 2-cup measure. MICROWAVE 3 to 4 MINUTES on '6', or until mushroom caps are almost tender.

Stir in onion salt, pepper, wine, sherry, sour cream, chives and cucumber, if desired. MICROWAVE 3 to 4 MINUTES on '6', or until heated through.

Pour over broccoli. MICROWAVE 1 to 2 MINUTES on '6', or until dish is bubbly hot.

For ovens without solid state heat control, to heat sour cream sauce, MICROWAVE 4 to 5 MINUTES on '5'. Pour over broccoli. MICROWAVE 1 MINUTE, 30 SECONDS to 2 MINUTES, 30 SECONDS on '5'.

Variation:
Substitute asparagus or green beans for broccoli.

BRUSSEL SPROUTS AU GRATIN

6 to 8 servings
1½-quart casserole
1-cup measure

2 *packages (10-ounces each) frozen brussel sprouts,*
  cooked and drained (page 148)
½ *cup process sharp cheese spread*
¼ *cup butter or margarine*
¼ *cup crushed dry bread crumbs*
⅓ *cup chopped walnuts*

Place hot cooked brussel sprouts in 1½-quart casserole. Dot with cheese spread. Set aside.

Place butter in 1-cup measure. MICROWAVE on HIGH until butter melts. Stir in bread crumbs and walnuts. Toss to coat. Scatter crumb mixture over brussel sprouts. MICROWAVE 30 SECONDS to 1 MINUTE on HIGH, or until cheese melts.

BRUSSEL SPROUTS IN CREAM SAUCE

3 to 4 servings
1-quart casserole

1 *package (10-ounces) frozen brussel sprouts, cooked*
  and drained (page 148)
½ *teaspoon onion salt*
1 *package (3-ounces) cream cheese, cut in ¼-inch*
  cubes

Place hot, cooked brussel sprouts in 1-quart casserole. Sprinkle with onion salt. Scatter cheese cubes over brussel sprouts. Cover. Let stand 3 minutes. Toss gently before serving.

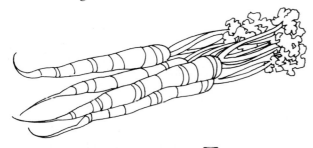

GRAPE GLAZED CARROTS

4 servings
1-quart casserole

2 *tablespoons butter or margarine*
2 *tablespoons honey*
1 *cup red grapes, halved and seeded*
2 *cups small carrots, cooked and drained (page 148)*
1 *tablespoon snipped parsley*

Combine butter and honey in 1-quart casserole. MICROWAVE 1 to 2 MINUTES on HIGH, or until mixture is bubbling.

Stir in grapes and carrots. MICROWAVE 2 MINUTES on HIGH, or until hot. Garnish with parsley.

SPICY CARROTS

4 servings
1-quart casserole

4 *or 5 large, fresh carrots, cut in julienne strips*
½ *cup sugar*
1 *teaspoon salt*
¼ *teaspoon cinnamon*
2 *tablespoons butter or margarine, cut in pieces*

Place carrots, sugar, salt and cinnamon in 1-quart casserole. Toss to combine. Dot with butter. Cover tightly. MICROWAVE 7 to 8 MINUTES on HIGH, or until carrots are tender-crisp.

GLAZED CARROT COINS

2 to 3 servings
1-quart casserole

¼ *cup water*
¼ *teaspoon salt*
3 *or 4 medium carrots, thinly sliced in rounds*
1½ *tablespoons butter or margarine*
⅓ *cup firmly packed brown sugar*
1 *tablespoon grated lemon rind*

Combine water, salt and carrots in 1-quart casserole. Cover tightly with plastic wrap. MICROWAVE 5 MINUTES on HIGH, or until carrots are tender-crisp.

Stir in butter, sugar and lemon rind. Cover. MICROWAVE 4 MINUTES on HIGH, or until hot and glazed.

DEVILED CAULIFLOWER

4 servings
1-quart measure

1 *pound fresh cauliflower, broken into flowerettes, or*
  1 *package (10-ounces) frozen cauliflower, cooked*
  and drained, (page 148)
1 *can (4½-ounces) deviled ham*
1 *teaspoon basil*
1 *teaspoon pepper*
1 *teaspoon prepared mustard*
1 *cup white sauce, (page 157)*

Stir ham, basil, pepper and mustard into white sauce. MICROWAVE 2 MINUTES on '8', or until heated through.

Pour deviled ham sauce over cooked and drained cauliflower. MICROWAVE 1 to 2 MINUTES on '8', or until sauce begins to bubble.

For ovens without solid state heat control, when preparing sauce, MICROWAVE 1 MINUTE, 30 SECONDS on HIGH. When reheating cauliflower MICROWAVE 45 SECONDS to 1 MINUTE, 30 SECONDS on HIGH.

BRAISED CELERY

4 servings
1-quart casserole

2 *cups celery, cut diagonally in ½-inch pieces*
½ *teaspoon basil*
¼ *teaspoon thyme*
¼ *cup red wine, or ¼ teaspoon instant beef bouillon*
dissolved in ¼ cup hot water

Place celery in 1-quart casserole. Season with basil and thyme. Pour wine over celery. Cover. MICROWAVE 5 to 7 MINUTES on HIGH, or until celery is tender crisp.

NOTE: On a diet? Tender crisp vegetables prepared by microwave add low-calorie flavor to diet menus. Experiment by adding dried herbs, such as sweet basil, tarragon, marjoram or rosemary, sprinkle with lemon or lime juice. Combine vegetables such as beans, peas and cauliflower or broccoli, onions and carrots, or mix with fresh fruit, such as fresh orange or grapefruit slices with beans, beets or broccoli.

WINE BRAISED CELERY AND MUSHROOMS

4 to 6 servings
2-quart casserole

1 *pound fresh mushrooms, cut in thick slices*
4 *cups diagonally sliced celery, 1 to 1½-inches thick*
½ *cup burgundy wine*
1 *teaspoon instant beef bouillon*
3 *tablespoons lemon juice*
2 *tablespoons butter or margarine, melted*
1 *teaspoon salt*
¼ *teaspoon pepper*
1 *tablespoon parsley flakes*

Spread half the mushrooms in bottom of 2-quart casserole. Cover with celery. Top with remaining mushrooms. Pour wine over vegetables. Sprinkle with instant bouillon, lemon juice, butter, salt, pepper and parsley flakes. Cover. MICROWAVE 6 to 8 MINUTES on HIGH, or until celery is tender crisp.

Fresh Vegetables when they are available, may be used for many of the recipes in this book which call for frozen vegetables. If you have favorite fresh vegetable dishes, prepare a double portion. Remove the extra amount when half cooked, chill and freeze for future use. When sweet corn is in season, buy it freshly picked. Husk it and blanch briefly. Chill, then seal individual ears in plastic pouches. Microwave frozen corn right in the pouch and you'll have fresh-tasting corn all winter long.

If you are a home gardener, pick vegetables right at the peak of flavor, even if you have only one serving. Blanch by microwave and freeze. It's easier and better to freeze vegetables as they ripen than to harvest everything at once, the unripe, the ripe and the over ripe. If you must do large lot canning or freezing, your conventional range will handle the large quantities better than the microwave oven.

To blanch small quantities (up to 4 cups), use ½ cup water for each cup of vegetables. Bring water to a boil in the microwave oven. Add vegetables and MICROWAVE 30 SECONDS to 1 MINUTE on HIGH, depending upon the quantity of vegetables. Stir until vegetables lose their raw appearance. Chill and freeze.

CORN BUBBLE

4 to 6 servings
1-quart casserole

2 tablespoons butter or margarine
1 small onion, finely chopped
2 tablespoons flour
1 teaspoon salt
½ teaspoon paprika
¼ teaspoon dry mustard
Pepper to taste
¾ cup milk
1 egg, slightly beaten with milk
1 can (16-ounces) whole kernel corn, drained

Place butter and onion in 1-quart casserole. MICROWAVE 1 to 2 MINUTES on HIGH, or until onion is transparent.

Add flour, salt, paprika, mustard and pepper. Blend well.

Add milk and egg mixture slowly, stirring until smooth. Stir in corn. Cover. MICROWAVE 8 to 10 MINUTES on '8', or until bubbly. Let stand 3 to 5 minutes, covered.

For ovens without solid state heat control, MICROWAVE 14 to 16 MINUTES on '5'.

ESCALLOPED CORN

4 to 6 servings
1-quart casserole

1 can (8-ounces) cream-style corn
1 can (8-ounces) whole kernel corn, drained
1 cup cracker crumbs
1 can (5¾-ounces) evaporated milk
1 egg, slightly beaten
2 tablespoons butter or margarine, cut in pieces

Combine cream-style and whole kernel corn, cracker crumbs and evaporated milk in 1-quart casserole. Mix well.

Stir in egg. Dot with butter. Cover. MICROWAVE 7 MINUTES, 30 SECONDS on '8', or until set. Let stand 3 to 5 minutes, covered. Garnish with paprika if desired.

For ovens without solid state heat control, MICROWAVE 12 MINUTES on '5'.

CREAMY BAKED EGGPLANT

4 servings
1-quart casserole

1 *medium eggplant*
1 *tablespoon whipping cream*
Salt and pepper

Cut stem from eggplant. Using a potato peeler, make a hollow in top of eggplant 1-inch in diameter and 2 to 3-inches deep. Stand eggplant upright in 1-quart casserole. Measure cream into cavity. Sprinkle with salt and pepper. Cover with plastic wrap. MICROWAVE 2 to 3 MINUTES on HIGH, or until cream begins to bubble.

Reduce setting. MICROWAVE 4 to 6 MINUTES on '6', or until eggplant is tender.

To serve, cut eggplant lengthwise in quarters.

For ovens without solid state heat control, during second cooking period, MICROWAVE 5 to 7 MINUTES on '5'.

SENSATIONAL ONION BAKE

4 servings
8 x 8-inch baking dish

4 *large white onions, peeled*
1 *can (5-ounces) boned chicken*
2 *tablespoons mayonnaise*
Salt and pepper
¼ *cup butter or margarine*
2 *cups catsup*

With a grapefruit knife, hollow out the center of each onion leaving a half-inch thick shell. Set aside.

Finely chop center portions. Combine onion, chicken and mayonnaise in medium bowl. Season with salt and pepper. Mix well.

Fill onion shells with stuffing and place in (8 x 8-inch) baking dish. Dot each onion with 1 tablespoon butter.

Pour catsup around onions. Cover with plastic wrap. MICROWAVE 9 MINUTES on HIGH, or until onions are tender-crisp.

For variety; substitute 1 can (10¾-ounces) double-strength chicken broth, undiluted, for catsup.

Can be prepared in advance and cooked later.

MINTED PEAS

3 to 4 servings
1-cup measure
1-quart casserole

2 *tablespoons butter or margarine*
1 *tablespoon chopped fresh mint leaves*
1 *teaspoon sugar*
1 *package (10-ounces) frozen peas*
½ *teaspoon salt*

Place butter in 1-cup measure. MICROWAVE on HIGH until butter melts.

Stir in mint leaves and sugar. Place frozen peas in 1-quart casserole. Sprinkle with salt. Pour minted butter over peas. Cover. MICROWAVE 3 to 5 MINUTES on HIGH, or until peas are tender. Stir well to coat with sauce.

MASHED POTATOES

6 to 8 servings
Paper towel
2-cup measure

6 *medium baking potatoes, baked (page 150)*
¾ *cup milk*
¼ *cup butter or margarine*
Salt and pepper to taste

Bake potatoes and let stand 5 minutes.

Combine milk and butter in 2-cup measure. MICROWAVE 1 MINUTE on HIGH to warm milk.

Cut potatoes in half. Scoop out cooked potato into medium bowl. Add milk and butter mixture. Season with salt and pepper. Beat with rotary or electric beater until fluffy.

NOTE: Potatoes may be prepared in advance. Omit heating milk and butter. To reheat mashed potatoes, MICROWAVE 3 MINUTES on HIGH, or until hot.

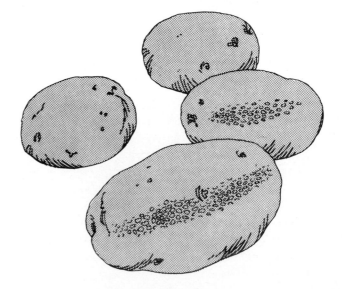

MATTERHORN VEGETABLE BAKE

6 servings
1½-quart casserole

¼ cup butter or margarine
1½ cups sliced summer squash
1 package (10-ounces) frozen, chopped broccoli,
 defrosted
1 egg
½ cup shredded Swiss cheese
¼ cup milk
1 teaspoon salt
¼ teaspoon dry mustard
3 tablespoons grated parmesan cheese

Place butter in 1½-quart casserole. MICROWAVE on HIGH until butter melts. Stir in squash and broccoli to coat with butter. Cover. MICROWAVE 6 to 8 MINUTES on HIGH, or until tender.

Beat egg lightly in small mixing bowl. Mix in cheese, milk, salt and mustard. Pour mixture over vegetables. Sprinkle with parmesan cheese. MICROWAVE 4 MINUTES on '6', or until cheese melts and is bubbly.
For ovens without solid state heat control, MICROWAVE 5 MINUTES on '5'.

CHEESE STUFFED POTATOES

8 servings
Paper towels
Serving plate

4 medium baking potatoes, baked (page 150)
¼ cup butter or margarine
½ cup milk
Salt and pepper to taste
1 cup grated cheddar cheese or finely diced American
 process cheese, ¼ cup reserved
1 tablespoon finely chopped onion

Bake potatoes. After standing time, halve potatoes lengthwise and carefully scoop out inside. Set shells aside. Combine potato, butter, milk, salt and pepper in medium mixing bowl. Mash until fluffy.

Stir in ¾ cup cheese and onion. Spoon mashed potato mixture into potato shells. Sprinkle remaining ¼ cup cheese on top.

Place stuffed potatoes on serving plate. MICROWAVE 1 MINUTE, 30 SECONDS to 2 MINUTES on HIGH, or until cheese melts and potatoes are hot. Garnish with paprika if desired.

NOTE: Potatoes may be prepared in advance and refrigerated without cheese topping. To reheat, MICROWAVE 4 to 5 MINUTES on HIGH, or until potatoes are hot. Top with reserved cheese. MICROWAVE 1 MINUTE on HIGH, until cheese melts.

AU GRATIN POTATOES

6 servings
2-quart casserole

1 box (5½-ounces) au gratin potatoes
2¼ cups boiling water
⅔ cup milk
2 tablespoons butter or margarine

Mix ingredients in order directed on box, using quantities and casserole size given here. Cover. MICROWAVE 18 to 20 MINUTES on '6', or until potatoes are tender and most of liquid is absorbed.

NOTE: Larger casserole is necessary to prevent over boiling. If drier potatoes are desired, use liquid as directed on box, a 2-quart casserole, and cook uncovered.
For ovens without solid state heat control, MICROWAVE 22 to 24 MINUTES on '5'.

SWEET POTATO MARSHAROLE

4 to 6 servings
1½-quart casserole

2 tablespoons butter or margarine
1 can (23-ounces) sweet potatoes, drained and mashed
2 tablespoons milk
2 tablespoons raisins
2 tablespoons orange marmalade
¼ teaspoon salt
¼ teaspoon cinnamon
¼ teaspoon nutmeg
½ cup miniature marshmallows

Place butter in 1½-quart casserole. MICROWAVE on HIGH until melted.

Add sweet potatoes, milk, raisins, marmalade, salt and spices. Mix well. Cover. MICROWAVE 7 MINUTES on HIGH, or until hot.

Top with marshmallows. Cover. MICROWAVE 1 MINUTE, 30 SECONDS to 2 MINUTES on HIGH until marshmallows begin to soften.

Let stand 5 minutes, covered.

SCALLOPED POTATOES

4 servings
1-quart casserole

2 *medium baking potatoes, peeled and thinly sliced*
1 *cup medium white sauce*
1 *teaspoon butter or margarine, cut in pieces*

Layer half of potato slices in 1-quart casserole. Mask with half of sauce. Repeat with potatoes and sauce. Dot with butter. MICROWAVE 25 to 30 MINUTES on '4', or until potatoes are fork tender. Let stand 5 minutes before serving.

For ovens without variable heat control, MICROWAVE 23 to 28 MINUTES on '5', with 2 minute rest periods every 10 minutes.

GERMAN POTATO SALAD

4 servings
1½-quart casserole

6 *slices bacon*
¾ *cup finely chopped onion*
2 *tablespoons flour*
⅓ *cup sugar*
1 *teaspoon salt*
Pepper to taste
½ *teaspoon celery seed*
⅔ *cup water*
5 *tablespoons cider vinegar*
4 *medium boiling potatoes, cooked, peeled and sliced*

Place bacon in 1½-quart casserole. MICROWAVE 3 to 4 MINUTES on HIGH, or until crisp. Remove bacon. Crumble and set aside.

Add onion to bacon drippings. MICROWAVE 2 to 3 MINUTES on HIGH, or until onion is transparent.

Stir in flour, sugar, salt, pepper and celery seed. MICRO-WAVE 1 MINUTE on HIGH. Stir in water and vinegar. MICROWAVE 3 to 4 MINUTES on HIGH, or until mixture boils. Add potatoes and bacon, stirring gently to coat with sauce.

NOTE: Salad may be prepared in advance. MICRO-WAVE 2 to 3 MINUTES on HIGH, or until potatoes are heated through.

SCALLOPED POTATOES FROM PACKAGE MIX

6 servings
2-quart casserole

1 *box (5½-ounces) scalloped potatoes*
2¼ *cups boiling water*
⅔ *cup milk*
2 *tablespoons butter or margarine*

Mix ingredients in order directed on box, using quantities and casserole size given here. Cover. MICROWAVE 18 to 20 MINUTES on '6', or until potatoes are tender and most of liquid is absorbed.

NOTE: Larger casserole is necessary to prevent over boiling. If drier potatoes are desired, use liquid as directed on box, a 2-quart casserole, and cook uncovered.

For ovens without solid state heat control, MICROWAVE 22 to 24 MINUTES on '5'.

ORANGE-POTATO SHELLS

4 servings
2-quart bowl

2 *oranges, reserve 2 tablespoons juice*
1 *can (23-ounces) vacuum packed sweet potatoes*
4 *portions instant mashed potatoes, prepared according to package directions*
1 *marshmallow, cut in quarters*

Cut oranges in half with sharp paring knife, making a saw-tooth pattern. Using a grapefruit knife, free fruit from shell carefully. Save juice.

With a fork, mash sweet potatoes in 2-quart bowl. Stir in 2 tablespoons reserved orange juice. Blend in mashed potatoes. Mix well.

Fill orange shells with potato mixture, using a pastry tube or spoon. Top with marshmallow quarters. MICRO-WAVE 1 MINUTE on HIGH, or until marshmallow softens.

SOUR CREAM & POTATO CASSEROLE

6 servings
1½-quart casserole

1 cup dairy sour cream
1 cup cottage cheese
2 cups mashed potatoes
3 tablespoons minced onion
1 jar (4-ounces) chopped pimientos, drained
2 eggs, lightly beaten
2 tablespoons butter or margarine, softened

Combine all ingredients in 1½-quart casserole. Beat with spoon until smoothly mixed. Cover with waxed paper. MICROWAVE 18 MINUTES on '6', rotating dish ½ turn after 9 minutes. Let stand 5 minutes, covered.

NOTE: When using leftover mashed potatoes from refrigerator, add 2 to 3 more minutes cooking time.

For ovens without solid state heat control, MICROWAVE 21 MINUTES on '5', rotating dish ½ turn after 10 minutes.

RATATOUILLE ✿

6 to 8 servings
3-quart casserole

¼ cup olive or salad oil
2 medium onions, thickly sliced
1 clove garlic, finely chopped
1 large green pepper, cut in strips
1 medium eggplant, peeled and cut into ½-inch cubes (about 1½-pounds)
2 medium zucchini, cut into ¼-inch slices (about 1½-pounds)
3 to 4 large tomatoes, peeled and cut in wedges, or 1 can (16-ounces) tomatoes
2 teaspoons basil
2 teaspoons parsley flakes
1 teaspoon marjoram
1 teaspoon salt
⅛ teaspoon pepper

Combine olive oil, onion, garlic and green pepper in 3-quart casserole. MICROWAVE 4 to 5 MINUTES on HIGH, or until onions are transparent.

Mix in eggplant and zucchini. Cover. MICROWAVE 4 to 5 MINUTES on HIGH, or until eggplant softens.

Gently stir in tomatoes, basil, parsley, marjoram, salt and pepper. MICROWAVE 10 MINUTES on '6', or until vegetables are tender.

For ovens without solid state heat control, MICROWAVE 12 MINUTES on '5'.

SAUERKRAUT WITH APPLES

4 servings
1-quart casserole

1 tablespoon butter or margarine
1 small onion, chopped
1 can (1-pound) sauerkraut, drained
1 cup tart apple slices
1 tablespoon flour
½ teaspoon instant beef bouillon dissolved in ½ cup hot water
1 tablespoon vinegar
⅛ teaspoon caraway seed

Combine butter and onion in 1-quart casserole. MICROWAVE on HIGH until butter melts. Stir in sauerkraut and apples. Sprinkle with flour. Pour in bouillon. Add vinegar and caraway seed. Mix gently. Cover. MICROWAVE 3 to 5 MINUTES on HIGH, or until apple is tender and sauce slightly thickened.

SPINACH COTTAGE PIE

6 to 8 servings
9-inch pie plate

Pastry for 9-inch pie shell
2 packages (10-ounces each) frozen chopped spinach, defrosted
1 carton (16-ounces) creamed cottage cheese
1 teaspoon sugar
1 teaspoon salt
½ teaspoon poultry seasoning, or basil and nutmeg, mixed
4 eggs, well beaten

Line (9-inch) pie dish with pastry.

Press excess liquid from spinach. Spread in pastry-lined dish.

Fold cottage cheese, sugar, salt and poultry seasoning into beaten eggs. Pour egg mixture over spinach. Cover. MICROWAVE 25 MINUTES on '8', or until set. Let stand 5 minutes to firm. Custard is done when metal knife inserted in center comes out clean.

NOTE: Standing time is necessary to complete cooking and firm custard.

For ovens without solid state heat control, MICROWAVE 20 to 25 MINUTES on HIGH, or until set, letting stand 1 minute after every 5 minutes. Rotate dish ¼ turn after each standing time.

SPINACH CASSEROLE

6 to 8 servings
1½ to 2-quart casserole

2 *packages (10-ounces each) frozen chopped spinach*
1 *can (10¾-ounces) condensed cream of mushroom*
  soup, undiluted
1 *small onion, finely chopped*
2 *tablespoons butter or margarine, cut in pieces*

Place spinach in a 1½ to 2-quart casserole. Cover. MICROWAVE 6 MINUTES on HIGH, or until spinach is defrosted thoroughly. Drain well.

Stir in soup and onion. Dot with butter. Cover. MICROWAVE 8 MINUTES on HIGH, or until hot.

SWEET-SOUR SPINACH

4 servings
1-quart casserole

4 *slices bacon*
1 *tablespoon flour*
1 *teaspoon sugar*
¼ *cup whipping cream*
1 *tablespoon cider vinegar*
1 *pound fresh spinach, or 1 package (10-ounces)*
  frozen leaf spinach cooked and drained (page 150)

Place bacon in 1-quart casserole. MICROWAVE 2 to 3 MINUTES on HIGH, or until crisp. Remove bacon. Crumble and set aside.

Drain all but 1 tablespoon bacon drippings from casserole. Add flour and mix until smooth. Stir in sugar and cream. MICROWAVE 1 MINUTE on HIGH, stirring once after 30 seconds. Stir in vinegar.

Add spinach and toss lightly to coat with sauce. MICROWAVE 1 MINUTE on HIGH, or until spinach is hot. Garnish with crumbled bacon.

BAKED SQUASH

2 servings
Paper towel

1 *medium acorn squash*
2 *tablespoons brown sugar*
2 *tablespoons butter or margarine, cut in pieces*

Pierce squash with fork several times. Place in oven on paper towel. MICROWAVE 8 MINUTES on HIGH, or until fork tender.

Cut in half and remove seeds. Place one tablespoon sugar in each cavity. Dot with butter. MICROWAVE 2 to 3 MINUTES on HIGH, or until butter and sugar are melted. NOTE: Piercing squash prevents it bursting in oven.

For 4 servings, use two small to medium squash or 1 large squash, cut in quarters. MICROWAVE 14 MINUTES on HIGH.

CARIBBEAN BAKED SQUASH

2 to 4 servings
1-quart casserole
2-cup measure

1 *pound winter squash (hubbard, acorn) peeled and*
  cut in 1-inch cubes
¼ *cup butter or margarine*
1 *can (8-ounces) crushed pineapple*
1 *teaspoon grated orange rind*
Dash nutmeg

Place squash in 1-quart casserole. Cover. MICROWAVE 8 to 10 MINUTES on HIGH, or until almost tender, stirring once. Set aside.

Place butter in 2-cup measure. MICROWAVE 30 SECONDS on HIGH, or until butter is melted. Add pineapple, orange rind and nutmeg. Mix well.

Spoon mixture over cooked squash. Cover. MICROWAVE 2 MINUTES on HIGH, or until hot.

Let stand 5 minutes to finish cooking and blend flavors. Garnish with parsley if desired.

STUFFED TOMATOES

4 servings
8 x 8-inch square baking dish
1-quart casserole

4 *large ripe tomatoes*
2 *tablespoons butter or margarine*
2 *tablespoons finely chopped onion*
1 *cup crushed dry bread crumbs*
½ *teaspoon salt*
¼ *teaspoon poultry seasoning*
⅛ *teaspoon pepper*
2 *tablespoons butter or margarine, cut in small pieces*
Paprika

Remove stem ends of tomatoes and scoop out center pulp and seeds. Place tomatoes in (8 x 8-inch) square baking dish. Set aside.

Combine butter and onion in a 1-quart casserole. Cover. MICROWAVE 4 MINUTES on HIGH, or until onion is transparent. Stir in bread crumbs, salt, poultry seasoning and pepper. Mix well.

Spoon stuffing mixture into tomatoes. Dot with remaining butter. Sprinkle with paprika. Cover. MICROWAVE 3 to 4 MINUTES on HIGH, or until skins begin to break and tomatoes are heated through.

SPEEDY ORANGE GLAZED YAMS

4 servings
1-quart casserole

1 *can (1-pound, 1-ounce) vacuum packed sweet*
   potatoes, cut in 2-inch pieces
½ *cup orange marmalade*

Combine sweet potatoes and marmalade in 1-quart casserole. MICROWAVE 3 to 4 MINUTES on HIGH, or until potatoes are hot and marmalade is melted, stirring after 1 minute, 30 seconds. Stir again before serving.

STUFFED ZUCCHINI

4 servings
2-cup measure
8 x 8-inch baking dish

4 *to 6 small zucchini, cut in half lengthwise*
1 *tablespoon olive or salad oil*
1 *medium onion, finely chopped*
1 *clove garlic, pressed or finely chopped*
¾ *cup dried bread crumbs, crushed*
⅓ *cup grated parmesan cheese*
2 *tablespoons snipped parsley*
1 *teaspoon basil*

Scoop out and discard seeds from zucchini. Set aside.

In 2-cup measure, combine oil, onions and garlic. MICROWAVE 2 to 3 MINUTES on HIGH, or until onions are transparent.

Mix in bread crumbs, cheese, parsley and basil. Spoon filling into zucchini shells. Arrange in (8 x 8-inch) baking dish. Cover with plastic wrap. MICROWAVE 6 to 8 MINUTES on HIGH, or until zucchini is tender.

ZUCCHINI PARMESAN

4 servings
1-quart casserole
Custard cup

1½ *pounds zucchini, sliced ¼-inch thick*
¼ *cup parmesan cheese*
½ *teaspoon basil*
¼ *teaspoon salt*
1 *tablespoon butter or margarine*

Arrange zucchini slices in the bottom of a 1-quart casserole. Mix parmesan cheese, basil and salt together. Sprinkle over zucchini.

Place butter in custard cup. MICROWAVE on HIGH until butter melts. Drizzle over top of zucchini. Cover. MICROWAVE 4 to 5 MINUTES on HIGH, or until zucchini is tender crisp.

BAKED ZUCCHINI AND ONIONS

4 servings
1½-quart casserole

4 *medium zucchini, sliced*
1 *medium onion, sliced*
2 *tablespoons wine vinegar*
¼ *cup salad oil*
1 *package (5-ounces) Italian salad dressing mix*
2 *tablespoons grated Parmesan cheese*

Alternate layers of zucchini and onions in a 1½-quart casserole.

Combine vinegar, oil and salad dressing mix in 2-cup measure. Mix well; pour over zucchini and onions.

Sprinkle top with cheese. Cover. MICROWAVE 9 to 11 MINUTES on HIGH, or until vegetables are tender-crisp.

Vegetable Cooking Chart

This cookbook recommends that vegetables be cooked tender crisp. This means that a vegetable is tender to bite but retains its texture. If you prefer softer vegetables, microwave a little longer.

Most vegetables cook on the HIGH setting, unless they are sauced or cheesed. For best results, cover vegetables tightly. If your casserole does not have a tight-fitting cover, substitute plastic wrap. Be careful when uncovering vegetables, as steam burns.

Blue areas indicate frozen items

VEGETABLE	AMOUNT	COOKING PROCEDURE	TIME	SETTING	STANDING TIME
Artichokes (fresh)	1 medium	1 tablespoon water in 8 x 8-inch dish, covered.	4 - 6 minutes	High	3 minutes, covered
	2 medium	¼ cup water, 1 teaspoon salt, in cake dish, covered	5 - 7 minutes	High	3 minutes, covered
	3 medium	½ cup water, ½ teaspoon salt in a round cake dish, covered.	7 - 9 minutes	High	3 minutes, covered
Asparagus (fresh)	15 4-inch pieces	¼ cup water, ½ teaspoon salt in 1½-quart covered casserole.	5 - 7 minutes	High	3 minutes, covered
Asparagus (frozen)	10 ounces	Use 1-quart covered casserole. Separate after 3 minutes.	5 - 7 minutes	High	3 minutes, covered
Beans, Butter (fresh)	1 pound (2 cups shelled)	½ cup water in 1-quart covered casserole. Stir.	6 - 8 minutes	High	3 minutes, covered
	2 pounds (4 cups shelled)	½ cup water in 1½-quart covered casserole. Stir.	9 - 11 minutes	High	3 minutes, covered

VEGETABLE	AMOUNT	COOKING PROCEDURE	TIME	SETTING	STANDING TIME
Beans, Green or Wax (fresh)	1 pound snapped or French cut	¼ cup water, ½ teaspoon salt in 1½-quart covered casserole.	7 - 9 minutes	High	3 minutes, covered
Beans, Green cut or wax French cut (frozen)	10 ounces	Use 1-quart covered casserole. Add 2 teaspoons hot water and stir.	6 - 8 minutes	High	3 minutes, covered
Beans, Lima (fresh)	1 pound (2 cups shelled)	½ cup water in 1-quart covered casserole. Stir.	6 - 8 minutes	High	3 minutes, covered
	2 pounds (4 cups shelled)	½ cup water in 1½-quart covered casserole. Stir.	9 - 11 minutes	High	3 minutes, covered
Beans, Pinto (fresh)	2 cups (1 pound)	Soak overnight. 3 cups water in 2-quart covered casserole. Stir.	20 - 25 minutes	High	3 - 5 minutes, covered
Beets (fresh)	4 whole, medium size	Barely cover with water, add ¼ teaspoon salt. Cook in 2-quart covered casserole	15 - 17 minutes	High	3 minutes, covered
	4 medium, sliced	½ cup water, ¼ teaspoon salt in 1-quart covered casserole.	12 minutes	High	3 minutes, covered

VEGETABLE	AMOUNT	COOKING PROCEDURE	TIME	SETTING	STANDING TIME
Broccoli (fresh)	1 small bunch (1½ pounds)	Cut away tough part of stalk, split tender ends. ½ cup water, ½ teaspoon salt in 1½-quart covered casserole.	7 - 9 minutes	High	3 minutes, covered
Broccoli (frozen)	10 ounces	Use 1-quart covered casserole. Separate after 4 minutes.	7 - 9 minutes	High	3 minutes, covered
Brussel Sprouts (fresh)	½ pound (2 cups)	2 tablespoons water in 1-quart covered casserole.	4 - 6 minutes	High	3 minutes, covered
	1 pound (4 cups)	3 tablespoons water in 1½-quart covered casserole.	5 - 7 minutes	High	3 minutes, covered
Brussel Sprouts (frozen)	10 ounce package	2 tablespoons water.	4 - 6 minutes	High	3 minutes, covered
	10 ounce pouch	Slit pouch with knife.	4½ - 5 minutes	High	3 minutes, covered
Cabbage (fresh)	1 small head chopped	Fill 1½-quart casserole with chopped cabbage, add ½ teaspoon salt, 2 tablespoons water. Cover.	10 - 12 minutes	High	3 minutes, covered
	1 medium head, whole	½ teaspoon salt, 2 tablespoons water in 2-quart covered casserole.	12 - 15 minutes	High	3 minutes, covered
Carrots (fresh)	4 medium sliced	2 tablespoons water in 1-quart covered casserole.	4 - 6 minutes	High	3 minutes, covered
	6 medium sliced	2 tablespoons water in 1½-quart covered casserole.	6 - 8 minutes	High	3 minutes, covered
Carrots (frozen)	10 ounce package	2 tablespoons water in 1-quart covered casserole.	5 - 7 minutes	High	3 minutes, covered
	10 ounce pouch	Slit pouch with knife.	4 - 6 minutes	High	3 minutes, covered
Cauliflower (fresh)	1 small head	½ cup water, ¼ teaspoon salt in 1½-quart covered casserole	5 - 7 minutes	High	3 minutes, covered
	1 medium head	½ cup water, ¼ teaspoon salt in 2-quart covered casserole	9 - 11 minutes	High	3 minutes, covered
Cauliflower (frozen)	10 ounces	2 tablespoons hot water in 1-quart covered casserole	4 - 6 minutes	High	3 minutes, covered

VEGETABLE	AMOUNT	COOKING PROCEDURE	TIME	SETTING	STANDING TIME
Celery (fresh)	4 cups coarsely chopped	¼ cup water, ½ teaspoon salt in 1½-quart covered casserole	6 - 8 minutes	High	3 minutes, covered
	6 cups coarsely chopped	¼ cup water, ½ teaspoon salt in 2-quart covered casserole	10 - 12 minutes	High	3 minutes, covered
Corn, cut off the cob (fresh)	1½ cups	¼ cup water, ½ teaspoon salt in 1-quart covered casserole	3 - 5 minutes	High	3 minutes, covered
Corn, cut off the cob (frozen)	10 ounces	¼ cup hot water in 1-quart covered casserole	4 - 6 minutes	High	3 minutes, covered
Corn on the cob (fresh)	2 ears	Put ears in open glass dish. Pour melted butter over corn. Turn ears 2 or 3 times during cooking.	4 - 6 minutes	High	3 minutes, covered
	4 ears	Same as above	8 - 10 minutes	High	3 minutes, covered
Corn on the cob (frozen)	2 ears	¼ cup hot water in 1-quart covered casserole. Turn ears after 3 minutes	6 - 8 minutes	High	3 minutes, covered
Eggplant (fresh) Not available for frozen	1 medium (4 cups, cubed)	Peel and dice eggplant. Put in 2-quart covered casserole. Add 2 tablespoons water, ¼ teaspoon salt	4 - 6 minutes	High	3 minutes, covered
Okra (frozen)	10 ounces	2 tablespoons hot water in 1-quart covered casserole	5 - 7 minutes	High	3 minutes, covered
Onions (fresh)	2 large, cut in quarters or eighths	½ cup water, ½ teaspoon salt in 1-quart covered casserole	5 - 7 minutes	High	3 minutes, covered
	4 large, cut in quarters or eighths	½ cup water, ½ teaspoon salt in 2-quart covered casserole	7 - 9 minutes	High	3 minutes, covered
Parsnips (fresh)	2 medium	2 tablespoons water in 1-quart covered casserole	5 - 7 minutes	High	3 minutes, covered
	4 medium	¼ cup water in 2-quart covered casserole	7 - 9 minutes	High	3 minutes, covered

VEGETABLE	AMOUNT	COOKING PROCEDURE	TIME	SETTING	STANDING TIME
Peas, Black Eyed (frozen)	10 ounce package	¼ cup water in 1-quart covered casserole	8 - 10 minutes	High	3 minutes, covered
Peas and Carrots (frozen)	10 ounces	2 tablespoons hot water in 1-quart covered casserole. Stir after 4 minutes	4 - 6 minutes	High	3 minutes, covered
Peas, Green (fresh)	2 cups shelled	2 tablespoons water in 1-quart covered casserole	4 - 6 minutes	High	3 minutes, covered
	3 cups shelled	2 tablespoons water in 1-quart covered casserole	5 - 7 minutes	High	3 minutes, covered
Peas, Tiny Green (frozen)	10 ounces	2 tablespoons hot water in 1-quart covered casserole	4 - 6 minutes	High	3 minutes, covered
Potatoes, baked (Irish) Idaho (fresh)	All medium size 1 2 3 4	Scrub potatoes and dry. Spread paper towel on oven shelf. Put potatoes on paper towel about 1-inch apart. Times are approximate and vary with size and variety. When baking more than 4 potatoes, rearrange after half the cooking time has expired	5 - 6 minutes 7 - 9 minutes 10 - 12 minutes 14 - 16 minutes	High High High High	Wrap in foil, let stand 5 - 10 minutes
Potatoes, boiled (fresh)	6 medium, cut in half, peeled	¼ cup water, ½ teaspoon salt in 2-quart covered casserole. Stir once after 6 minutes	12 - 16 minutes	High	3 - 5 minutes, covered
Potatoes, buttered (Irish) (fresh)	4 medium, sliced	2 tablespoons butter in 1½-quart glass casserole. Sprinkle potatoes with ½ teaspoon salt, dot with butter	12 - 14 minutes	High	5 minutes, covered
	6 medium, sliced	2 tablespoons butter in 2-quart glass casserole. Stir after 5 minutes	17 - 19 minutes	High	5 minutes, covered
Rutabaga (fresh)	One (1 lb.)	Wash, peel and cube rutabaga. ½ cup water, 3 tablespoons butter, salt and pepper to taste. Use 1-quart covered casserole	7 - 9 minutes	High	3 minutes, covered
Spinach (fresh)	4 cups (1 lb.)	Wash. Cook in water that clings to the leaves. 2-quart covered casserole.	3 - 5 minutes	High	3 minutes, covered

VEGETABLE	AMOUNT	COOKING PROCEDURE	TIME	SETTING	STANDING TIME
Spinach, leaf or chopped (frozen)	10 ounces	Use 1-quart covered casserole	4 - 6 minutes	High	3 minutes, covered
	10 ounce package	2 tablespoons water in 1-quart covered casserole	4 - 6 minutes	High	3 minutes, covered
Squash, Acorn or Butternut (fresh)	One (1 lb.)	Cook whole. Pierce skin with sharp knife in several places. Cook on paper towel.	4 - 6 minutes	High	5 minutes, covered
Squash, Hubbard (frozen)	10 ounce package	2 tablespoons water in 1-quart casserole	4 - 6 minutes	High	3 minutes, covered
Sweet Potatoes (fresh)	4 medium, cut in half length-wise, peeled	¼ cup water, ½ teaspoon salt in 1½-quart covered casserole	8 - 10 minutes	High	3 minutes, covered
	6 medium, cut in half length-wise, peeled	¼ cup water, ½ teaspoon salt in 2-quart covered casserole. Stir after 5 minutes	12 - 14 minutes	High	3 minutes, covered
Sweet Potatoes, baked whole (fresh)	All medium size 1 2 4	Scrub and dry potatoes. Cover oven shelf with paper towel, put potatoes on towel about 1-inch apart	5 - 7 minutes 7 - 9 minutes 14 - 16 minutes	High High High	Wrap in foil after cooking, let stand 5 - 10 minutes
Zucchini (fresh)	One (1 lb.)	Wash, remove stems. Cut into thin slices. Add ¼ cup water in 1-quart covered casserole	5 - 5½ minutes	High	3 minutes, covered
Tomatoes (fresh)	4 large 2½ - 3-inch dia. (1 lb.)	Clean, peel and halve tomatoes. Place in 1½-quart covered casserole. Add 2 tablespoons water	4 - 6 minutes	High	3 minutes, covered Add ½ teaspoon salt
Turnips (fresh)	2 or 3 medium (1 lb.)	Peel and cube. Add 3 tablespoons water, ¼ teaspoon salt in 1½-quart covered casserole	7 - 9 minutes	High	3 minutes, covered
Vegetables, Mixed (frozen)	10 ounce package	Add ¼ cup hot water in 1-quart covered casserole	4 - 6 minutes	High	3 minutes, covered
	10 ounce pouch	Split pouch with knife	4 - 6 minutes	High	3 minutes, covered

Rice, Pasta & Cereals

Spanish Rice

Rice and pasta are dry foods, and need time to absorb moisture. Since only a little time is saved by microwave cooking, you may prefer to cook rice and pasta conventionally while you prepare the sauce or main dish in the microwave oven. Rice and pasta reheat easily in a covered casserole and need no additional water. If they have been refrigerated, stir once or twice during heating.

Use rice and pasta to create your own quick-and-easy dinners. Add chopped onion, green pepper or celery, canned shrimp, chopped luncheon meat or leftover roast. For variety, add 1 teaspoon instant chicken or beef bouillon for each cup of water when cooking rice.

Hot cooked cereals are so easy by microwave that children can cook their own breakfast right in the cereal bowl, and there won't be a messy pan left to soak in the sink.

QUICK SHRIMP RICE

4 to 6 servings
1½-quart casserole

3 *cups hot cooked rice*
1 *can (8-ounces) small cooked shrimp, drained*
1 *can (6-ounces) water chestnuts, drained and sliced*
½ *cup finely chopped onion*
½ *cup finely chopped celery*
⅓ *cup butter, cut in bits*
¼ *cup dry sherry*
1 *clove garlic, pressed or finely chopped*
½ *teaspoon salt*

Combine all ingredients in a 1½-quart casserole. Mix well. Cover. MICROWAVE 4 MINUTES on HIGH, or until heated through, stirring after 2 minutes.

RICE VERDE

3 to 4 servings
1½-quart casserole

¼ *cup butter or margarine*
1 *small onion, finely chopped*
1 *cup hot cooked rice*
1 *package (10-ounces) chopped spinach, defrosted*
1 *cup milk*
1 *egg, slightly beaten*
½ *teaspoon salt*
1 *cup grated sharp cheddar cheese*

Combine butter and onion in 1½-quart casserole. MICROWAVE 2 to 3 MINUTES on HIGH, or until onion is transparent. Stir in rice, spinach, milk, beaten egg, salt and cheddar cheese, mixing well with fork. Cover. MICROWAVE 4 to 6 MINUTES on HIGH, or until mixture is hot and cheese is melted.

NOTE: If using cold leftover rice, microwave 1 to 2 minutes longer.

152

RICE PILAF

6 to 8 servings
2-quart casserole

¼ cup butter or margarine
1 medium onion, finely chopped
½ cup finely chopped celery
1½ cups uncooked regular rice
¼ cup snipped parsley
¼ teaspoon salt
Dash pepper
⅓ bay leaf
⅛ teaspoon thyme
1 can (10½-ounces) condensed chicken broth
1⅓ cups water

Combine butter, onion and celery in 2-quart casserole. MICROWAVE 3 to 4 MINUTES on HIGH, or until onion is transparent.

Add rice, parsley, salt, pepper, bay leaf, thyme, broth and water. Cover. MICROWAVE 5 to 6 MINUTES on HIGH, or until mixture begins to boil.

Reduce setting. MICROWAVE 16 to 18 MINUTES on '5', or until rice is tender. Let stand 3 to 5 minutes, covered. Remove bay leaf before serving.

Variations:

ITALIAN RICE

Substitute ⅓ cup dry white wine for ⅓ cup water. Add ⅛ teaspoon powdered or crushed saffron threads to water. Just before serving, stir in 2 tablespoons soft butter and ⅓ cup grated parmesan cheese.

INDIAN PILAF

Substitute ¼ teaspoon allspice and ¼ teaspoon curry powder for bay leaf and thyme. Add ⅓ cup raisins.

MINNESOTA WILD RICE CASSEROLE ▣ ▣

4 to 6 servings
1-quart casserole

1 package (12-ounces) frozen white and wild rice
4 ounces fresh mushrooms, chopped
1 medium onion, chopped
2 tablespoons butter or margarine

Place pouch of rice in oven. MICROWAVE 5 MINUTES on HIGH, or until hot, flexing pouch after 3 minutes. Set aside.

Combine mushrooms, onions and butter in casserole with butter on top. MICROWAVE 2 MINUTES, 30 SECONDS to 3 MINUTES on HIGH, stirring after 1 minute.

Add rice to mushroom mixture. If necessary, MICROWAVE 30 SECONDS to warm.

SPANISH RICE

6 servings
1-quart casserole

1 package (7-ounces) instant rice
1¾ cups water
1 can (8-ounces) tomato sauce
¼ cup finely chopped green peppers
1 tablespoon onion flakes
2 tablespoons chili powder
2 tablespoons bacon drippings
¾ teaspoon salt

Combine all ingredients in 1-quart casserole. Cover. MICROWAVE 10 to 12 MINUTES on HIGH, or until water is absorbed. Fluff rice with fork.

RICE PUDDING

4 servings
1-quart measure
2-quart casserole

1 cup cooked rice
2 cups milk
2 eggs, beaten
½ cup sugar
⅛ teaspoon salt
½ cup raisins
¼ teaspoon cinnamon
½ teaspoon vanilla

Measure milk in 1-quart measure. MICROWAVE 2 to 3 MINUTES on HIGH, or until almost boiling.

Combine eggs, sugar and salt in 2-quart casserole. Stir in scalded milk. Mix in rice, raisins, cinnamon and vanilla thoroughly. MICROWAVE 5 to 7 MINUTES on '6', or until set.

For ovens without solid state heat control, MICROWAVE 6 to 8 MINUTES on '5'.

LONG GRAIN RICE

4 to 6 servings
2-quart casserole

2½ cups water
1 teaspoon salt
1 teaspoon salad oil, butter, or margarine
1 cup long grain rice

Combine all ingredients in 2-quart casserole. Stir. Cover. MICROWAVE 5 MINUTES on HIGH.

Reduce setting. MICROWAVE 10 to 12 MINUTES on '5', or until rice is tender and water is absorbed.

PREPARATION INSTRUCTIONS FOR PASTA

ITEM	COOKING DISH	HOT WATER	BRING WATER TO BOIL ON HIGH	Add Pasta, 1 teaspoon salt, 1 teaspoon oil	REDUCE SETTING TO '5' AND HEAT	SPECIAL INSTRUCTIONS
Egg Noodles 8 oz. (4 cups)	3-quart casserole	1½-quart	5 - 7 min. covered		6 - 8 min. uncovered	Drain and rinse if desired
Lasagna 8 oz.	2-quart utility dish	1-quart	4 - 6 min. covered		8 - 10 min. uncovered	Drain and rinse if desired
Macaroni 7 oz. (2 cups)	3-quart casserole	1½-quart	5 - 7 min. covered		8 - 10 min. uncovered	Drain and rinse if desired
Spaghetti 7 oz.	2-quart utility dish	1-quart	4 - 6 min. covered		6 - 8 min. uncovered	Drain and rinse if desired

PERFECT EGG NOODLES

4 to 6 servings
3-quart casserole

1½ *quarts water*
1 *teaspoon salt*
1 *teaspoon oil*
1 *package (8-ounces) egg noodles (approximately 4 cups)*

Pour water into casserole. Cover. MICROWAVE 5 to 7 MINUTES on HIGH, or until water is boiling.

Stir in salt, oil and noodles. Do not cover. MICROWAVE 6 to 8 MINUTES on '5', or until tender. Drain. Rinse if desired.

ONE MAN OATMEAL

1 serving
Cereal bowl

¼ *cup quick-cooking oats*
½ *cup water*
Dash salt

Stir oats, water and salt together in cereal bowl. MICROWAVE 1 MINUTE, 15 SECONDS on HIGH. Stir. Let stand 3 minutes, covered. Serve with milk and sugar.

FAMILY OATMEAL

4 to 6 servings
1½ to 2-quart casserole

1½ *cups regular oatmeal*
3 *cups water*
¾ *teaspoon salt*

Stir oatmeal, water and salt together in 1½-quart casserole. MICROWAVE 6 to 8 MINUTES on HIGH, or until creamy, stirring once. Let stand 3 to 5 minutes, covered. Serve with milk and granulated or brown sugar.

PREPARATION INSTRUCTIONS FOR RICE

ITEM	COOKING DISH	HOT WATER	ADD RICE TO WATER PLUS:	HEAT ON HIGH	REDUCE SETTING TO '5'	SPECIAL INSTRUCTIONS
Brown Rice 1 cup	2-quart casserole	3 cups	1 tsp. salt	6 min. covered	11 - 13 min. covered	Let stand if necessary
Long Grain 1 cup	2-quart casserole	2 cups	1 tsp. oil or butter	5 min. covered	10 - 12 min. covered	Let stand if necessary
Quick Cooking 1½ cup	1-quart casserole	1½ cups	1 tsp. salt	2 - 4 min. covered		Let stand 3 - 5 min. fluff with fork
Wild Rice 1 cup	2-quart casserole	2½ cups	1 tsp. salt, 2 tsp. butter	6 min. covered	16 - 18 min. covered	Let stand if necessary
Wild and White Rice Mix 6 oz. package	2-quart casserole	2 cups	1 tsp. salt, 1 tsp. butter	5 min. covered	12 - 14 min. covered	Let stand if necessary

GRITS ROYALE

4 servings
1½-quart casserole

⅔ cup grits
3 cups water
¾ teaspoon salt

Stir grits and water together in 1½-quart casserole. MICROWAVE 5 MINUTES to 5 MINUTES, 30 SECONDS on HIGH, or until desired doneness. Stir in salt. Serve with butter or margarine, or with milk and sugar as a hot cereal. Grits may be substituted for rice as a side dish.

For fried grits, make as above. Preheat micro-browner 3 to 4 MINUTES on HIGH, add butter or margarine and grits. MICROWAVE 30 SECONDS on HIGH. Turn if desired.

One serving of grits may be made in 1-quart casserole following method above. Use 3 tablespoons grits, 1 cup water, dash salt. MICROWAVE 3 MINUTES to 3 MINUTES, 30 SECONDS on HIGH.

QUICK CREAM OF WHEAT 🔳

1 serving
Cereal bowl

2 tablespoons cream of wheat
¾ cup water
Dash salt

Stir cream of wheat, water and salt together in cereal bowl. MICROWAVE 1 MINUTE, 30 SECONDS on HIGH, stirring once. Let stand 3 minutes.

Sauces & Toppings

Sauces are easy to make in the microwave oven. Add variety to meals with sauced meats, fish or vegetables. Make old-fashioned cooked salad dressing with modern ease. Create a quick dessert with sauce and fruit, cake or ice cream.

With microwave cooking, sauces heat more evenly, so they require less attention. An occasional stir with a wire whip is all they need to prevent scorching and lumping.

Make sauces right in the cup you use to measure. For small quantities, halve the recipe and cook for the same amount of time on '5'. Small amounts do better on the lower setting.

CURRANT-RAISIN SAUCE

2 cups
1-quart measure or casserole

½ cup orange juice
½ cup water
⅓ cup currant jelly
⅓ cup raisins
½ teaspoon grated orange rind
1 tablespoon corn starch
1 tablespoon water
2 tablespoons firmly packed brown sugar
Dash of allspice
Dash of salt

Combine orange juice, water, jelly, raisins and orange rind in 1-quart measure or casserole. MICROWAVE 3 to 4 MINUTES on HIGH, or until boiling.

Blend corn starch with water in a small bowl to make a smooth paste. Add brown sugar, allspice and salt. Mix well. Stir into hot mixture. MICROWAVE 4 MINUTES on HIGH, or until thick and clear, stirring after 2 minutes. Serve with ham or duck.

BECHAMEL SAUCE

1 cup
Glass custard cup
1-quart measure or bowl

2 tablespoons butter or margarine
1 tablespoon flour
½ cup light cream
½ cup chicken broth, or ½ teaspoon instant chicken bouillon dissolved in ½ cup water
2 teaspoons grated onion, or ½ teaspoon instant minced onion
½ teaspoon salt
Pepper
Pinch thyme

Place butter in custard cup. MICROWAVE on HIGH until butter is melted. Blend in flour to make a smooth paste. Set aside.

Combine cream, chicken broth and onion in 1-quart measure or bowl. MICROWAVE 2 MINUTES, 30 SEC-

ONDS on HIGH, or until mixture is about to boil. Beat in butter-flour paste, using a wire whip. MICROWAVE 2 MINUTES on '8', or until thickened, stirring after 1 minute. Stir in salt, pepper and thyme.

For ovens without solid state heat control, use HIGH for second cooking period, beating every 30 seconds.

MORNAY SAUCE

Stir in ¼ to ½ cup grated Swiss cheese. Serve with eggs, fish, poultry, pasta, vegetables.

NEWBURG SAUCE

Follow directions for Bechamel Sauce, substitute fish stock for chicken broth. After cooking, add ¼ cup chopped cooked shrimp and a pinch of cayenne. Serve with eggs, fish, rice or toast.

FLUFFY HOLLANDAISE

⅔ cup
1-quart mixing bowl

¼ *cup butter or margarine*
¼ *cup whipping cream*
2 *egg yolks, well beaten*
1 *tablespoon lemon juice*
½ *teaspoon dry mustard*
¼ *teaspoon salt*

Place butter in 1-quart bowl. MICROWAVE on HIGH until melted. Add remaining ingredients. Mix well. MICROWAVE 1 MINUTE to 1 MINUTE, 30 SECONDS on '5', or until thickened, stirring halfway through. Beat with wire whip or rotary beater until light and fluffy.

Serve with eggs, fish or vegetables.

NOTE: Over cooking will curdle sauce.

BARBECUE SAUCE

1½ cups
1-quart measure or bowl

1 *cup catsup*
¼ *cup cider vinegar*
1 *tablespoon Worcestershire sauce*
2 *tablespoons finely chopped onion*
2 *tablespoons firmly packed brown sugar*
1 *tablespoon paprika*
1 *teaspoon sugar*
1 *teaspoon salt*
Pepper to taste

Combine all ingredients in a 1-quart measure or bowl. Mix well. MICROWAVE 5 MINUTES on HIGH, or until sauce is hot and thick enough to coat a spoon, stirring after three minutes.

TERIYAKI SAUCE

2¼ cups
1-quart bowl or casserole

2 *tablespoons corn starch*
¼ *cup soy sauce*
1 *can (10½-ounces) beef broth, diluted with water to make 2 cups, or 2 teaspoons instant beef bouillon dissolved in 2 cups water*
2 *tablespoons dry white wine*
2 *teaspoons finely chopped fresh ginger, or ⅛ teaspoon ground ginger*
1 *clove garlic, pressed or finely minced*

Blend corn starch with soy sauce in a 1-quart bowl to make a smooth paste. Add beef broth, wine, ginger and garlic. Mix well. MICROWAVE on HIGH 4 to 5 MINUTES, or until clear, stirring after 3 minutes. Serve with pork, poultry or as a rumaki dip.

WHITE SAUCE

1 cup
Glass custard cup
1-quart measure or bowl

2 *tablespoons butter or margarine*
2 *tablespoons flour*
½ *teaspoon salt*
1 *cup milk*

Place butter in custard cup. MICROWAVE on HIGH until butter is melted. Blend in flour and salt to make a smooth paste. Set aside.

Place milk in 1-quart measure or bowl. MICROWAVE 2 MINUTES, 30 SECONDS on HIGH, or until milk is about to boil.

Beat in butter-flour paste, using a wire whip. MICROWAVE 2 MINUTES on '8', or until thickened, stir after 1 minute. Mix well before using.

NOTE: To double recipe, heat 2 cups milk 4 to 5 minutes on HIGH.

For ovens without solid state heat control, use HIGH for second cooking period, beating every 30 seconds.

CHEDDAR CHEESE SAUCE

Add ½ cup grated sharp cheddar cheese and pinch of cayenne to white sauce. Stir until melted.

CURRY SAUCE

Add 1 teaspoon or more curry powder to white sauce.

MAUNA LOA SAUCE

About 1 cup
1-quart measuring cup or bowl

1 tablespoon corn starch
¼ cup water
⅓ cup pineapple juice
3 tablespoons soy sauce
2 tablespoons salad oil
2 tablespoons cider vinegar
1 tablespoon sugar
1 teaspoon salt

Dissolve corn starch in water. Add pineapple juice, soy sauce, salad oil, vinegar, sugar and salt. Mix well. Cover with waxed paper. MICROWAVE 3 to 4 MINUTES on HIGH, or until thickened. Stir once after first 2 minutes. Serve with pork, chicken, lamb or beef.

SALSA DI VONGOLE (White Clam Sauce)

3 cups
1-quart measure

2 tablespoons butter or margarine
1 clove garlic, pressed or finely chopped
1 tablespoon flour
1 egg, beaten
1 cup milk
1 can (6½-ounces) minced clams, drained
¼ cup snipped fresh parsley
¾ teaspoon thyme
¾ teaspoon basil
¼ teaspoon salt
⅛ teaspoon pepper

Combine butter and garlic in 1-quart measure. MICROWAVE on HIGH until butter melts. Blend in flour to make a smooth paste. Stir in remaining ingredients. MICROWAVE 4 MINUTES on '8', or until slightly thickened. Stir half way through.

For ovens without solid state heat control, MICROWAVE 3 MINUTES, 30 SECONDS on HIGH, stirring halfway through.

Serve with pasta or fish.

GRAVY

2 cups
1-quart measure

½ cup all-purpose flour
1½ cups water
½ cup pan drippings
Salt and pepper

Combine flour and water in 1-quart measure. Beat with wire whip until smooth. Beat in drippings. MICROWAVE 3 to 4 MINUTES on HIGH, or until mixture boils, stirring once. Season with salt and pepper.

OLD-FASHIONED COOKED SALAD DRESSING

3 cups
1½-quart bowl

1½ cups water
1 cup cider vinegar
½ cup sugar
3 tablespoons flour
1 teaspoon salt
1 teaspoon dry mustard
6 egg yolks, well beaten

Combine 1 cup water, vinegar and sugar in 1½-quart bowl. MICROWAVE 3 to 4 MINUTES on HIGH, or until sugar is dissolved.

Blend flour, salt and mustard with remaining ½ cup water in 1-cup measure. Stir into hot vinegar mixture. Mix well. MICROWAVE 4 MINUTES on HIGH, or until slightly thickened. Stir.

Pour ¼ cup hot sauce into beaten egg yolks. Mix well. Pour into remaining sauce and stir until well blended. MICROWAVE 5 MINUTES on HIGH, or until thickened, beating well after 3 minutes.

NOTE: Keeps well in refrigerator.

FRUIT SALAD DRESSING

2 cups
1-quart bowl

¼ cup lemon juice
¼ cup pineapple juice
½ cup sugar
2 eggs, well beaten
1 cup whipping cream, whipped

Combine lemon and pineapple juices in 1-quart bowl. MICROWAVE 1 to 2 MINUTES on HIGH, or until hot.

Fold sugar into beaten eggs. Slowly add egg mixture to hot fruit juice, beating well after each addition. MICROWAVE 1 MINUTE on HIGH, or until thickened. Stir.

Chill at least 20 minutes in refrigerator. Before serving, fold in whipped cream.

TIPSY FRUIT SAUCE ▦

1¼ cups
1-quart measure

1 package (10-ounces) frozen berries or peaches, defrosted
2 tablespoons liqueur or sweet wine

Pour berries and their juice into 1-quart measure. MICROWAVE 1 MINUTE, 30 SECONDS on HIGH, or until berries are warm. Stir in liqueur.

Serve warm over ice cream, cake or sherbet.

HOT FUDGE SAUCE

1 cup
1-quart measure or bowl

2 *squares unsweetened chocolate*
¼ *cup butter or margarine*
¼ *cup evaporated milk*
½ *cup powdered sugar*
1 *teaspoon vanilla*

Place chocolate and butter in 1-quart measure or bowl. MICROWAVE 2 MINUTES on HIGH, or until chocolate and butter are melted. Stir.

Stir in milk. Add sugar and beat until smooth and creamy. Add vanilla.

NOTE: Can be reheated easily. Excellent over ice cream, cake or fruits.

CHOCOLATE MINT TOPPING

2 cups
1½-quart casserole

3 *squares unsweetened chocolate*
¼ *cup water*
1 *cup sugar*
½ *cup light corn syrup*
Pinch salt
⅔ *cup heavy cream or evaporated milk*
⅛ *teaspoon peppermint extract*

Combine chocolate and water in 1½-quart casserole. MICROWAVE 1 MINUTE, 30 SECONDS on HIGH, or until chocolate is melted.

Add sugar, corn syrup and salt. Blend well, MICROWAVE 1 MINUTE on HIGH, or until a little dropped in cold water forms a soft ball. If necessary, MICROWAVE 1 MINUTE more. Stir, test again.

Gradually stir in cream and peppermint extract. Serve warm or cold.

LEMON DESSERT SAUCE

1½ cups
2-cup measure

1 *cup water*
½ *cup sugar*
1 *tablespoon corn starch*
2 *tablespoons butter or margarine*
1½ *teaspoons lemon juice*
½ *teaspoon lemon rind*
⅛ *teaspoon salt*

Measure water into 2-cup measure. Stir in sugar and corn starch until dissolved. MICROWAVE 4 MINUTES on HIGH, or until slightly thickened.

Add butter, lemon juice, rind and salt. Stir until butter is melted. Serve warm or cold over pudding or cake.

Hot Fudge Sauce.

NOTE: Sauce will be the consistency of light cream.
Variations:
Add fresh blueberries, raspberries or halved and pitted cherries before serving.

VELVET CUSTARD SAUCE

2 cups
1-quart bowl or casserole

½ *cup sugar*
2 *tablespoons corn starch*
1 *teaspoon salt*
2 *cups milk*
4 *egg yolks, well beaten*
1 *teaspoon vanilla, sherry, rum or lemon extract*

Combine sugar, corn starch and salt in 1-quart bowl. Mix well.

Gradually add milk to dry ingredients, stirring until mixture is smooth. Add egg yolks, beating until well combined.

MICROWAVE 4 to 5 MINUTES on '8', or until mixture coats a metal spoon, stirring after 8 minutes.

Stir in vanilla or other flavoring and chill thoroughly.

Serve over cake or ice cream.

For ovens without solid state heat control, MICROWAVE 3 to 4 MINUTES on HIGH.

159

Baking

With microwave's short cooking times you can have fresh hot muffins and coffeecakes whenever you want them, as a surprise for breakfast or an impromptu coffee break with a neighbor. Save time by proofing fresh or frozen yeast breads in the microwave oven. Warm rolls.

Treat yourself to dressed-up French breads for a party touch at a family meal. Use the microwave oven set at '5' to dry bread crumbs and toast croutons. To make seasoned croutons, spread butter and seasonings on bread slices, cut in cubes and dry on a microwave roasting rack.

Clockwise, starting from basket, Corn Muffins, Sticky Buns, Date Nut Bread, Onion-Cheese Sticks. Recipes on following pages.

BAKING BASICS

With microwave cooking, muffins and coffeecakes will be ready in one-sixth to one-third the time needed conventionally. As they will not brown in this time, they need toppings, frostings or ingredients which supply color, such as spices, brown sugar or corn meal.

Baked goods rise more in the microwave oven, so fill muffin cups half full. Use an 8 x 8-inch baking dish for coffeecakes. If you want a round coffeecake, use the extra batter for muffins.

Use the microwave oven for proofing fresh or frozen yeast breads. If you wish to bake yeast breads in the microwave oven, use a recipe with corn meal, whole wheat or rye flour for color.

Breads and rolls should be heated only until warm to the touch. A few seconds is sufficient. Overheating makes bread tough or rubbery.

Heat breads on a paper napkin or towel to absorb excess moisture, or use the microwave roasting rack.

PROOFING FROZEN BREAD

1 pound loaf
9 x 5-inch loaf dish

1 *loaf (1-pound) frozen white bread dough*

Place dough in greased (9 x 5-inch) loaf dish. Cover loosely with plastic wrap. MICROWAVE 55 to 60 MINUTES on '1' (low), or until double.

Heat conventional oven to 425°. Bake loaf 20 to 25 minutes, or until golden brown and loaf sounds hollow when tapped.

Remove from loaf dish. Brush with soft butter. Cool on wire rack.

NOTE: This recipe is not suitable for ovens without variable heat control.

WHOLE WHEAT BREAD

1 loaf
Medium mixing bowl
9 x 5-inch loaf dish

¾ cup milk
¼ cup sugar
1 teaspoon salt
2 tablespoons shortening
1 package active dry yeast
¼ cup warm water (105° to 115°)
1 egg, slightly beaten
1½ cups all-purpose flour
2 cups whole wheat flour
Soft butter or margarine

Measure milk into large mixing bowl. MICROWAVE 3 to 4 MINUTES on HIGH, or until bubbles form around edge. Stir in sugar, salt and shortening. Let stand until lukewarm.

Dissolve yeast in warm water. Stir yeast into lukewarm milk mixture. Add egg, all-purpose flour and ½ cup whole wheat flour. Beat until smooth. Mix in remaining flour. Turn dough out onto well-floured board. Knead until smooth and elastic (about 5 minutes). Place in greased bowl. Turn greased side up. Cover with plastic wrap. Let rise until double in bulk. (See note.)

Punch dough down. Knead lightly on floured board. Shape into loaf. Place in greased (9 x 5-inch) loaf dish. Brush lightly with butter. Let rise until double. (See note.) MICROWAVE 6 to 8 MINUTES on '5'.

NOTE: To proof bread in microwave ovens with variable or solid state heat control. MICROWAVE 15 to 20 MINUTES on '1'.

SODA BREAD

1 loaf
2½-quart casserole

4 *cups all-purpose flour*
⅓ *cup sugar*
1 *tablespoon baking powder*
1 *teaspoon soda*
1 *teaspoon salt*
½ *cup butter or margarine*
1½ *cups raisins*
½ *cup chopped nuts*
1⅓ *cups sour milk (add 1 teaspoon vinegar to regular milk)*
1 *egg*
1 *tablespoon water*
1 *egg yolk*

Stir together flour, sugar, baking powder, soda and salt in large mixing bowl. Cut in butter with a pastry blender until mixture is well blended to a coarse grainy texture. Stir in raisins and nuts. Thoroughly mix in milk and egg.

Set into lightly greased 2½-quart casserole. With a sharp knife, cut an X in top. Mix water and egg yolk together. Brush surface of bread. MICROWAVE 14 to16 MINUTES on '8', or until center is firm.

Turn out of pan on rack. Cool completely before serving.

For ovens without solid state heat control, MICROWAVE 11 to 13 MINUTES on HIGH.

DEPENDABLE DUMPLINGS

8 servings
1½ to 2-quart casserole

2½ *cups stock or lightly salted water*
1 *cup flour*
1½ *teaspoons baking powder*
½ *teaspoon salt*
3 *tablespoons shortening*
⅔ *cup milk*

Pour stock into 1½-quart casserole. MICROWAVE 6 to 8 MINUTES on HIGH, or until boiling.

Measure flour, baking powder and salt into mixing bowl. Cut in shortening until mixture looks like corn meal. Stir in milk until mixture is moistened but not smooth. Drop dough by rounded teaspoonfuls onto boiling stock. Do not cover. MICROWAVE 6 MINUTES on HIGH.

Cover. MICROWAVE 5 MINUTES on HIGH, or until dumplings are firm. Remove dumplings to serving dish with slotted spoon.

ONION-CHEESE STICKS

16 pieces
Microwave roasting rack in
12 x 8-inch utility dish or,
Paper towels

1 *cup quick biscuit mix*
⅓ *cup milk*
⅓ *cup grated American cheese*
1 *package (1¼-ounces) dry onion soup mix*

Measure biscuit mix into 1-quart bowl. Stir in milk to make soft dough. Mix in cheese. Turn out on lightly floured pastry cloth. Knead lightly several times.

Pinch off 1-inch balls of dough. Roll into sticks. Roll sticks in soup mix to coat. Arrange 6 to 8 at a time on microwave roasting rack in (12 x 8-inch) utility dish, or paper towels. MICROWAVE 3 to 4 MINUTES on '8', or until firm to touch.

For ovens without solid state heat control, MICROWAVE 2 to 3 MINUTES on HIGH, watching carefully.

STICKY BUNS

8 pieces
8-inch cake dish

1 *cup quick biscuit mix*
⅓ *cup milk*
2 *tablespoons butter or margarine, melted*
¼ *cup sugar*
1 *teaspoon cinnamon*
2 *tablespoons butter or margarine, softened*
2 *tablespoons firmly packed brown sugar*
¼ *cup walnut or pecan pieces*

Measure biscuit mix into 1-quart bowl. Stir in milk to make a soft dough. Turn out on lightly floured pastry cloth. Knead lightly several times. Roll out in 8-inch square. Brush with melted butter. Mix together sugar and cinnamon. Sprinkle on dough. Roll up. Cut in 1-inch pieces.

Combine softened butter and brown sugar in 8-inch cake dish. Spread to cover bottom. Scatter nuts over sugar mixture. Arrange rolls in dish. MICROWAVE 5 to 6 MINUTES on HIGH, or until wooden pick inserted in center comes out clean. Let stand 5 minutes. Invert onto serving plate.

BUTTERMILK BRAN MUFFINS

20 to 24 pieces
Medium mixing bowl
Doubled paper baking cups

½ cup hot water
1½ cups all bran cereal
¼ cup butter or margarine
¾ cup sugar
¼ cup brown sugar
2 eggs
2 cups all-purpose flour
3 teaspoons baking powder
¼ teaspoon salt
1 cup buttermilk

Measure water into medium mixing bowl. MICRO-WAVE 2 MINUTES on HIGH, or until water boils. Stir in cereal. Add butter. Let stand until butter is softened. Beat in sugars and egg. Blend in flour, baking powder, salt and buttermilk until well mixed. Spoon into baking cups, filling them half full. See chart for cooking times.

NOTE: This recipe can be doubled, stored in refrigerator for 1 month to 6 weeks, and used as needed. Add 12 to 15 seconds additional time when using chilled batter.

DOWN HOME STREUSEL COFFEE CAKE

9 to 12 servings
8 x 8-inch baking dish

⅓ cup butter or margarine
¾ cup sugar
2 eggs
1 teaspoon almond or vanilla extract
1½ cups all-purpose flour
2½ teaspoons baking powder
½ teaspoon salt
½ cup milk
Streusel, below

Place butter in large mixing bowl. If necessary, MICRO-WAVE 20 SECONDS on '5' to soften. Cream sugar with butter until fluffy. Beat in eggs and almond extract. Stir in flour, baking powder, salt and milk.

Pour all coffee cake mixture in pan. MICROWAVE 6 MINUTES on '8'. Then sprinkle on streusel topping and MICROWAVE 4 to 5 MINUTES on '8' or until wooden pick inserted in center comes out clean.

For ovens without solid state heat control, MICROWAVE 5 MINUTES on HIGH and 3 to 4 MINUTES on HIGH.

STREUSEL TOPPING

1 cup firmly packed brown sugar
¼ cup flour
¼ cup granulated sugar
½ teaspoon cinnamon
½ cup chopped nuts
2 tablespoons butter or margarine, melted
Blend all ingredients in small bowl.

GARLIC BREAD

24 ½-inch slices
Custard cup
Waxed paper

1 loaf (1-pound) French or Vienna bread
⅓ cup butter or margarine
1 teaspoon parmesan cheese
½ teaspoon garlic salt

Cut bread in ½-inch slices, leaving bottom crust intact. Set aside on piece of waxed paper large enough to wrap bread.

Place butter in custard cup. MICROWAVE 30 SEC-ONDS on HIGH, or until butter melts. Stir in cheese and garlic salt. Pour between bread slices.

Bring sides of waxed paper up over top of loaf. Twist ends to close loosely. MICROWAVE 45 SECONDS on HIGH, or until bread is warm. Cut slices free. Serve.

Variation:

ONION HERB BREAD

Substitute for cheese-garlic butter:

½ cup butter
2 teaspoons snipped parsley
½ teaspoon salt
¼ teaspoon onion salt
¼ teaspoon thyme
¼ teaspoon paprika

CORN BREAD

9 to 12 pieces
8 x 8-inch baking dish

1 cup corn meal
1 cup flour
¼ cup sugar
1 teaspoon baking powder
1 teaspoon salt
½ teaspoon soda
1 cup sour milk
1 egg, well beaten
2 tablespoons melted shortening

Blend all ingredients in mixing bowl. Beat thoroughly. Pour into (8 x 8-inch) baking dish. MICROWAVE 5 to 6 MINUTES on HIGH, or until wooden pick inserted in center comes out clean.

Variation:

Spoon batter into doubled paper baking cups or custard cups with paper liners. Fill cups ½ full. Bake according to muffin chart.

PREPARATION INSTRUCTIONS
FOR MUFFINS

NUMBER OF MUFFINS	SETTING	TIME
1	High	35 - 40 sec.
2	High	45 - 60 sec.
4	High	45 sec. - 1½ min.
6	High	1½ - 2 min.

Prepare mix according to package directions. Microwave in paper muffin cups (double thickness).

FAST CHEESE FRENCHIES ⊞

24 ½-inch slices
Waxed paper

1 *loaf (1-pound) French bread*
French or Italian salad dressing
Grated parmesan cheese

Cut bread diagonally in 1-inch slices, leaving bottom crust intact. Place on sheet of waxed paper large enough to wrap loaf. Spread dressing between slices and over top of loaf. Sprinkle generously with parmesan cheese. Bring sides of paper up over top of loaf. Twist ends to close loosely. MICROWAVE 45 SECONDS on HIGH, or until bread is warm.

STREUSEL COFFEE CAKE

9 servings
8 x 8-inch baking dish

1 *package (14½-ounces) streusel coffee cake mix*

Prepare coffee cake as directed on package. Pour all the batter into (8 x 8-inch) baking dish. Sprinkle all streusel topping on top. MICROWAVE 7 to 9 MINUTES on '6', or until wooden pick inserted in center comes out clean, rotating dish once. Let stand 5 minutes.

For ovens without solid state heat control, MICROWAVE 8 to 10 MINUTES on '5'.

DRESSED UP GINGERBREAD

9 servings
8 x 8-inch baking dish

1 *package gingerbread mix*
Sweetened whipped cream or ice cream
¼ *cup crushed peppermint candy*

Prepare gingerbread as directed on package. Pour into (8 x 8-inch) baking dish. MICROWAVE 5 to 7 MINUTES on '8', or until top is slightly firm to touch.

Cool slightly. Serve warm topped with whipped cream or ice cream. Sprinkle with crushed candy.

For ovens without solid state heat control, MICROWAVE 4 to 6 MINUTES on HIGH.

DATE NUT BREAD

1 loaf
9 x 5-inch loaf dish

1 *package (17-ounces) Date Nut Bread mix*

Prepare bread as directed on package. Grease loaf dish and line bottom with waxed paper. Pour batter into loaf dish. MICROWAVE 8 to 9 MINUTES on '8', or until top is slightly moist and wooden pick inserted in center comes out clean, rotating dish once. Let stand 10 minutes. Remove from loaf dish.

NOTE: Top will be slightly irregular.

For ovens without solid state heat control, MICROWAVE 6 to 7 MINUTES on HIGH, rotating dish once.

Desserts

Glamorous party desserts, traditional family favorites, spur-of-the-moment treats, all become quick and easy with your microwave oven. Desserts make even a simple meal something special.

Use the microwave oven to soften toppings, warm sauces or toast nuts to dress up cakes or ice cream. Warm pie or cake a few seconds by microwave for fresh from the oven flavor.

Be creative. Using these recipes as inspiration, invent some new desserts of your own with package mixes, toppings, fresh or canned fruits, or new combinations with canned pudding and pie filling.

MOCHA TORTE

8 to 10 servings
3 (8-inch) round cake dishes, lined with waxed paper

1 *package (18½-ounces) chocolate cake mix*
2 *tablespoons cinnamon*
½ *teaspoon cloves*
Mocha Filling, below

Blend dry cake mix, cinnamon and cloves in large mixing bowl. Prepare cake according to package directions. Divide batter among 3 (8-inch) round cake dishes. One at a time, MICROWAVE 4 MINUTES, 30 SECONDS to 5 MINUTES on '6', or until wooden pick inserted in center comes out clean.

Let stand 5 minutes. Immediately turn out on cake rack. Cool

For ovens without solid state heat control, MICROWAVE 5 MINUTES, 20 SECONDS to 6 MINUTES on '5'.

Mocha Filling

Fill and frost 3 (8-inch) round cake layers
1-quart bowl

1 *package (3¾-ounces) instant vanilla pudding mix*
2 *tablespoons instant coffee*
2 *cups prepared whipped topping mix*

Blend dry pudding mix and coffee in 1-quart bowl. Prepare pudding according to package directions. Let stand 20 minutes to set.

Gently fold pudding into topping.

Fill layers and frost top of Mocha Torte, using ⅓ of filling for each layer. Garnish with shaved semi-sweet or unsweetened chocolate. Refrigerate until ready to serve.

DESSERT BASICS

Cakes cook in the microwave oven in one-sixth to one-third the time needed conventionally. If the cake is to be turned out for layering and frosting, line the bottom of the baking dish with waxed paper for easy removal.

To line a round cake dish, tear off an 8 or 9-inch length of waxed paper. Fold and cut as shown.

A waxed paper lining is not necessary if the cake is to be served from the dish.

A few moist spots may appear on the surface of the cake, but the cake is done if the top springs back lightly when touched, or when a wooden pick inserted in the center comes out clean.

When baking conventionally, use your microwave oven to scald milk, soften butter, melt chocolate and prepare cooked frostings and fillings.

Pastry shells cooked by microwave are especially tender and flaky, but they do not brown.

Since they cook from all sides, smooth puddings, fillings and custards can be made quickly with only occasional, rather than frequent or constant stirring.

Baked fresh fruits and compotes keep their fresh flavor and texture when cooked.

APPLESAUCE-SPICE CAKE

2-layer cake
8-inch cake dish, lined with waxed paper

½ *cup shortening*
2 *cups sugar*
2 *eggs*
2½ *cups all-purpose flour*
1½ *teaspoons soda*
1½ *teaspoons salt*
¼ *teaspoon baking powder*
¾ *teaspoon cinnamon*
½ *teaspoon cloves*
¼ *teaspoon nutmeg*
1 *cup raisins*
½ *cup chopped walnuts*
1½ *cups applesauce*
½ *cup water*

Cream shortening and sugar together. Beat in eggs. Add flour, soda, salt, baking powder, cinnamon, cloves, nutmeg, raisins and nuts. Stir in applesauce and water.

Place half of the batter into 8-inch cake dish lined with waxed paper. MICROWAVE 6 MINUTES, 30 SEC-ONDS to 7 MINUTES on HIGH, or until cake springs back when touched lightly. Let stand 5 minutes before turning out onto cake rack.

Repeat with second layer.

GERMAN CHOCOLATE CAKE

2 8-inch layers
1-cup measure
8-inch round cake dish,
lined with waxed paper

3 *squares semi-sweet chocolate, melted*
¾ *cup butter or margarine, softened*
1¾ *cups granulated sugar*
4 *eggs*
1 *teaspoon vanilla*
2½ *cups sifted cake flour*
1¼ *teaspoons soda*
½ *teaspoon salt*
1¼ *cups ice water*

Place chocolate in 1-cup measure. MICROWAVE on HIGH, or until melted. Set aside to cool.

Cream together butter, sugar, eggs and vanilla in large mixing bowl, beat until light and fluffy. Blend in chocolate.

Mix in flour, soda and salt alternately with ice water, beating after each addition until mixture is smooth.

Pour half of the batter into 8-inch cake dish. MICRO-WAVE 6 MINUTES, 30 SECONDS to 7 MINUTES on HIGH, or until a wooden pick inserted in center comes out clean. Let stand 5 minutes before turning out onto cake rack. Cool.

Repeat with second layer.

GERMAN CHOCOLATE CAKE TOPPING

Fills and frosts top of 8-inch layer cake
1-quart measure

1 *cup evaporated milk*
1 *cup firmly packed brown sugar*
3 *tablespoons butter or margarine*
1 *teaspoon vanilla*
1 *cup flaked coconut*
1 *cup chopped nuts*

Measure milk into 1-quart measure. Stir in sugar. MICRO-WAVE 2 MINUTES on HIGH, or until sugar melts. Add butter and vanilla. Stir until butter melts. Stir in coconut and nuts.

Fill cake with half the frosting. Use remainder to frost top of cake. Place assembled cake in oven. MICROWAVE 30 SECONDS on HIGH, to glaze and fluff frosting.

CAKES AND CUPCAKES FROM A MIX ⊞

Microwave cakes usually rise higher than those cooked conventionally, so it is important not to fill containers over half full. Use any extra batter for cupcakes. Often cakes will have a slightly uneven top. This will vary with the type of cake and the brand of cake mix used. Most types of mixes bake well on high, but generally chocolate cakes do better at a lower setting. Below you will find some sample recipes using cake mixes, as well as a chart to guide you to times and settings.

PREPARATION INSTRUCTIONS FOR CAKE MIXES

SIZE OF CAKE	CHOCOLATE		OTHER FLAVORS	
	Setting	Time	Setting	Time
8" round	6	8-10 min.	High	5 - 6 min.
	5	9-11 min.		
8 x 8" square	6	8-10 min.	High	5½ - 6½ min.
	5	9-11 min.		
1 cupcake	6	45 sec. 60 sec.	High	25 - 35 sec.
	5	50 sec. 70 sec.		
2 cupcakes	6	1-1¼ min.	High	35 - 45 sec.
	5	1¼-1¾ min.		
4 cupcakes	6	1½-2 min.	High	1 - 1½ min.
	5	1¾-2½ min.		
6 cupcakes	6	2½-3 min.	High	1½ - 2½ min.
	5	3-3½ min.		

YELLOW CAKE MIX

Two 8-inch layers
8-inch baking dish,
lined with waxed paper

1 package (18½-ounces) yellow cake mix

Prepare cake according to directions on package. Pour cake mix into 8-inch cake dish, lined with waxed paper, filling half full. MICROWAVE 5 to 6 MINUTES on HIGH, or until wooden pick inserted in center comes out clean. Let stand 5 minutes before turning out on cake rack. Line dish with waxed paper. Bake remaining batter.

NOTE: Remaining batter can be frozen for future use.

CAKE MIX CUPCAKES

Doubled paper baking cups
or paper-lined custard cups

1 package cake mix

Prepare batter according to directions on package. Fill baking cups ½ full.

Arrange cupcakes in center of oven with 1-inch spaces between. Follow cooking time on chart. Cupcakes are done when wooden pick inserted in center comes out clean.

NOTE: Some cupcakes may be done sooner than others.

RASPBERRY SWIRL BUNDT CAKE

9-inch cake
9-inch pottery bundt cake dish

1 package (23½-ounces) Raspberry Swirl Bundt Cake mix

Prepare cake according to package directions. Pour batter into bundt cake dish. MICROWAVE 16 to 18 MINUTES on '6', or until wooden pick inserted in center comes out clean, rotating dish once during cooking period. Let stand 8 to 10 minutes before turning out on cake rack.

Prepare glaze according to directions on package. Drizzle over cooled cake.

NOTE: Follow directions above when preparing Pound and Lemon-Blueberry Bundt cakes.

For ovens without solid state heat control, MICROWAVE 19 to 21 MINUTES on '5', rotating dish once.

TRIPLE FUDGE BUNDT CAKE WITH GLAZE

9-inch cake
9-inch pottery bundt cake dish

1 package (23½-ounces) Triple Fudge Bundt Cake mix

Prepare cake according to package directions. Reserve ¼ cup batter to make 2 cup cakes. Pour remaining batter into bundt cake dish. MICROWAVE 25 to 30 MINUTES on '4', or until wooden pick inserted in center comes out clean, rotating dish twice during cooking period. Let stand 8 to 10 minutes before turning out on cake rack.

Prepare glaze according to directions on package. Drizzle over cooled cake.

For ovens without variable heat control, MICROWAVE 20 to 25 MINUTES on '5'. Rotate dish twice.

CHOCOLATE FUDGE CAKE

2 8-inch layers
1-cup measure
8-inch round cake dish
lined with waxed paper

3 *squares unsweetened chocolate*
⅔ *cup butter or margarine, softened*
2 *cups sugar*
4 *eggs*
1 *teaspoon vanilla*
2½ *cups cake flour*
1¼ *teaspoons soda*
½ *teaspoon salt*
1⅓ *cups ice water*

Place chocolate in 1-cup measure. MICROWAVE on HIGH, or until melted. Set aside to cool.

Cream together butter, sugar, eggs and vanilla in large mixing bowl, beat until light and fluffy. Blend in chocolate.

Mix in flour, soda and salt alternately with ice water, beating after each addition until mixture is smooth.

Pour half the batter into 8-inch cake dish. MICROWAVE 6 MINUTES, 30 SECONDS to 7 MINUTES on HIGH, or until a wooden pick inserted in center comes out clean. Let stand 5 minutes. Turn out on cake rack. Cool.

Prepare and bake second layer. Cool.

CHOCOLATE ICING

Frosts 2 8-inch layers or 1 dozen cupcakes
2-quart batter bowl

¼ *cup cocoa*
⅔ *cup milk*
2 *cups sugar*
⅓ *cup butter or margarine*
1 *teaspoon almond or vanilla extract*

Blend cocoa and milk in 2-quart bowl to make a smooth paste. Mix in sugar and butter. MICROWAVE 8 MINUTES on HIGH, stirring after every 2 minutes. Cool thoroughly.

Add almond extract. Beat vigorously until frosting reaches spreading consistency.

CHOCOLATE FROSTING

Fills and frosts two 8 or 9-inch layers
1-quart bowl

2 *squares unsweetened chocolate*
1 *tablespoon water*
⅓ *cup butter or margarine*
3 *tablespoons light cream*
1 *teaspoon vanilla*
2 to 2½ *cups confectioner's sugar*

Combine chocolate and water in 1-quart bowl. MICROWAVE 30 SECONDS on HIGH, or until chocolate melts. Stir until smooth. Mix in butter, cream and vanilla. Beat in sugar until frosting is desired consistency.

Variation:

MARSHMALLOW MIST ICING

2 *cups marshmallow sundae topping, at room temperature*
½ *cup shaved sweet or semi-sweet chocolate*
Finely chopped nuts

Fill and frost cake with chocolate frosting. Carefully place heaping teaspoonfuls of marshmallow around edge of cake, letting it trickle down sides. Swirl remaining marshmallow on top of cake. Sprinkle with shaved chocolate and nuts.

PINEAPPLE UPSIDE DOWN CAKE

9 servings
8 x 8-inch baking dish

¼ *cup butter or margarine*
½ *cup firmly packed brown sugar*
1 *can (8½-ounces) sliced pineapple, drained and juice reserved*
Maraschino cherries
1 *package (9-ounces) yellow cake mix (1-layer size)*
½ *cup (reserved) pineapple juice*
2 *eggs*

Combine butter and brown sugar in (8 x 8-inch) baking dish. MICROWAVE 1 MINUTE, 30 SECONDS to 2 MINUTES on HIGH, or until butter and sugar melt. Stir.

Arrange pineapple rings in syrup. Place maraschino cherry in center of each pineapple ring.

Blend cake mix, pineapple juice and eggs in medium mixing bowl on low speed of electric mixer. Beat on medium speed two minutes. Pour evenly over fruit. MICROWAVE 8½ to 10 MINUTES on HIGH, or until wooden pick inserted in center comes out clean, rotating dish ½ turn after 5 minutes. Immediately invert onto serving plate and remove dish.

Serve warm or cooled to room temperature, with whipped cream, if desired.

BUTTERSCOTCH FROSTING

Frosts 8 or 9-inch layer cake
2-quart casserole

1½ *cups firmly packed brown sugar*
½ *cup granulated sugar*
½ *cup cream*
1 *teaspoon vanilla*
2 *tablespoons butter or margarine*

Blend sugars and cream in 2-quart casserole. MICRO-WAVE 5 to 6 MINUTES on HIGH, or until sugar is dissolved and mixture is no longer grainy, stirring after 3 and 4 minutes.

Immediately add butter and vanilla. Stir until butter melts. Cool thoroughly. Beat to spreading consistency. Thin with a little cream if necessary.

STRAWBERRY MACAROON TORTE

8 to 12 servings
8-inch round cake dish

½ *cup butter or margarine, melted*
1 *package (13-ounces) coconut macaroon mix*
1 *package (18½-ounces) yellow cake mix*
Strawberry Cream Filling, below

Blend butter with macaroon mix in medium bowl. Press one quarter of mixture firmly and evenly in bottom of 8-inch cake dish. Set remaining mixture aside.

Prepare cake mix according to package directions. Pour half the batter into cake dish. Sprinkle one quarter of macaroon mixture evenly over batter, making sure it goes all the way to the edge. MICROWAVE 4 MINUTES to 4 MINUTES, 30 SECONDS on HIGH, or until a wooden pick inserted in center comes out clean. Turn out on cake rack. Cool.

Prepare and bake second layer. Cool.

STRAWBERRY CREAM FILLING

1 *package (12-ounces) frozen sliced strawberries,*
 defrosted, drained and mashed
2 *cups whipping cream*
¼ *cup confectioner's sugar*

In a chilled bowl, whip cream and confectioner's sugar until stiff. Carefully fold in strawberries.

Split cake layers in half. Place top slice of first cake layer on plate macaroon side down. Spread with one-third filling. Top with bottom slice macaroon side up. Spread with one-third filling. Top with bottom slice of second layer, macaroon side down. Spread with one-third filling. Cover with top slice.

Refrigerate for at least 2 hours.

PEACH SPICE PUDDING CAKE

12 servings
12 x 8-inch baking dish

1 *package lemon pudding*
1 *can (16-ounces) sliced peaches, drained*
1 *package (9-ounces) spice cake mix (one-layer size)*

Prepare pudding according to directions on page 176.

Pour pudding in (12 x 8-inch) baking dish. Arrange peach slices over pudding.

Prepare cake mix according to package directions. Pour over peaches and pudding. MICROWAVE 10 MINUTES on HIGH, or until a wooden pick inserted in cake center comes out clean, rotating dish ½ turn after 5 minutes.

Serve warm or cool, with whipped cream if desired.

BLACK BOTTOM PIE

9-inch pie
2-quart bowl or casserole

9-*inch baked chocolate wafer crumb crust*
½ *cup sugar*
1 *tablespoon corn starch*
2 *cups milk or cream*
4 *egg yolks, slightly beaten*
1 *package (6-ounces) semi-sweet chocolate bits*
1 *teaspoon vanilla*
1 *tablespoon unflavored gelatin*
¼ *cup cold water*
4 *egg whites*
½ *cup sugar*
1 *cup whipping cream, whipped*
Shaved bitter chocolate

Combine sugar and corn starch in 2-quart bowl. Gradually stir in milk. MICROWAVE 8 MINUTES on '8', or until slightly thickened, stirring twice with wire whip.

Stir half the hot mixture into egg yolks. Blend warmed yolks into hot mixture. MICROWAVE 2 to 3 MINUTES on '8', or until mixture lightly coats a metal spoon, stirring once.

Pour 1 cup hot custard into 1-quart measure. Add chocolate bits to custard in measure. Stir until chocolate melts. Stir in vanilla. Pour into baked crumb crust. Chill.

Soften gelatin in cold water. Add to remaining hot custard. Stir until gelatin is completely dissolved. Cool.

Beat egg whites until foamy. Gradually beat in sugar. Continue beating until stiff peaks form. Fold into cooled custard-gelatin mixture. Spread over chilled chocolate layer. Refrigerate pie until set. Top with whipped cream and shaved chocolate just before serving.

For ovens without solid state heat control, MICROWAVE 6 MINUTES on HIGH, stirring 3 times. After adding egg yolks, MICROWAVE 1 MINUTE, 30 SECONDS to 2 MINUTES, 30 SECONDS on HIGH, stirring twice.

STRAWBERRY PIE

9-inch pie
1-quart bowl
9-inch pie plate

9-*inch baked pastry shell*
1½ *quarts fresh strawberries*
3 *tablespoons corn starch*
¾ *to 1 cup sugar*
1 *cup water*
1 *teaspoon butter or margarine*

Clean and hull berries. Measure ⅔ cup of berries and mash in 1-quart measure. Add water and ¾ to 1 cup sugar, depending on sweetness of berries. MICROWAVE 5 to 6 MINUTES on HIGH, or until mixture is boiling.

Soften corn starch in small amount of water and add to mixture. MICROWAVE 2 to 3 MINUTES on HIGH, or until mixture thickens, stirring once. Stir in butter. Cool.

Fill baked pie shell with remaining strawberries. Pour cooled glaze over top. Garnish with whipped cream.

Variation:
Soften 1 package (8-ounces) cream cheese. Spread evenly in bottom of pie shell before adding strawberries.

PASTRY FOR ONE-CRUST PIE

9-inch pie crust
9-inch pie plate

1 *cup all-purpose flour*
½ *teaspoon salt*
⅓ *cup plus 1 tablespoon shortening*
3 *to 4 tablespoons cold water*
Yellow food coloring

Measure flour and salt into mixing bowl. Cut in shortening thoroughly. Add a few drops of yellow food coloring to water. Sprinkle water over mixture, one tablespoon at a time, stirring lightly with fork.

Roll out pastry to fit 9-inch pie plate. Trim and flute edge. Prick sides and bottom with fork. MICROWAVE 4 to 5 MINUTES on '8', or until crust appears flaky. Cool.

For ovens without solid state heat control, MICROWAVE 4 to 5 MINUTES on HIGH, turning halfway through.

PASTRY SHELL FROM MIX

1 *pie crust stick or mix*

Using pie crust stick or mix, prepare recommended amount for one 9-inch single pastry shell as directed on package. Follow above directions.

LEMON MERINGUE PIE

9-inch pie
9-inch pie plate
1-quart measure

9-inch baked pastry shell or graham cracker crust
1½ cups sugar
⅓ cup corn starch
1½ cups boiling water
3 egg yolks, slightly beaten
3 tablespoons butter or margarine
1 tablespoon grated lemon rind
3 tablespoons lemon juice
3 egg whites
¼ teaspoon cream of tartar
6 tablespoons sugar

Combine sugar, corn starch and boiling water in 1-quart measure. MICROWAVE 3 to 4 MINUTES on HIGH, or until thick and clear, stirring once with wire whip.

Stir a little of the hot mixture into egg yolks. Add warmed yolks to hot filling. MICROWAVE 1 MINUTE on HIGH. Add butter, lemon rind and lemon juice. Cool. Pour into baked pie shell.

Beat egg whites with cream of tartar until foamy. Gradually beat in sugar. Continue beating until stiff peaks form. Gently spread meringue over lemon filling, sealing meringue to edges of crust. Brown under conventional broiler.

PECAN PIE

9-inch pie
9-inch pie plate

9-inch baked pastry shell
3 eggs, slightly beaten
⅔ cup sugar
½ teaspoon salt
⅓ cup butter or margarine, melted
1 cup light corn syrup
1 cup pecan halves

Beat eggs, sugar, salt, butter and corn syrup in medium bowl using a rotary beater. Stir in pecan halves. Pour into 9-inch baked pastry shell. MICROWAVE 5 to 6 MINUTES on '6', or until filling is set, rotating dish ½ turn after 3 minutes. Let cool. Garnish with whipped cream if desired.

For ovens without solid state heat control, MICROWAVE 6 to 7 MINUTES on '5'.

VANILLA CREAM PIE

9-inch pie
2-quart bowl or casserole

9-inch baked pastry shell
¾ cup sugar
3 tablespoons corn starch
Pinch salt
2 cups milk or half-and-half
3 egg yolks, slightly beaten
2 tablespoons butter or margarine
1 teaspoon vanilla
3 egg whites
¼ teaspoon cream of tartar
6 tablespoons sugar

Combine sugar, corn starch and salt in 2-quart bowl. Gradually stir in milk. MICROWAVE 8 MINUTES on '8', or until thickened, stirring twice with wire whip.

Stir a little of the hot mixture into egg yolks. Blend warmed yolks into hot mixture. MICROWAVE 2 MINUTES on '8', or until custard coats a metal spoon, stirring once.

Stir in butter and vanilla until butter melts. Cool. Pour into baked pie shell.

Beat egg whites with cream of tartar until foamy. Gradually beat in sugar. Continue beating until stiff peaks form. Gently spread meringue over cream filling, sealing meringue to edges of crust. Brown under conventional broiler.

NOTE: Sweetened whipped cream may be substituted for meringue.

For ovens without solid state heat control, MICROWAVE 6 MINUTES on HIGH, stirring three times. After adding egg yolks, MICROWAVE 1 MINUTE, 30 SECONDS on HIGH, stirring twice.

Variations:

BANANA CREAM PIE

Slice 2 ripe bananas into bottom of baked pie shell, or graham cracker crust. Pour Vanilla Cream filling over bananas. Top with meringue.

CHOCOLATE CREAM PIE

Follow above recipe, but increase sugar to 1 cup. Melt 2 squares (1-ounce each) unsweetened chocolate. Add with vanilla.

COCONUT CREAM PIE

Stir in 1 cup flaked coconut with butter. Sprinkle ⅓ cup coconut over meringue before browning.

BUTTERSCOTCH PIE

Substitute ¾ cup firmly packed brown sugar for granulated sugar. Increase butter to ⅓ cup.

GRAHAM CRACKER CRUST

9-inch crust
1-quart bowl
9-inch pie plate

⅓ cup butter or margarine
1½ cups graham cracker crumbs
⅓ cup firmly packed brown sugar

Place butter in 1-quart bowl. MICROWAVE on HIGH until butter is melted. Add graham cracker crumbs and sugar. Mix thoroughly. Press mixture firmly and evenly against bottom and sides of (9-inch) pie plate. MICROWAVE 1 MINUTE, 30 SECONDS to 2 MINUTES, 30 SECONDS on HIGH, or until hot. Cool.

Variations:

VANILLA WAFER CRUST

Substitute 1½ cups vanilla wafer crumbs for graham cracker crumbs.

CHOCOLATE WAFER CRUMB CRUST

Substitute 1½ cups chocolate wafer crumbs for graham cracker crumbs.

COCONUT CRUST

2 tablespoons butter or margarine, softened
1½ cups flaked coconut

Spread softened butter evenly on bottom and sides of (9-inch) pie plate. Sprinkle coconut over butter. Press firmly to form even crust. MICROWAVE 1 MINUTE to 1 MINUTE, 30 SECONDS on HIGH.

PUMPKIN PIE

9-inch pie
9-inch pie plate

1 baked pastry shell, (page 172)
2 whole eggs
1 can (15-ounces) pumpkin
½ cup firmly packed brown sugar
1 teaspoon cinnamon
½ teaspoon nutmeg
¼ teaspoon ginger
¼ teaspoon cloves
1¼ cup half-and-half or evaporated milk

Break eggs into 1½-quart bowl. Beat lightly. Add pumpkin and mix thoroughly. Add remaining ingredients, one at a time, beating well after each addition.

Pour mixture into baked pastry shell. MICROWAVE 12 MINUTES on '6', or until almost set. Let stand 30 minutes. Garnish with swirl of whipped cream, if desired.

NOTE: Standing time is important, as center of pie will continue to cook until firm.

For ovens without solid state heat control, MICROWAVE 14 MINUTES, 25 SECONDS on '5'.

WAIKIKI PINEAPPLE PIE

6 to 8 servings
1½-quart mixing bowl

9-inch baked pastry shell
1 tablespoon flour
1 can (15½-ounces) crushed pineapple and juice
3 tablespoons corn starch
2 tablespoons sugar
1 tablespoon grated lemon rind
1 tablespoon lemon juice
¼ teaspoon salt
1 tablespoon butter

Dust baked pie shell with flour. Set aside.

Combine pineapple and juice in 1½-quart bowl. MICROWAVE 4 MINUTES on HIGH, or until mixture is hot.

Add corn starch, sugar, rind, lemon juice and salt. MICROWAVE 3 MINUTES on HIGH, or until mixture thickens, stirring every minute. Stir in butter. Let stand 15 minutes. Pour into baked pie shell.

QUICK CHERRY PIE ⬛

9-inch pie
9-inch pie plate

2 teaspoons almond extract
1 can (21-ounces) cherry pie filling
9-inch baked pastry shell (page 172)

Add almond extract to cherry pie filling in can. Pour into baked pastry shell. MICROWAVE 8 MINUTES on HIGH, or until cherries are bubbling hot.

CHERRY-PEACH MOUNDS

6 servings
12 x 8-inch baking dish

1 can (16-ounces) cherry pie filling
½ teaspoon cinnamon
⅛ teaspoon ground cloves
½ cup water
2 tablespoons lemon juice
1 can (16-ounces) sliced peaches, drained
1½ cups biscuit mix
1 egg, beaten, mixed with milk to make ½ cup liquid

Combine pie filling, cinnamon, cloves, water and lemon juice in (12 x 8-inch) baking dish. Stir in sliced peaches. MICROWAVE 8 MINUTES on HIGH, or until mixture boils, stirring twice.

Blend biscuit mix and egg-milk mixture in a 1-quart bowl to make a soft dough. Drop dough by tablespoons into hot cherry-peach mixture. MICROWAVE 5 to 6 MINUTES on HIGH, or until biscuits are no longer doughy, rotating dish once during cooking.

Let stand 5 minutes.

CHERRY CRUMBLE

12 servings
12 x 8-inch baking dish

1 package (18½-ounces) yellow cake mix (2-layer size)
1 can (21-ounces) cherry pie filling
½ cup water
1 teaspoon lemon juice
½ teaspoon cinnamon

Sprinkle ¾ package cake mix in (12 x 8-inch) baking dish. Pour pie filling over cake mix. Sprinkle remaining cake mix over pie filling.

Combine water and lemon juice. Pour evenly over mix. Sprinkle with cinnamon. MICROWAVE 12 to 13 MINUTES on HIGH, or until topping is set like streusel, rotating dish ½ turn after 5 minutes.

CHERRY DESSERT

10 to 12 servings
12 x 8-inch baking dish

2 cans (21-ounces each) cherry pie filling
½ teaspoon cinnamon
1½ teaspoons almond extract
1 package (9-ounces) yellow cake mix (one-layer size)
½ cup (¼-pound) butter, or margarine
½ cup sliced almonds

Combine pie filling, cinnamon and almond extract in (12 x 8-inch) baking dish.

Spread evenly. Sprinkle cake mix over top.

Drizzle with butter, sprinkle with almonds. MICROWAVE 15 MINUTES on HIGH, rotating dish ½ turn after 7 minutes. Serve hot or cold.

FROZEN CHERRY PIE

1 package (33-ounces) frozen cherry pie

Remove lid from aluminum foil baking pan. Cut slits in top of pie. MICROWAVE 10 MINUTES on '4'.

Increase setting. MICROWAVE 5 to 6 MINUTES on '8'.

Place pie 3 inches from preheated conventional broiler for 1½ to 2 minutes to brown top.

NOTE: To defrost frozen pies before cooking in conventional oven, MICROWAVE 10 MINUTES on '4'. Transfer pie to conventional oven. Reduce baking time by one third.

For ovens without solid state heat control, to defrost pie, MICROWAVE 8 MINUTES on '5'. Increase setting. MICROWAVE 2 MINUTES on HIGH. Let stand 1 minute. MICROWAVE 2 to 3 MINUTES on HIGH.

CRANBERRY CRISP

8 servings
6-cup souffle dish

1 can (16-ounces) cranberry sauce
1 cup sugar
Grated rind of 2 oranges
Juice of 1 orange
¼ cup butter or margarine, softened
¾ cup old-fashioned rolled oats
⅓ cup firmly packed brown sugar
⅓ cup all-purpose flour
1 cup whipping cream, whipped and flavored with 1 teaspoon vanilla and 1 tablespoon confectioner's sugar

Combine cranberry sauce, sugar, rind and juice in 6-cup souffle dish.

Mix butter, oats, brown sugar and flour until crumbly. Sprinkle mixture evenly over berries. MICROWAVE 9 MINUTES on HIGH, or until juices begin to bubble.

Cool to lukewarm. Serve with whipped cream.

CHOCOLATE PUDDING

6 servings
Custard cup
1½-quart casserole

1 tablespoon butter or margarine
2 squares unsweetened chocolate
½ cup sugar
3 tablespoons corn starch
¼ teaspoon salt
1¾ cups milk
1 egg yolk, slightly beaten
1 egg white
1 teaspoon vanilla or almond extract

Combine butter and chocolate in custard cup. MICROWAVE 45 SECONDS to 1 MINUTE on HIGH, or until melted. Set aside.

Mix sugar, corn starch and salt together in 1½-quart casserole. Gradually stir in milk. Blend in melted chocolate mixture. MICROWAVE 6 to 7 MINUTES on '8', or until thickened, stirring once with wire whip.

Stir a little of the hot mixture into egg yolk. Blend warmed yolk into hot mixture. MICROWAVE 1 MINUTE, 30 SECONDS on '8', or until custard coats a metal spoon.

Beat egg white in small bowl until stiff peaks form. Gently fold into custard. Fold in vanilla. Cool.

For ovens without solid state heat control, MICROWAVE 5 to 6 MINUTES on HIGH, stirring three times. After adding egg yolk MICROWAVE 1 MINUTE on HIGH, stirring once.

BUTTERSCOTCH PUDDING

6 servings
2-quart casserole

1 *cup firmly packed brown sugar*
3 *tablespoons corn starch*
¼ *teaspoon salt*
1¾ *cups milk*
2 *egg yolks, slightly beaten*
1 *tablespoon butter or margarine*
2 *egg whites*
1 *teaspoon vanilla*

Combine sugar, corn starch and salt in 2-quart casserole. Gradually stir in milk. MICROWAVE 6 to 7 MINUTES on '8', or until thickened, stirring once with wire whip.

Stir a little of the hot mixture into egg yolks. Blend warmed yolks into hot mixture. MICROWAVE 1 MINUTE, 30 SECONDS on '8', or until custard coats a metal spoon. Stir in butter.

Beat egg whites in small bowl until stiff peaks form. Gently fold into custard. Fold in vanilla. Cool.

For ovens without solid state heat control, MICROWAVE 5 to 6 MINUTES on HIGH and 1 MINUTE on HIGH.

VANILLA FLUFF PUDDING

6 servings
1-quart casserole

⅓ *cup sugar*
3 *tablespoons corn starch*
¼ *teaspoon salt*
2 *cups milk*
1 *egg yolk, slightly beaten*
1 *egg white*
½ *teaspoon vanilla*

Blend sugar, corn starch and salt in 1-quart casserole. Gradually stir in milk. Mix well. MICROWAVE 8 MINUTES on '8', or until thickened, stirring twice with a wire whip.

Stir a little of the hot mixture into egg yolk. Add warmed yolk to hot mixture. Mix well. MICROWAVE 1 MINUTE, 30 SECONDS on '8', or until custard coats a metal spoon.

Beat egg white in small bowl until stiff peaks form. Gently fold into custard. Fold in vanilla. Cool.

For ovens without solid state heat control, MICROWAVE 5 to 6 MINUTES on HIGH, stirring three times. After adding egg yolk, MICROWAVE 1 MINUTE on HIGH, stirring once.

PUDDING OR CUSTARD MIX

4 servings
1-quart measure

2 *cups milk*
1 *package (3¾-ounces) pudding or custard mix*

Measure milk into 1-quart measure. Add mix, stirring until dissolved. MICROWAVE 4 MINUTES on HIGH, or until pudding starts to boil, stirring every minute. Pudding thickens as it cools.

NOTE: Pudding may be cooked without stirring, and then beaten with wire whip until smooth.

6 serving package:
Mix in 1½-quart bowl and MICROWAVE 7 MINUTES on HIGH, or until mixture starts to boil.

TAPIOCA FLUFF

5 servings
1½-quart casserole

1 *egg, separated*
3 *tablespoons sugar*
⅛ *teaspoon salt*
2 *cups milk*
3 *tablespoons minute tapioca*
2 *tablespoons sugar*
¾ *teaspoon vanilla*

Combine egg yolk, 3 tablespoons sugar, salt, milk and tapioca in 1½-quart casserole. Let stand 3 minutes to soften tapioca.

Beat egg white until foamy in 2-quart bowl. Gradually beat in sugar. Continue beating until egg white holds soft peaks. Set aside.

Place tapioca mixture in oven. MICROWAVE 8 to 10 MINUTES on '8', or until mixture has thickened, stirring twice.

Fold tapioca mixture into meringue carefully but thoroughly. Stir in vanilla. Cool slightly and chill.

For ovens without solid state heat control, MICROWAVE 6 to 8 MINUTES on HIGH, stirring 3 times.

BAKED CUSTARD

6 servings
1½-quart casserole
1-quart measure
8 x 8-inch baking dish

3 *eggs*
4 *tablespoons sugar*
¼ *teaspoon salt*
½ *teaspoon vanilla*
1⅔ *cup milk*
Nutmeg

Beat eggs lightly in 1½-quart casserole. Mix in sugar, salt and vanilla, stirring well.

Measure milk into 1-quart measure. MICROWAVE 3 to 4 MINUTES on HIGH, or until about to boil. Stir gradually into egg mixture. Sprinkle with nutmeg.

Place casserole in (8 x 8-inch) baking dish. Pour 1 cup very hot water into baking dish. MICROWAVE 9 MINUTES on '6', or until custard is almost set. Custard will become firm as it cools. Serve chilled.

For ovens without solid state heat control, MICROWAVE 10 to 30 SECONDS on '5'.

PEARS IN RED WINE

4 servings
1-quart measure
Serving dish or casserole large enough
to hold pears upright

4 *ripe pears, d'Anjou or Comice*
1 *cup red wine*
½ *cup water*
1 *cup sugar*
1 *teaspoon ginger*

Arrange pears in serving dish so that they stand upright. Set aside. Combine wine, water, sugar and ginger in 1-quart measure. MICROWAVE 3 to 5 MINUTES on HIGH, or until boiling.

Pour sauce over pears. Cover with plastic wrap. MICROWAVE 4 to 5 MINUTES on HIGH, or until pears have softened but still hold their shape. Let stand 5 minutes, covered.

Pears in Red Wine

FRUIT COCKTAIL TORTE

6 to 8 servings
8 x 8-inch baking dish

¾ *cup sugar*
1 *egg*
1 *can (16-ounces) fruit cocktail, drained*
1 *cup flour*
1 *teaspoon soda*
¼ *teaspoon salt*
½ *cup firmly packed brown sugar*
½ *cup chopped nuts*

Combine sugar and egg in medium bowl. Beat well. Stir in fruit, flour, soda and salt until mixed. Spread in (8 x 8-inch) baking dish. Combine brown sugar and nuts. Sprinkle over torte. MICROWAVE 8 to 10 MINUTES on HIGH, or until top springs back when lightly touched, rotating dish ½ turn after 5 minutes.

SPICED APRICOTS

6 servings
2-quart casserole

1 *pound dried apricots*
½ *cup sugar*
2 *cups water*
½ *teaspoon cinnamon*
6 *whole cloves*

Wash apricots. Place in 2-quart casserole. Add sugar, water and spices. Cover. MICROWAVE 15 to 20 MINUTES on HIGH, or until fruit is tender and flavors have blended.

HOLIDAY FRUIT PUDDING

16 servings
3-quart casserole or bowl

1 *package (8-ounces) dried apples*
1 *package (12-ounces) dried pears*
1 *package (12-ounces) dried peaches*
1 *package (16-ounces) dried prunes, pitted*
1 *can (20-ounces) pineapple chunks and juice*
⅓ *cup red wine*
½ *cup water*
1 *can (21-ounces) cherry pie filling*
1 *cup chopped walnuts*

Combine dried fruits, pineapple chunks and juice, red wine and water in 3-quart casserole.

Spread cherry pie filling over mixture. Sprinkle with chopped walnuts. Cover. MICROWAVE 20 to 25 MINUTES on HIGH, or until fruits are tender. Serve warm or chilled.

NOTE: Fruit pudding may be stored in refrigerator up to two weeks, tightly covered.

GINGER PEARS

6 servings
Shallow 1-quart casserole or baking dish

6 canned Bartlett pear halves, drained
¼ teaspoon ginger
¼ teaspoon nutmeg
¼ teaspoon cinnamon
2 tablespoons butter or margarine
2 tablespoons sugar

Arrange pears in a single layer, cut sides up, in a 1-quart casserole. Combine ginger, nutmeg and cinnamon. Sprinkle over pears.

Cream butter and sugar together. Divide evenly between pears, placing mixture in cavities. MICROWAVE 2 MINUTES on HIGH, or until butter is melted and pears hot. Garnish with whipped cream and maraschino cherries, if desired.

BEAUTIFUL BAKED APPLE

1 serving
Custard cup

1 cooking apple
1 to 1½ tablespoons brown sugar
2 teaspoons butter or margarine
Cinnamon

Peel a rim of apple skin from top of apple to allow steam to escape. Core apple. Combine brown sugar and butter. Fill cavity. Place apple in custard cup. Sprinkle cinnamon over cavity and peeled portion of apple. MICROWAVE 2 MINUTES on HIGH, or until apple is almost tender. Let stand 5 minutes to complete cooking.

NOTE: When cooking several apples at a time, add 1 additional minute per apple.

HOT AMBROSIA COMPOTE

6 servings
2-quart casserole

½ cup flaked coconut (plain or toasted)
¼ cup graham cracker crumbs
1 can (13-ounces) pineapple chunks, drained
1 can (16-ounces) sliced peaches, drained
1 can (11-ounces) mandarin oranges, drained
½ cup sliced fresh green grapes, or 1 can
  (8-ounces) green grapes, drained
8 to 10 maraschino cherries, halved
1 can (13-ounces) apricots, drained

Combine all ingredients in 2-quart casserole. MICROWAVE 5 to 6 MINUTES on HIGH, or until bubbly. Spoon into serving dishes. Garnish with whipped cream, if desired.

RHUBARB CRISP

9 servings
8 x 8-inch baking dish

1 cup all-purpose flour
½ cup rolled oats
1 cup firmly packed brown sugar
½ cup butter or margarine
1¾ pounds rhubarb, cut in ½-inch pieces (4 cups)
1 cup sugar
¼ cup all-purpose flour
½ teaspoon cinnamon
½ cup water

Mix together flour, oats and sugar in large bowl. Stir in butter with fork to make a crumbly mixture. Set aside.

Combine rhubarb, sugar, flour, cinnamon and water in (8 x 8-inch) baking dish. Stir to mix well. Cover with plastic wrap. MICROWAVE 3 MINUTES on HIGH.

Sprinkle topping evenly over rhubarb mixture. Do not cover. MICROWAVE 8 MINUTES on HIGH, or until topping is golden and crusty, and rhubarb is tender.

BANANAS FOSTER

4 servings
1-quart casserole

2 tablespoons butter or margarine
2 large bananas, quartered
2 tablespoons brown sugar
½ teaspoon cinnamon
2 tablespoons banana or orange liqueur
2 tablespoons rum

Place butter in 1-quart casserole. MICROWAVE on HIGH until butter melts. Roll bananas in butter.

Mix brown sugar and cinnamon together. Sprinkle over bananas. MICROWAVE 2 MINUTES, 30 SECONDS to 3 MINUTES on HIGH, or until sugar begins to melt. Remove from oven.

Pour liqueur and rum over hot bananas. Ignite. When flame dies down serve bananas and sauce on ice cream or a thin slice of pound cake.

FANTASTIC CHOCOLATE FONDUE 🔲

2 cups
1-quart bowl or ceramic fondue pot

¾ cup whipping cream
1 package (11½-ounces) milk-chocolate chips
3 tablespoons kirsch or brandy
¼ to ½ teaspoon cinnamon
1½ cups fresh strawberries
2 medium bananas cut into ½-inch slices
1½ cups fresh pineapple cubes
6 slices pound cake, ¾-inch thick, cut in 1-inch
   squares

Pour cream in bowl or fondue pot. Add 1½ cups chocolate chips. MICROWAVE 1 MINUTE on HIGH, or until chocolate melts. Stir to blend chocolate and cream.

Add remaining chocolate chips. MICROWAVE 30 SECONDS on HIGH. Stir in liqueur and cinnamon. Keep mixture warm in fondue pot or chafing dish, or reheat as needed.

Serve with fruits and cake on bamboo skewers or fondue forks.

BANANA BOATS 🔲

4 servings
8 x 8-inch baking dish

2 ripe bananas, peeled
3 tablespoons brown sugar
1 tablespoon butter or margarine, cut in pieces
1 tablespoon chopped walnuts

Split bananas lengthwise and place in (8 x 8-inch) baking dish, cut sides up. Sprinkle brown sugar over bananas. Dot with butter. Scatter nuts on top. MICROWAVE 30 SECONDS on HIGH, or until sugar melts. Garnish with whipped cream or chocolate syrup, if desired.

APPLESAUCE

6 servings
1½-quart casserole

4 medium cooking apples, peeled, cored and quartered
½ cup water
¾ cup sugar
½ teaspoon cinnamon

Place apples and water in 1½-quart casserole. Cover. MICROWAVE 10 MINUTES on HIGH, or until apples are tender, stirring well after 5 minutes.

Mash apples with fork. Stir in sugar and cinnamon. Cool.

Variation:
RHUBARB SAUCE

Substitute 4 cups rhubarb cut in ½-inch pieces for apples. Adjust sugar to taste.

INSTANT CHOCOLATE FONDUE

2½ cups sauce
1-quart bowl or casserole

1 tablespoon butter or margarine
2 squares semi-sweet baking chocolate
2 cups marshmallow creme
½ cup Kahlua
Assorted fresh fruits and pound cake squares

Place butter and chocolate in 1-quart bowl. MICROWAVE 45 SECONDS to 1 MINUTE on HIGH, or until butter and chocolate are melted.

Add marshmallow creme. MICROWAVE 35 to 40 SECONDS on HIGH, or until melted. Stir in Kahlua until smooth.

Serve with chunks of fresh fruit or cake squares on forks.

CURRIED FRUIT

8 servings
2-quart casserole

1 package (12-ounces) mixed dried fruits
1 can (20-ounces) pineapple chunks
1 can (21-ounces) strawberry or cherry pie filling
¼ cup dry sherry
½ cup water
1 to 2 teaspoons curry powder

Combine dried fruits, pineapple chunks and juice in 2-quart casserole.

Combine pie filling, sherry, water and curry powder in 1-quart measure and pour over fruits. Cover with plastic wrap. MICROWAVE 13 MINUTES on HIGH, or until fruits are fork tender, stirring after 5 minutes. Let stand 15 minutes before serving with pork, ham or poultry.

FRUIT BRULE

6 to 8 servings
10 x 6-inch baking dish

1 can (16-ounces) pitted black cherries, drained
1 can (17-ounces) figs, drained
1 can (16-ounces) pears, drained
1 can (16-ounces) apricots, drained
Juice and grated rind of one orange
Juice and grated rind of one lemon
1½ cups firmly packed brown sugar

Combine fruits, juices and rinds in (10 x 6-inch) baking dish. Sprinkle brown sugar over top. MICROWAVE 15 MINUTES on HIGH, or until mixture is hot and syrupy, stirring once after 7 minutes.

Serve hot or cold, garnished with dairy sour cream, if desired.

Candy & Cookies

Candy making is easy and fast with a microwave oven. Because microwave heats from all sides, candies need only minimum attention. They cook smooth and creamy without constant stirring. With a heat control microwave oven, you can bring mixtures to a boil on high, then reduce the settings so they bubble without boiling over.

Bar cookies cook quickly by microwave, whether you bake them from a mix or from 'scratch'. Have them often for desserts, a coffee break or snacks. They're the perfect choice when you're asked to bake something for a meeting or potluck supper. Use our recipes as a guide, and adapt your favorite bar cookies to microwave baking.

Two recipes for individual cookies are given in this section. Some cookie doughs are not suitable for microwave baking because they cook unevenly or do not set. If you wish to convert cookie recipes to microwave, test one cookie when you are baking conventionally. Large batches of cookies should be done conventionally.

Top tier: Peanut Brittle
Middle tier: Fantastic Fudge and Nature's Own Candy
Bottom tier: Sunshine Divinity and Penuche
Recipes on following pages.

CANDY BASICS

Sugar becomes very hot when boiled. Be sure to use a container which can withstand high temperatures, and be careful when removing the bowl from the oven.

Traditional candy recipes call for a temperature test. If you test with a candy thermometer, do not use it in the oven while cooking. You may prefer to use the cold water tests given in our recipes.

PEANUT BRITTLE

1½ pounds
2-quart batter bowl

2 *cups sugar*
1 *cup light corn syrup*
1 *cup water*
2 *cups shelled unroasted peanuts*
¼ *teaspoon salt*
1 *teaspoon butter or margarine*
1 *teaspoon soda*

Combine sugar, corn syrup and water in 2-quart batter bowl. MICROWAVE 18 to 20 MINUTES on HIGH, or until a small amount dropped in very cold water forms a soft ball (240°).

Stir in peanuts and salt. MICROWAVE 7 to 9 MINUTES on HIGH, or until a small amount dropped in very cold water separates into hard, brittle threads (290°). Immediately stir in butter and soda. Mix well. Spread evenly and thinly on large buttered cookie sheet. Cool, lifting occasionally with spatula to prevent sticking. Break into pieces when cool.

NOTE: Do not use candy thermometer in microwave oven.

NEVER-FAIL FUDGE ▣

2 dozen pieces
10 x 8-inch utility dish

1 *package (1-pound) confectioner's sugar*
½ *cup cocoa*
½ *cup butter or margarine*
¼ *cup milk*
½ *cup finely chopped nuts*
1 *teaspoon vanilla*

Mix sugar and cocoa together in (10 x 8-inch) utility dish. Drop butter onto sugar mixture in 4 or 5 pieces. Pour in milk. MICROWAVE 2 to 3 MINUTES on HIGH, or until bubbly. Stir lightly.

Thoroughly stir in nuts and vanilla so nuts are evenly distributed. Spread fudge evenly in dish. Refrigerate 1 hour. Cut into squares.

FANTASTIC FUDGE

64 pieces
2-quart batter bowl

¾ *cup evaporated milk or light cream*
1 *tablespoon butter or margarine*
1½ *cups sugar*
16 *marshmallows, cut in half*
1 *package (12-ounces) chocolate chips*
1 *cup chopped nuts*
1 *teaspoon vanilla*

Combine evaporated milk, butter, sugar and marshmallows in 2-quart bowl. MICROWAVE 3 to 4 MINUTES on HIGH, or until marshmallows puff and mixture begins to boil. Stir.

Reduce setting. MICROWAVE 3 to 4 MINUTES on '6', or until mixture boils and sugar dissolves completely. Stir in chocolate chips, nuts and vanilla. Beat until smooth. Spread in buttered (8 x 8-inch) baking dish. Cool. Cut into 1-inch squares.

For ovens without solid state heat control, after mixture boils MICROWAVE 2 MINUTES, 30 SECONDS to 3 MINUTES, 30 SECONDS on '5'.

PENUCHE

1½ dozen pieces
3-quart casserole

2½ *cups firmly packed brown sugar*
¾ *cup milk*
1 *tablespoon butter or margarine*
1 *tablespoon light corn syrup*
Pinch salt
1 *teaspoon vanilla*
⅓ *cup chopped nuts*

Blend together sugar, milk, butter, corn syrup and salt in a 3-quart casserole. MICROWAVE 5 MINUTES on HIGH, or until sugar is dissolved. Stir well. MICROWAVE 6 MINUTES on HIGH, or until a small amount dropped in very cold water forms a soft ball (240°).

Cool to lukewarm. Using a wooden spoon, beat vigorously until mixture begins to thicken. Stir in vanilla and nuts. Continue beating until candy is thick and difficult to work. Spread evenly in buttered (8 x 8-inch) pan. Cool until firm. Cut in squares.

NOTE: Do not use candy thermometer in the microwave oven.

NATURE'S OWN CANDY

5 dozen pieces
10 x 8-inch baking dish

½ cup (1 stick) butter or margarine
¾ cup firmly packed light brown sugar
1½ cups quick-cooking oatmeal
1 cup flaked coconut
1 cup coarsely chopped walnuts
½ cup toasted wheat germ
⅓ cup sesame seeds
½ cup snipped dried apricots
⅓ cup honey
1 teaspoon cinnamon

Combine butter and brown sugar in (10 x 8-inch) baking dish. MICROWAVE 1 MINUTE, 30 SECONDS on HIGH, or until melted.

Add all remaining ingredients and mix thoroughly. Spread evenly in baking dish. MICROWAVE 6 MINUTES on HIGH, or until bubbly, stirring every 2 minutes.

Turn mixture out onto a sheet of waxed paper. Spread evenly to 1-inch thickness. Allow candy to cool completely and break into bite-sized pieces, or cool only until mixture can be handled comfortably. Form into 1-inch balls. Cool.

FONDANT

3 dozen 1-inch pieces
3½ to 4-quart casserole

2 cups sugar
1½ cups, plus 2 tablespoons water
⅛ teaspoon cream of tartar
2 tablespoons light corn syrup
1 tablespoon butter or margarine
1 teaspoon vanilla

Butter the sides of a 3½-quart casserole. Combine sugar, water, cream of tartar and corn syrup in casserole. MICROWAVE 22 to 26 MINUTES on HIGH, or until a small amount dropped in very cold water forms a soft ball (238°).

Immediately pour syrup into large platter. Let cool until warm to touch. Using a wooden spoon, work fondant from outside toward center until it forms a creamy white mass.

Work in butter and vanilla. Continue working until fondant begins to harden. Drop by teaspoonfuls onto wax paper. Let stand until firm. Store in closed container.

NOTE: Do not use candy thermometer in the microwave oven.

SUNSHINE DIVINITY

2½ dozen pieces
3-quart bowl or casserole

2 cups sugar
½ cup light corn syrup
⅓ cup water
2 egg whites
1 teaspoon vanilla
¾ cup finely chopped candied cherries
¾ cup chopped nuts

Combine sugar, corn syrup and water in 3-quart bowl. Stir until sugar dissolves. MICROWAVE 5 MINUTES on HIGH, or until mixture is clear.

Stir thoroughly. MICROWAVE 8 MINUTES on HIGH, or until a small amount dropped in very cold water forms a hard ball (260°).

While syrup is cooking, beat egg whites until stiff peaks form. When syrup is ready, beat egg whites with electric mixer while slowly pouring in a thin stream of hot syrup. Add vanilla. Beat until candy loses its gloss. (About 6 to 8 minutes.) Fold in fruit and nuts.

Drop from buttered teaspoon onto waxed paper or spread in a buttered (10 x 8-inch) pan. Cut into squares when cooled.

NOTE: Do not make divinity when humidity is high, as it will not set. Do not use candy thermometer in the microwave oven.

TOFFEE TEMPTERS

16 small pieces
8 x 8-inch baking dish

¼ cup butter or margarine, softened
¼ cup vegetable shortening
½ cup firmly packed brown sugar
1 cup flour
1 package (6-ounces) semi-sweet chocolate pieces
½ cup chopped nuts (optional)

Thoroughly mix butter, shortening and sugar in medium bowl. Blend in flour.

Spread evenly in (8 x 8-inch) baking dish. MICROWAVE 2 MINUTES, 30 SECONDS on HIGH, or until set, rotating dish ¼ turn after each minute. Immediately sprinkle chocolate pieces on crust. Let stand 2 to 3 minutes until chocolate softens. Spread evenly. Sprinkle with nuts, if desired. Cut into squares while warm.

COOKIE BASICS

Individual cookies and bars do not brown when baked by microwave. Select recipes with ingredients which add color, such as spices or chocolate. You may also use toppings, frostings or a sprinkling of powdered sugar. Over-baked bar cookies are hard and dry. A few moist spots may appear on the surface, but bars are done when a wooden pick inserted in the center comes out clean, or when a light touch on the center leaves no imprint.

PUMPKIN BARS ❈

36 bars
Two 8 x 8-inch glass baking dishes

4 *eggs*
1 *cup salad oil*
2 *cups sugar*
1 *can (15-ounces) pumpkin*
2 *cups all-purpose flour*
2 *teaspoons baking powder*
1 *teaspoon soda*
½ *teaspoon salt*
2 *teaspoons cinnamon*
½ *teaspoon ginger*
½ *teaspoon cloves*
½ *teaspoon nutmeg*

Blend eggs, oil, sugar and pumpkin together in large mixing bowl. Measure flour, baking powder, soda, salt, cinnamon, ginger, cloves and nutmeg into 1-quart measure. Mix together lightly with a fork. Stir into pumpkin mixture.

Divide batter equally into two (8 x 8-inch) glass baking dishes. One at a time, MICROWAVE 5 MINUTES, 30 SECONDS to 6 MINUTES on HIGH, or until wooden pick inserted in center comes out clean. Let stand until thoroughly cooled. Top with Cream Cheese Frosting.

CREAM CHEESE FROSTING

2 *packages (3-ounces each) cream cheese*
½ *cup butter or margarine*
1 *tablespoon cream or milk*
1 *teaspoon vanilla*
4 *cups confectioner's sugar (sift if lumpy)*

Combine cream cheese and butter in medium mixing bowl. MICROWAVE 1 to 2 MINUTES on '2', or until soft but not melted.

With a fork, stir in cream and vanilla. Gradually add sugar until frosting reaches spreading consistency. Frost pumpkin bars. Cut into 2-inch squares.

For ovens without variable heat control, to soften cheese and butter, MICROWAVE 30 SECONDS on '5' and watch carefully.

LEMON BUTTER DESSERT SQUARES

6 to 8 servings
8 x 8-inch baking dish

1 *cup all-purpose flour*
½ *cup butter or margarine*
¼ *cup powdered sugar*
2 *eggs*
1 *tablespoon all-purpose flour*
½ *teaspoon baking powder*
1 *cup granulated sugar*
Grated rind and juice of 2 *lemons*

Blend flour, butter and powdered sugar together. Press lightly into bottom of (8 x 8-inch) baking dish. MICROWAVE 3 MINUTES on HIGH, or until firm.

Beat eggs until light. Stir in flour, baking powder, granulated sugar, lemon rind and juice. Pour over baked layer. MICROWAVE 6 MINUTES on HIGH, or until top is set and custard like.

CANDIED ORANGE DATE BARS ❈

20 bars
2-quart bowl
8 x 8-inch baking dish

Filling:
½ *pound candied orange slices, cut in thirds*
½ *cup pitted dates, cut up*
¼ *cup sugar*
1 *tablespoon all-purpose flour*
½ *cup boiling water*

Batter:
½ *cup butter or margarine*
1 *cup firmly packed brown sugar*
2 *eggs*
1¾ *cups all-purpose flour*
1 *teaspoon baking soda*
Pinch salt
1 *teaspoon vanilla*
1 *cup chopped walnuts*

Combine orange slices, dates, sugar and flour in 2-quart bowl. Toss lightly to distribute sugar and flour. Pour boiling water over fruit. MICROWAVE 2 MINUTES, 30 SECONDS to 3 MINUTES on HIGH, or until thick. Set aside.

Mix butter, sugar and eggs thoroughly. Blend in flour, soda, salt and vanilla. Beat well. Stir in nuts.

Spread half of batter in (8 x 8-inch) baking dish. Cover evenly with filling. Top with remaining batter. (It will not cover completely.) MICROWAVE 7 MINUTES, 30 SECONDS to 8 MINUTES on HIGH, or until almost no imprint remains when touched in center.

GINGER PEOPLE

About 2 dozen
12 x 8-inch baking dish

2½ cups all-purpose flour
1 teaspoon salt
1 teaspoon ginger
¼ teaspoon nutmeg
¼ teaspoon cloves
½ teaspoon cinnamon
½ cup margarine or vegetable shortening
½ cup sugar
½ cup molasses
¼ cup water

Combine flour, salt, ginger, nutmeg, cloves and cinnamon in 1-quart measure. Mix together lightly. Set aside.

In large mixing bowl. Cream shortening and sugar together until light and fluffy. Stir in molasses and water. Blend in flour mixture until smooth. Chill dough at least 3 hours.

Roll dough ⅛-inch thick on floured pastry cloth. Cut into gingerbread boys or girls with 3 to 4-inch cookie cutters.

Place sheet of waxed paper on inverted (12 x 8-inch) baking dish. 4 at a time, MICROWAVE 2 MINUTES, 30 SECONDS to 4 MINUTES on '6', or until cookies are set. Cool. Decorate as desired.

For ovens without solid state heat control, MICROWAVE 3 to 5 MINUTES on HIGH.

SCOTCH ROCKY ROAD CANDY

24 pieces
1-quart measure

¼ cup butter or margarine
1 package (6-ounces) semi-sweet chocolate chips
1 package (6-ounces) butterscotch chips
1 package (10-ounces) miniature marshmallows
½ cup coarsely chopped nuts

Combine butter, chocolate and butterscotch chips in 1-quart measure. MICROWAVE 2 to 3 MINUTES on HIGH, or until chips have softened and can be stirred easily. Beat with a fork until well blended.

Mix marshmallows and nuts in 2-quart casserole. Pour in melted mixture. Mix thoroughly. Drop by spoonfuls onto waxed paper. Refrigerate until firm.

BROWNIES

16 to 18 squares
8 x 8-inch baking dish

1 package (13-ounces) brownie mix

Prepare batter as directed on package. Spread into (8 x 8-inch) baking dish. MICROWAVE 7 MINUTES to 8 MINUTES, 30 SECONDS on '6', or until firm to touch. Cool. Cut in 2-inch squares.

For ovens without solid state heat control, MICROWAVE 8 to 10 MINUTES on '5'.

GINGER JOYS

3 to 4 dozen
1-quart casserole
12 x 8-inch baking dish

½ cup vegetable shortening
½ cup sugar
½ cup light molasses
1½ teaspoons vinegar
1 egg, well beaten
3 cups all-purpose flour
½ teaspoon soda
½ teaspoon ginger
½ teaspoon cinnamon
¼ teaspoon salt

Blend shortening, sugar, molasses and vinegar together in 1-quart casserole. MICROWAVE 2 MINUTES on HIGH, or until mixture begins to boil, stirring once. Let stand ½ hour to cool.

Stir in egg. Combine flour, soda, ginger, cinnamon and salt in 1-quart measure. Mix together lightly. Stir into cooled mixture. Mix thoroughly. Refrigerate several hours.

Place a sheet of waxed paper on inverted (12 x 8-inch) baking dish. Form dough in 1-inch balls. Place 6 to 8 on waxed paper. MICROWAVE 2 MINUTES on HIGH, or until set. Let stand 1 minutes. Cool.

BUTTERSCOTCH CRISPS

2 dozen 1½-inch squares
Large mixing bowl

1 package (12-ounces) butterscotch bits
3 cups crisp unsweetened cereal

Pour butterscotch bits into large mixing bowl. MICROWAVE 2 MINUTES, 30 SECONDS on HIGH, or until very soft. Stir in cereal gently but thoroughly. Spread in well-buttered rectangular pan. Refrigerate until completely cooled and set. Cut into squares.

Jams, Preserves & Relishes

The microwave oven makes small batches of jams preserves or relishes quickly and easily. You can always have fresh jam or jelly. Reducing the setting after the mixture boils prevents over-boiling and eliminates the need of constant watching.

Preserves and jellies are traditional at breakfast, but try serving savory ones with hot dinner rolls as a complement to meats.

Use hot strawberry jam as an ice cream topping.

By following the methods given in these recipes, you can prepare your favorite preserves and jellies in the microwave oven.

FRESH STRAWBERRY REFRIGERATOR JAM

1½ cups
2-quart batter bowl

2 cups (1-pint) strawberries, washed and hulled
1½ cups sugar
2 teaspoons powdered fruit pectin

Slice strawberries into 2-quart bowl. Mash well. Stir in sugar and pectin thoroughly. MICROWAVE 3 to 4 MINUTES on HIGH, or until mixture comes to a full rolling boil.

Reduce setting. MICROWAVE 5 MINUTES on '6', or until mixture is slightly thickened. It will thicken more as it cools. Pour into glasses. Cover with plastic wrap. Store in refrigerator. For a thicker jam, add 1 teaspoon pectin.

NOTE: Fresh strawberry jam in a pretty glass makes a thoughtful gift for your hostess, a new neighbor or a good friend. The recipe makes enough jam to fill a large coffee mug or 2 wine glasses.

1 package (10 to 12-ounces) frozen strawberries may be substituted for fresh. Add 1 teaspoon pectin.

For ovens without solid state heat control, after mixture boils MICROWAVE 6 MINUTES on '5'.

MILD PEACH CHUTNEY

Two 1-pint jars
3-quart casserole

1 *large unpeeled apple, cored and chopped*
1 *cup chopped celery*
¼ *cup chopped green pepper*
1 *tablespoon finely chopped onion*
2 *cans (16-ounces each) sliced cling peaches with juice*
½ *cup seedless raisins*
¾ *cup cider vinegar*
½ *cup sugar*
½ *teaspoon salt*
¼ *teaspoon ginger*
Dash cayenne pepper

Combine all ingredients in 3-quart casserole. Stir well. Cover. MICROWAVE 5 MINUTES on HIGH, or until mixture boils.

Reduce setting. MICROWAVE 45 MINUTES on '5', or until syrup is thickened and chutney is desired consistency, stirring 2 or 3 times.

Ladle into hot sterilized jars. Cover tightly. Cool. Store in refrigerator. Serve with meats.

NOTE: Be sure mixture is boiling before reducing setting to '5'.

PICKLED BEETS

2 cups
1-quart measure

1 *can (16-ounces) sliced beets*
Water
1 *tablespoon sugar*
½ *teaspoon salt*
½ *teaspoon celery seed*
1 *to 2 whole cloves*
Small cinnamon stick

Drain liquid from beets into 1-quart measure. Set beets aside. Add equal amount of water to beet juice. MICROWAVE 1 to 2 MINUTES on HIGH, or until boiling.

Stir in sugar, salt, celery seed, cloves and cinnamon. MICROWAVE 1 MINUTE on HIGH, or until sugar is dissolved. Add beets. Refrigerate at least 12 hours to blend flavors.

Variation:
Add ½ to 1 cup sliced onions with beets. Stir in 1 tablespoon dairy sour cream just before serving.

ANTIPASTO RELISH 🔲

6 servings
3-quart casserole

½ *small head cauliflower, cut in flowerets and sliced*
2 *carrots, pared, cut in 2-inch strips*
2 *stems celery, cut diagonally in 1-inch pieces (1 cup)*
1 *small onion, cut in ¾-inch squares*
1 *green pepper, cut in 2-inch strips*
1 *jar (3-ounces) stuffed green olives, drained*
¾ *cup wine vinegar*
½ *cup olive or salad oil*
1 *to 2 tablespoons sugar*
1 *teaspoon salt*
½ *teaspoon oregano leaves*
¼ *teaspoon pepper*
¼ *cup water*

Combine all ingredients in 3-quart casserole. MICROWAVE 8 to 10 MINUTES on HIGH, or until mixture has come to a rapid boil, stirring twice.

Reduce setting. MICROWAVE 4 to 6 MINUTES on '6'. Cool. Refrigerate at least 24 hours. Drain well before serving.

Will keep several days in refrigerator, covered. Serve as appetizer, salad, or garnish for meats.

NOTE: Pitted ripe olives, medium zucchini cut in 1-inch pieces, or other crisp, fresh vegetables may be substituted for part of ingredients above.

For ovens without solid state heat control, after mixture boils MICROWAVE 5 to 7 MINUTES on '5'.

EASY SPICED PEACHES

2 to 3 pint jars
2-quart batter bowl
12 x 8-inch baking dish

2 *cans (1-pound, 13-ounces each) peach halves*
2 *tablespoons cider vinegar*
1 *teaspoon whole allspice*
1 *teaspoon whole cloves*
4 *cinnamon sticks (2½-inches)*

Drain peaches well, reserving 1½ cups syrup. In 2-quart bowl, combine reserved syrup, vinegar; allspice, cloves and cinnamon sticks. MICROWAVE 4 to 6 MINUTES on HIGH, or until mixture boils.

Reduce setting. MICROWAVE 4 MINUTES on '6'. Remove and discard cloves.

Arrange peach halves in (12 x 8-inch) baking dish. Pour hot syrup over peaches. MICROWAVE 5 MINUTES on '6', basting peaches several times.

Serve hot or cold. Peaches will keep in jars several days, refrigerated.

For ovens without solid state heat control, MICROWAVE 5 MINUTES on '5'. Pour syrup over peaches. MICROWAVE 6 MINUTES on '5'.

GRAPEFRUIT AND SAVORY JELLY

Three ½-pint jars
2-quart batter bowl

½ cup boiling water
2 teaspoons dried summer savory
1 cup grapefruit juice
1 package (1¾-ounces) powdered fruit pectin
Green food color
3¼ cups sugar

Pour boiling water over savory in small bowl. Cover. Let stand 15 minutes. Strain through cheese cloth into measuring cup. Add more water, if needed, to make ½ cup.

Combine savory water, grapefruit juice and pectin in 2-quart bowl. MICROWAVE 5 to 7 MINUTES on HIGH, or until mixture boils. Tint light green with food color. Stir in sugar.

Reduce setting. MICROWAVE 6 to 8 MINUTES on '6', or until slightly thickened, stirring once to dissolve sugar. Skim. Pour into hot sterilized jars. Seal.

For ovens without solid state heat control, after adding sugar, MICROWAVE 7 to 9 MINUTES on '5'.

AROMATIC APPLE JELLY

Four ½-pint jars
2-quart batter bowl

2 cups apple juice
1 package (1¾-ounces) powdered fruit pectin
1 tablespoon aromatic bitters
2 tablespoons lemon juice
Red food color
3½ cups sugar

Stir apple juice and pectin together in 2-quart batter bowl. MICROWAVE 5 to 7 MINUTES on HIGH, or until mixture boils. Add bitters, lemon juice and a few drops red food color. Stir in sugar.

Reduce setting. MICROWAVE 6 to 8 MINUTES on '6', or until mixture is slightly thickened, stirring once to dissolve sugar. Skim. Pour into hot sterilized jars. Seal.

For ovens without solid state heat control, after adding sugar, MICROWAVE 7 to 9 MINUTES on '5'.

GRAPE-AND-BASIL JELLY

Four ½-pint jars
2-quart batter bowl

½ cup boiling water
1 tablespoon dried basil
1½ cups grape juice
1 package (1¾-ounces) powdered fruit pectin
3 cups sugar

Pour boiling water over basil in small bowl. Cover. Let stand 5 to 10 minutes. Strain through cheese cloth into measuring cup. Add more water, if necessary, to make ½ cup. Combine basil water, grape juice and pectin in 2-quart bowl. MICROWAVE 5 to 7 MINUTES on HIGH, or until mixture boils. Stir in sugar.

Reduce setting. MICROWAVE 6 to 8 MINUTES on '6', or until mixture is slightly thickened, stirring once to dissolve sugar. Skim. Pour into hot sterilized jars. Seal.

NOTE: Dried thyme may be substituted for basil.

For ovens without solid state heat control, after adding sugar, MICROWAVE 7 to 9 MINUTES on '5'.

HOT GINGERED PEARS

2 to 3 pint jars
2-quart batter bowl
12 x 8-inch baking dish

2 cans (1-pound, 13-ounces each) pear halves
24 whole cloves
2 cinnamon sticks (2-inches)
¼ teaspoon nutmeg
4 teaspoons lemon juice
1 teaspoon grated lemon peel
1 teaspoon grated orange peel
2½ tablespoons chopped crystallized ginger
⅛ teaspoon ground ginger
2 tablespoons butter or margarine

Drain pears well, reserving 1½ cups syrup. In 2-quart bowl, combine reserved syrup, 10 cloves, cinnamon sticks and nutmeg. MICROWAVE 4 to 6 MINUTES on HIGH, or until mixture boils.

Reduce setting. MICROWAVE 4 MINUTES on '6'. Remove and discard cloves. Add lemon juice, lemon and orange peels, gingers and butter. Mix well. MICRO-WAVE 4 to 6 MINUTES on '6', or until slightly thickened.

Arrange pear halves in (12 x 8-inch) baking dish. Insert 1 or 2 cloves in each. Pour hot syrup over pears. MICRO-WAVE 5 MINUTES on '6', basting pears with syrup several times.

Serve hot or cold. Will keep in jars several days, refrigerated.

For ovens without solid state heat control, after mixture boils MICROWAVE 5 to 7 MINUTES on '5'. Pour syrup over pears. MICROWAVE 6 MINUTES on '5'.

Convenience Foods

Microwave cooking makes convenience foods even more convenient. Mixes, ready-prepared frozen and canned foods save you preparation time. The microwave oven saves you cooking and heating time.

Some convenience foods have become so basic to the American cooking style that they are considered ingredients. Canned and frozen soups and sauces, meats, fish and vegetables, evaporated and condensed milks, gravy and seasoning mixes appear in recipes throughout this cookbook.

In the casserole section there are sample recipes for the preparation of dehydrated mixes, such as "add-meat" dinners and macaroni and cheese. The vegetable section includes charts for cooking frozen vegetables and sample recipes for dehydrated potato mixes. Directions and time charts for cooking macaroni, spaghetti and noodles are in the rice and pasta chapter.

In the dessert and baking sections you'll find basic instructions for preparing mixes in the microwave oven, sample recipes to illustrate the method and time charts for different types of mix cakes, cupcakes, quick breads and muffins. There are also recipes which call for mixes as ingredients.

The charts on the following pages list some readily available frozen, canned and dehydrated convenience foods. Instructions are given for defrosting, heating or cooking them. Time and setting charts are provided for

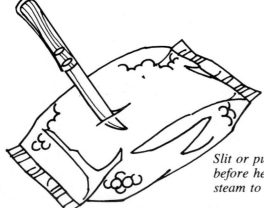

Slit or puncture frozen food pouches before heating or defrosting to allow steam to escape.

different heat control microwave ovens. Standing times are important since foods will continue to heat after removal from the oven.

These charts can serve as guide lines for handling similar convenience foods, as well as frozen or canned foods prepared in the home. A special chart for defrosting homemade frozen casseroles follows the convenience food guide.

Convenience foods come in several types of packages. Foods frozen in pouches may be defrosted or heated right in the pouch. Slit or puncture the pouch before heating to allow steam to escape, and open carefully when done. You may also remove pouched foods from the package and heat them in casseroles or serving dishes covered with plastic wrap.

Foods frozen or canned in glass jars may be heated right in the jar with the lid removed. Foods frozen in aluminum foil trays need not be removed to another dish, although you may wish to do so for faster heating. If the lid is foil, remove it and replace with plastic wrap. Non-foil lids can be loosened and left resting on top of the tray to cover lightly. Check paper lids for foil linings. Turn down any rough edges on the tray.

Remove foil lids from foil trays and cover tray with plastic wrap before heating.

Remove lids from glass jars before heating.

Convenience Foods

Frozen Foods/Defrosting

ITEM	SIZE	COOKING CONTAINER	MINUTES	SETTING	SPECIAL INSTRUCTIONS
Beef pattie in bun (2 per package)	8¼ oz.	Place on paper napkin	2 - 3	4	
			2 - 3	4	
			1½ - 2½	5	
Brownies	13 oz.	Original tray, loosen lid	1 - 1½	4	Let stand 3 minutes
			1 - 1½	4	
			¾ - 1¼	5	
Cake, frosted	20½ oz.	Original tray	2 - 2½	4	Let stand 3 - 5 minutes
			2 - 2½	4	
			1½ - 2	5	
Coffee cake (streusel type)	10⅞ oz.	Original package, loosen lid	2 - 2½	4	Let stand 3 minutes
			2 - 2½	4	
			1½ - 2	5	
Donuts	2 donuts	Place on paper plate or napkin	1	4	Let stand 3 minutes
			1	4	
			¾	5	
Eggs, frozen	8 fl. oz.	Original carton, open	4 - 5	4	Shake well, let stand 10 minutes
			4 - 5	4	
			3 - 4	5	
Hamburger buns	8 buns	Original package, open	2 - 3	4	Let stand 2 minutes
			2 - 3	4	
			1½ - 2½	5	
Pancake batter	7 oz.	Original carton, open	3 - 5	4	Shake, let stand 10 minutes
			3 - 5	4	
			2½ - 4	5	
Strawberries, whole	16 oz.	Covered casserole	2 - 3	High	Let stand 5 minutes
			2 - 3	High	
			2 - 3	High	

Frozen Foods/Reheating

ITEM	SIZE	COOKING CONTAINER	MINUTES	SETTING	SPECIAL INSTRUCTIONS
Chicken Ala King	5 oz.	Plastic pouch, slit	3 - 4	High	
			3 - 4	High	
			3 - 4	High	
Chicken, batter fried	16 oz.	Original tray, loosen lid	13	High	Turn after 8 minutes
			13	High	
			13	High	
Corn, Peas, Beans, in butter sauce	10 oz.	Plastic pouch, slit, or 1-qt. casserole	5 - 6	High	
			5 - 6	High	
			5 - 6	High	
Fish Fillets, fried	14 oz.	Place on roasting rack	5 - 6	High	Rearrange after 3 minutes
			5 - 6	High	
			5 - 6	High	
Fondue, Swiss	10 oz.	Plastic pouch, slit	6	6	Stir well before serving
			7	5	
			7	5	
Green Peppers, stuffed	14 oz.	Original pkg. cover with plastic wrap	18 - 20	8	
			14½ - 16	High	
			14½ - 16	High	
Lasagna	50 oz.	Original tray, loosen lid	20 - 22	8	
			16 - 17½	High	
			16 - 17½	High	
Meatballs, with gravy and mashed potatoes	9¼ oz.	Original tray, loosen lid	6 - 7	8	
			4½ - 5½	High	
			4½ - 5½	High	
Mexican style dinner	11 oz.	Original tray, loosen lid	6 - 7	8	
			4½ - 5½	High	
			4½ - 5½	High	

Convenience Foods *continued*

Frozen Foods/Reheating *continued*

ITEM	SIZE	COOKING CONTAINER	MINUTES	SETTING	SPECIAL INSTRUCTIONS
Omelets, Western	10 oz. (two omelets)	Glass or pottery plate	4 - 5	6	Turn once
			5 - 6	5	
			5 - 6	5	
Pizza Roll appetizers	6 oz.	Browning dish, preheat 4 min. on High, add 1 Tbsp. oil	1 - 2	High	Turn once
			1 - 2	High	
			1 - 2	High	
Pork Ribs, (cooked)	32 oz.	Original pkg. cover with plastic wrap	15	8	Rearrange after 10 minutes
			12	High	
			12	High	
Potatoes, baked, stuffed	12 oz.	Original pkg. Open one end	8 - 9	High	
			8 - 9	High	
			8 - 9	High	
Potatoes and Celery in white sauce	10 oz.	Plastic pouch, slit or 1-qt. covered casserole	5 - 6	High	
			5 - 6	High	
			5 - 6	High	
Potatoes, shoestring	10 oz.	Plastic pouch, slit or 1-qt. covered casserole	5 - 6	High	
			5 - 6	High	
			5 - 6	High	
Salisbury Steak with gravy	32 oz.	Original tray, loosen lid	23 - 25	8	Rearrange after 8 minutes
			18 - 20	High	
			18 - 20	High	
Spaghetti and sauce	14 oz.	Remove from pouch, place in 1-qt. casserole	8 - 9	6	
			9½ - 11	5	
			9½ - 11	5	
Tuna-Noodle Casserole	11½ oz.	Original pkg. loosen lid	10 - 12	8	Stir before serving
			8 - 9½	High	
			8 - 9½	High	
Turkey or Beef dinner	11½ oz.	Original pkg. remove cover from tray	9 - 10	High	
			9 - 10	High	
			9 - 10	High	

Frozen Foods/Reheating

ITEM	SIZE	DIRECTIONS	MINUTES	SETTING	SPECIAL INSTRUCTIONS
Potatoes, fried	10 oz.	Preheat browning dish on High 4 min. add 1 Tbsp. oil and potatoes	5 - 6	High	Stir after 2 minutes
			5 - 6	High	
			5 - 6	High	
Tater Tots	16 oz.		3 - 5	High	Stir after 2 minutes
			3 - 5	High	
			3 - 5	High	

Frozen Foods/Cooking

ITEM	SIZE	COOKING CONTAINER	MINUTES	SETTING	SPECIAL INSTRUCTIONS
Chicken Kiev	6½ oz.	8x8 baking dish lightly covered with plastic wrap	15 - 18	6	Rearrange after 10 minutes
			18 - 22	5	
			18 - 22	5	
Mixed Vegetables	16 oz.	Covered casserole	8 - 10	High	Stir before serving
			8 - 10	High	
			8 - 10	High	
Spinach Souffle	12 oz.	Original pkg. loosen lid	13 - 15	8	
			11 - 12	High	
			11 - 12	High	

Canned Foods

ITEM	SIZE		MINUTES	SETTING	SPECIAL INSTRUCTIONS
Beans, baked	21 oz.	Covered casserole	6 - 7	8	Stir before serving
			5 - 6	High	
			5 - 6	High	
Beef Ravioli	40 oz.	Covered casserole	10	8	
			8	High	
			8	High	

Convenience Foods *continued*

Canned Foods continued

ITEM	SIZE	COOKING CONTAINER	MINUTES	SETTING	SPECIAL INSTRUCTIONS
Beef Stew	24 oz.	Covered casserole	10	8	Stir once
			8	High	
			8	High	
Cabbage, stuffed with beef, soy	16 oz.	Covered casserole	7 - 8	8	Rearrange once
			5½ - 6½	High	
			5½ - 6½	High	
Chili with beans	15 oz.	Covered casserole	5 - 6	High	Stir once
			5 - 6	High	
			5 - 6	High	
Corn, Peas, Cut Beans	17 oz.	Covered casserole	3 - 4	High	Stir before serving – Larger cans, increase time 1-1½ min.
			3 - 4	High	
			3 - 4	High	
Ham, patties (refrigerated)	4 patties	Plate	3 - 3½	8	Turn once
			3 - 3½	High	
			3 - 3½	High	
Hash, Corned Beef	15 oz.	Covered casserole	5 - 6	High	Stir before serving
			5 - 6	High	
			5 - 6	High	
Pork, sliced with gravy	12½ oz.	Covered casserole	5 - 6	8	Stir before serving
			4 - 5	High	
			4 - 5	High	
Potato Salad, German style	15 oz.	Covered casserole	5 - 6	High	Stir before serving
			5 - 6	High	
			5 - 6	High	
Soup, chunky style	19 oz.	Covered casserole	5 - 6	High	Stir before serving
			5 - 6	High	
			5 - 6	High	

Canned Foods *continued*

ITEM	SIZE	COOKING CONTAINER	MINUTES	SETTING	SPECIAL INSTRUCTIONS
Soup, condensed cream style (diluted)	10¼ oz.	Covered casserole	5 - 6	High	Stir before serving
			5 - 6	High	
			5 - 6	High	
Spaghetti	15 oz.	Covered casserole	5 - 6	High	Stir before serving
			5 - 6	High	
			5 - 6	High	

Dehydrated Foods

ITEM	SIZE	COOKING CONTAINER	MINUTES	SETTING	SPECIAL INSTRUCTIONS
Onion soup, dry mix	1¼ oz.	Medium mixing bowl, covered	13 - 14	High	Stir before serving
			13 - 14	High	
			13 - 14	High	
Wine sauce mix	1 oz.	Medium mixing bowl, covered	4½ - 5	High	Stir before serving
			4½ - 5	High	
			4½ - 5	High	
Hamburger Helper	See recipes in Casserole section (page 108 - 123)				
Tuna Helper					
Macaroni and Cheese					
Scalloped potatoes					
Hash browns					

Homemade Casseroles Frozen - Precooked

		MINUTES	SETTING	SPECIAL INSTRUCTIONS
1-quart		12 - 18	4	Cover
		12 - 18	4	Stir once
		10 - 15	5	
2-quart		25 - 30	4	Cover
		25 - 30	4	Stir once
		20 - 24	5	

Drying Flowers

The microwave oven dries flowers in minutes, with a fresher appearance and color than flowers dried by traditional methods. Microwave-dried flowers are also less perishable.

Microwave-drying of flowers requires a drying agent to absorb moisture and hold the flower in its natural shape. Three different agents may be used.

1. Silica Gel, available in most hobby shops, is best for drying smooth petals, such as orchids or daisies.
2. An equal mixture of borax and corn meal can be used.
3. Kitty litter is inexpensive and easiest to use.

All three drying agents can be used over again. Rubber or plastic gloves will protect your hands from the drying agents.

1. Select fresh flowers or leaves. Flowers should be just at the peak of bloom. Flowers which have passed their prime will continue to turn brown. Clip stem of flower to ½-inch long.

2. Select a glass or paper container large enough to hold the flower and deep enough so that the drying agent covers the entire bloom. Small flowers may be dried individually in small bowls; up to three may be dried in the oven at once. Use a casserole for large flowers.

3. Spread a ½-inch layer of drying agent in the bottom of container. Place flower in agent, bloom up. With a spoon, carefully sprinkle drying agent between and over the petals, making sure that each petal is covered, but not bent out of shape by the weight of the agent. All petals should be completely covered.

4. Place a 1-cup measure full of water and the flower container in the microwave oven. The separate container of water provides moisture and keeps the flowers from becoming too dry.

   MICROWAVE 1 to 3 MINUTES on HIGH, depending upon the size and type of flower. Large flowers, such as chrysanthemums may take as long as 5 to 6 minutes.

   Let flower stand in the agent at least 10 hours. When removing flower from the agent, tap flower gently until all granules of the drying agent are removed. Tape wires or floral sticks to the remaining ½-inch of flower stem.

DRYING LEAVES

   Fall leaves dried in the microwave oven retain their beautiful color. Select a branch of 3 leaves, with the largest leaf about 4 inches wide. Clean leaves carefully. Invert a 12 x 8-inch baking dish on the oven floor. Cover with a layer of paper towel. Place the branch on the towel. Cover with another layer of towel. MICROWAVE 1 MINUTE, 30 SECONDS on HIGH. Turn branch over and cover with towel. MICROWAVE 1 MINUTE, 30 SECONDS on HIGH. To dry larger branches, increase oven time.

Recipe Index

A

After Christmas Quiche, 129
All-American Cheeseburger, 44
All In One Beef Dinner, 112
American Pork, 87
Antipasto Relish, 188
Appetizers, 34. See also Canapés,
    Hors D'Oeuvres, Dips
  Baby Burgers, 37
  Bacon-Bleu Cheese Hors D'Oeuvres, 40
  Bacon Oysters, 36
  Bacon Stuffed Mushrooms, 43
  Bacon Wands, 36
  Bleu Cheese Mushrooms, 43
  Bourbon Wieners, 36
  Butterflied Wieners, 35
  Cheese Nachoes, 39
  Chestnut Celery Mushrooms, 43
  Chicken 'N Bacon Bits, 40
  Cocktail Nibbles, 38
  Crab or Lobster Stuffed Mushrooms, 43
  Easy-Does-It Canapés, 39
  Escargot, 38
  Florentine Mushrooms, 43
  Ham and Pineapple Kabobs, 37
  Ham Roll Ups, 37
  Herbed Scallops, 38
  Hot Cheese Dip, 41
  Hot Cheese-Clam Dip, 41
  Hot Cheese Dip with Fruit, 41
  Italian Mushrooms, 43
  Italian Shrimp, 37
  Liverwurst Pate on Toast, 39
  Marinated Chicken Wings, 38
  Mexican Mushrooms, 43
  Mini Meatballs, 37
  Mushroom-Cheddar Canapés, 41
  Mushroom Kabobs, 37
  Olives in Bacon Blankets, 36
  Party Appetizer Pie, 38
  Patio Dip, 40
  Polynesian Mushrooms, 43
  Quick and Easy Clam Dip, 41
  Rarebit Dip, 35
  Rumaki, 36
  Saucy Shrimp Hors D'Oeuvre, 40
  Seafood Tantalizers, 39
  Sea Salad Canapés, 40
  Shrimp in Bacon, 36
  Shrimp Stuffed Mushrooms, 43
  Stroganoff Stuffed Mushrooms, 43
  Stuffed Mushrooms, 43
Apples
  Baked, 178
  Jelly, 189
  Pie (defrosting), 23
  Spiced Cider, 59
Applesauce, 179
Applesauce-Spice Cake, 168
Apricots, Spiced, 177
Aromatic Apple Jelly, 189
Artichokes, 146
Asparagus, 146
  Ham Birds, 117
Asparanuts, 134
Au Gratin Potatoes, 141
Australian Beef, 79
Australian Lamb, 94

B

Baby Burgers, 37
Bacon, 13
  Basics, 96
  Bleu Cheese Hors D'Oeuvre, 40
  Oysters, 36
  Stuffed Mushrooms, 43
  Wands, 36
Bacon, Sausage and Specialty Meats, 96
Baked. See also specific foods.
  Beans, 135
  Custard, 176
  Fish, 67
  Ham, 91
  Potato, 15
  Salmon with Mushrooms, 69
  Squash, 144
  Torsk, 67
  Zucchini and Onions, 145
Baking, 160
  Basics, 162
  Buttermilk Bran Muffins, 164
  Cornbread, 164
  Date Nut Bread, 165
  Dependable Dumplings, 163
  Down Home Streusel Coffeecake, 164
  Dressed Up Gingerbread, 165
  Fast Cheese Frenchies, 165
  Onion Cheese Sticks, 163
  Onion Herb Bread, 164
  Proofing of Frozen Bread, 162
  Soda Bread, 163
  Sticky Buns, 163
  Streusel Coffeecake, 165
  Whole Wheat Bread, 162
Bananas
  Boats, 179
  Cream Pie, 173
  Foster, 178
Barbecued
  Crab Sandwiches, 49
  Pork Chops, 88
  Sauce, 157
  Spareribs, 89
Barbecues, 47
Basic Beef Casserole, 79
Basic Lamb Casserole, 94
Basic Pork Casserole, 87
Beans, 146
  and Burgundy, 135
  Baked, 195
  Butter, 146
  Cut, 147, 196
  Lima, 147
  Pinto, 147
Beautiful Baked Apple, 178
Bechamel Sauce, 156
Beef, 70
  Australian, 79
  Basic Casserole, 79
  Basics, 74
  Belgian, 79

  Birds, 78
  Bouquetiere Dinner, 25
  Bourguignonne, 77
  Casserole-Steak, 78
  Chinese, 79
  Cooking Times
    Tender Cuts, 74
    Less Tender Cuts, 75
  Corned, 97
  Country Style Short Ribs, 76
  Defrosting, 20
  Dinner, frozen, 194
  Easy Beef Stew Supreme, 110
  English, 79
  Every Day Pot Roast, 76
  Fiji Beef Chunks, 111
  Flank Steak Roll-Up, 76
  Freezer to Table Pot Roast, 83
  Freezer to Table Rump Roast, 83
  Freezer to Table Swiss Steak, 83
  Fried Liver and Onion, 97
  Frontier Pot Roast, 75
  Goulash, 110
  Hamburger Creole, 82
  Hungarian, 79
  Indian, 79
  Lazy Beef Casserole, 111
  Oven Stew, 110
  Pattie in Bun, frozen, 192
  Pepper Steak, 77
  Roast, 71
  Sirloin Steak, 75
  Stew, 196
  Stroganoff, 112
  Stroganoff Spectacular, 78
  Stuffed Cabbage Rolls, 82
  Stuffed Pepper Pots, 82
  Swiss Steak, 76
  With Onions, 78
Beets, 147
  Harvard, 136
  Pickled, 188
  Tangy Creamed, 136
Belgian Pork, 87
Beverages, 58
  Café Au Lait, 58
  Café Brulot, 59
  Coffee House Varieties, 58
  Elegant Egg Nog, 59
  Espresso Royale, 58
  Hot Chocolate, 59
  Hot Mulled Wine, 58
  Hot Toddy, 58
  Killarney Coffee, 59
  Parisian Mocha, 58
  Quick Cocoa, 59
  Spiced Cider, 59
Black Bottom Pie, 171
Bleu Cheese Mushrooms, 43
Bologna Cheese Bake, 118
Bologna, Scalloped Bake, 118
Bolognese, 50
Borscht, 53
Bourbon Wieners, 36
Braised Celery, 138
Bran Muffins, 164
Bratwurst, smoked, 97
Breads. Also see Baking.
  Corn, 164
  Date Nut, 165
  Defrosting, 22
  Onion Herb, 164
  Proofing of Frozen, 162

Soda, 163
Whole Wheat, 162
Broccoli, 148
Italian Style, 136
and Mushrooms in Sour Cream, 136
Brown Sugar Ham, 90
Brownies, 185
Brownies, frozen, 17, 192
Browning, 19
Browning Dish Hamburgers, 16
Brussel Sprouts, 148
Au Gratin, 137
in Cream Sauce, 137
Buns, Sticky, 163
Burger-Dogs, 46
Busy Day Casserole, 120
Busy Day Supper, 31
Butter, Whipped Herb, 111
Butterflied Wieners, 35
Buttermilk Bran Muffins, 164
Butterscotch
Crisps, 185
Frosting, 171
Pie, 173
Pudding, 176

C

Cabbage, 148
Cabbage, stuffed, 196
Café Au Lait, 58
Café Brulot, 59
Cake Mix Cupcakes, 169
Candy, 181
Basics, 182
Fantastic Fudge, 182
Fondant, 183
Nature's Own Candy, 183
Never-Fail Fudge, 182
Peanut Brittle, 182
Penuche, 182
Scotch Rocky Road Candy, 185
Sunshine Divinity, 183
Toffee Tempters, 183
Cantonese Shrimp and Pea Pods, 62
Caribbean Baked Squash, 144
Carrots, 148
Glazed, 137
Grape Glazed, 137
Spicy, 137
Cakes
Applesauce-Spice, 168
Cake Mix Cupcakes, 169
Cherry Crumble, 175
Cherry Dessert, 175
Chocolate Fudge, 170
Defrosting, 23
Frosted, frozen, 192
German Chocolate, 168
Mocha Torte, 167
Peach Spice Pudding, 171
Pineapple Upside Down, 170
Raspberry Swirl Bundt, 169
Strawberry Macaroon Torte, 171
Triple Fudge Bundt Cake with Glaze, 169
Yellow Cake Mix, 169
Canapés, 39
Easy-Does-It, 39
Mushroom-Cheddar, 41
Sea Salad, 40

Candied Orange Date Bars, 184
Casserole Beefsteak, 78
Casseroles, 108
All In One Beef Dinner, 112
Asparagus Ham Birds, 117
Australian Beef, 79
Australian Lamb, 94
Basic Beef, 79
Basic Lamb, 94
Beef Birds, 78
Beefsteak, 78
Belgian Beef, 79
Bologna Cheese Bake, 118
Busy Day Casserole, 120
Cantonese Shrimp and Pea Pods, 62
Chicken and Wild Rice Casserole, 121
Chicken-Tuna Bake, 120
Chili, 113
Chinese Beef, 79
Chow Mein, 119
Confetti, 117
Cooked-Beef, 112
Cooked Pork and Sauerkraut, 119
Country Pie, 115
Crab Gumbo, 121
Dried Beef Bake, 115
Easy Beef Stew, 110
English Beef, 79
Fiji Beef Chunks, 111
Fillet of Sole, 69
French Lamb, 94
Garbanzo, 114
Goulash, 110
Greek Lamb, 94
Ground Beef "Add Meat" Dinner, 114
Hamburger Creole, 82
Ham 'N Oyster, 117
Hawaiian Sweet Sour Ham, 116
Heavenly Ham Loaf, 116
Homemade, Reheating from frozen, 197
Hungarian Beef, 79
Indian Beef, 79
Indian Lamb, 94
Irish Lamb, 94
Italian Lamb, 94
Italian Liver Bake, 115
Johnny Marzetti, 114
Lamb Riblets in Tomato Honey Sauce, 94
Lasagna for Four, 113
Lazy Beef, 111
Leftover Ham, 116
Luncheon Shrimp, 63
Macaroni and Cheese Dinner Mix, 123
Matterhorn Vegetable Bake, 141
Mom's Tater Tot Hot Dish, 115
Mushroom-Barley, 123
Noodles Almondine, 123
Noodles Bolognese, 113
Noodles Romano, 122
One Dish Spaghetti, 113
Oriental Frankfurters, 119
Oriental Hash, 119
Oriental Tuna, 122
Oven Stew, 110
Oysters and Macaroni Au Gratin, 121
Pork and Bean, 119
Potato-Cheese, 121
Quick Beef Chip, 115
Roast Beef Stew, 111
Saturday Special, 114
Saucy Beef Hash, 111
Saucy Turkey and Rice, 120

Sausage Noodle, 116
Scalloped Bologna Bake, 118
Speedy Macaroni and Cheese, 123
Spinach Casserole, 144
Stroganoff Spectacular, 78
Stuffed Cabbage Rolls, 82
Stuffed Pepper Pots, 82
Sweet-Sour Spinach, 144
Tasty Tuna Bake, 122
Top the Taters Dinner, 114
Tuna "Add Meat" Dinner, 122
Tuna Chow Mein, 122
Turkey Special, 120
Weenie-Mac, 116
Whipped Herb Butter, 111
Cauliflower, 148
Deviled, 137
Celery, 149
Braised, 138
Wine Braised with Mushrooms, 138
Cereals, 154
Family Oatmeal, 154
Grits Royale, 155
One Man Oatmeal, 154
Quick Cream of Wheat, 155
Cheese, 124
Cheddar Cheese Sauce, 157
and Onion Quiche, 129
Basics, 130
B.L.T. Sandwich, 50
Classic Cheese Strata, 130
Fondue, 131
Nachoes, 39
'N Tuna Buns, 48
Scrambled Eggs, 127
Souffle, 125
Soup Canadienne, 54
Sandwich, Grilled, 45
Stuffed Potatoes, 141
Swiss Luncheon Bake, 130
Tomato Beans, 135
Toppers, 131
Welsh Rarebit, 130
Cherry
Crumble, 175
Dessert, 175
Peach Mounds, 174
Pie, frozen, 175
Chestnut-Celery Mushrooms, 43
Chicken
A La King, 105
A La King, frozen, 193
and Wild Rice Casserole, 121
Barbecue, 103
Braised in Wine, 103
Butterfried, frozen, 193
Bechamel Sauce, 156
Cacciatori, 102
Coq Au Vin, 102
Creamy Chicken 'N Ham Soup, 57
Defrosting, 21
Easy-Bake, 104
Kiev, 195
Livers Chablis, 105
Majorca, 104
Marengo, 102
Marinated Wings, 38
'N Bacon Bits, 40
Parisienne, 103
Roast, 104
Saltimbocca, 103
Sherried Breasts, 103

Soup with Little Dumplings, 55
Tuna Bake, 120
Children's Luncheon, 28
Chili, 113
Chili Con Queso Soup, 54
Chili with Beans, 196
Chinese Beef, 79
Chinese Pork, 87
Chocolate
Cream Pie, 173
Frosting, 170
Fudge Cake, 170
German Chocolate Cake, 168
Hot Chocolate, 59
Hot Fudge Sauce, 159
Icing, 170
Mint Topping, 159
Mocha Torte, 167
Pudding, 175
Quick Cocoa, 59
Wafer Crumb Crust, 174
Chowder
Fish, 56
Manhattan Clam, 56
New England Clam, 56
Quickie Corn, 56
Chow Mein, 119
Chuck Roast, 83
Clams
Hot-Cheese Dip, 41
Manhattan Chowder, 56
New England Chowder, 56
Quick and Easy Dip, 41
Salsa Di Vongole, 158
Classic Cheese Strata, 130
Cocktail Nibbles, 38
Cocoa, Parisian, 58
Cocoa, Quick, 59
Coconut
Cream Pie, 173
Crust, 174
German Chocolate Cake Topping, 168
Coffee
Café Au Lait, 58
Café Brulot, 59
Cake
Down Home Streusel, 164
Frozen, 192
Streusel, 165
House Varieties, 58
Killarney, 59
Cognac, Espresso Royale, 58
Colossal Baked Limas, 135
Company Chicken Dinner, 31
Coney Islands, 48
Confetti Casserole, 117
Convenience Foods, 190
Cooked Beef Stroganoff, 112
Cooked Pork and Sauerkraut, 119
Cookies, 184
Basics, 184
Brownies, 185
Butterscotch Crisps, 185
Candied Orange Date Bars, 184
Cream Cheese Frosting, 184
Ginger Joys, 185
Ginger People, 185
Lemon Butter Dessert Squares, 184
Pumpkin Bars, 184
Cooking Beef at Other Settings, 75

Cooking Utensils, 10
Coq Au Vin, 102
Coquilles Saint Jacques, 64
Corn
Bread, 164
Bubble, 139
Canned, 196
Escalloped, 139
On The Cob, 133, 149
Off The Cob, 149
Quickie Corn Chowder, 56
Corned Beef, 97
Defrosting, 20
Hash, canned, 196
Reuben Sandwich, 49
Roast, 97
Wide-Open Reuben Sandwich, 50
Cornish Hens for Two, 107
Country Pie, 115
Country Style Short Ribs, 76
Covering, 19
Crab
Barbecued Sandwiches, 49
Gumbo, 121
Key West Sandwich, 50
Mornay, 64
Spaghetti with Crab Sauce, 63
Stuffed Mushrooms, 43
Cranberry Crisp, 175
Cranberry Sauce, 104
Cream
Cheese Frosting, 184
Curry Beans, 134
of Turkey Soup, 55
of Wheat, Quick, 155
Baked Eggplant, 140
Chicken 'N Ham Soup, 57
Tomato Soup, 54
Velvet Veal, 85
Cucumber Sauce, 68
Currant-Raisin Sauce, 156
Curry
Eggs, 127
Eggs and Shrimp, 128
Fruit, 179
Meat Loaf, 81
Sauce, 157

D

Date Bars, Candied Orange, 184
Date Nut Bread, 165
Defrosting and Defrosting Charts, 20
Delectable Duckling, 101
Denver Sandwich, 47
Desserts, 166
Applesauce, 179
Applesauce-Spice Cake, 168
Baked Custard, 176
Banana Boats, 179
Banana Cream Pie, 173
Bananas Foster, 178
Beautiful Baked Apple, 178
Black Bottom Pie, 171
Butterscotch Frosting, 171
Butterscotch Pie, 173
Butterscotch Pudding, 176
Cake Mix Cupcakes, 169
Cherry Crumble, 175
Cherry Dessert, 175
Cherry-Peach Mounds, 174
Chocolate Cream Pie, 173

Chocolate Frosting, 170
Chocolate Fudge Cake, 170
Chocolate Icing, 170
Chocolate Pudding, 175
Chocolate Wafer Crumb Crust, 174
Coconut Cream Pie, 173
Coconut Crust, 174
Cranberry Crisp, 175
Curried Fruits, 179
Fantastic Chocolate Fondue, 179
Frozen Cherry Pie, 175
Fruit Brule, 179
Fruit Cocktail Torte, 177
German Chocolate Cake, 168
German Chocolate Cake Topping, 168
Ginger Pears, 178
Graham Cracker Crust, 174
Holiday Fruit Pudding, 177
Hot Ambrosia Compote, 178
Instant Chocolate Fondue, 179
Lemon Meringue Pie, 173
Marshmallow Mist Icing, 170
Mocha Filling, 167
Mocha Torte, 167
Pastry for One-Crust Pie, 172
Pastry Shell from Mix, 172
Peach Spice Pudding Cake, 171
Pears in Red Wine, 177
Pecan Pie, 173
Pineapple Upside Down Cake, 170
Pudding or Custard Mix, 176
Pumpkin Pie, 174
Raspberry Swirl Bundt Cake, 169
Rhubarb Crisp, 178
Rhubarb Sauce, 179
Spiced Apricots, 177
Strawberry Cream Filling, 171
Strawberry Macaroon Torte, 171
Strawberry Pie, 172
Tapioca Fluff, 176
Triple Fudge Bundt Cake with Glaze, 169
Vanilla Cream Pie, 173
Vanilla Fluff Pudding, 176
Vanilla Wafer Crust, 174
Waikiki Pineapple Pie, 174
Yellow Cake Mix, 169
Deviled Cauliflower, 137
Dinner Rolls, Defrosting, 22
Dips
Hot and Creamy Shrimp Dip, 15
Hot Cheese-Clam Dip, 41
Hot Cheese Dip, 41
Hot Cheese Dip with Fruit, 41
Mushroom Cheese Fondue Dip, 131
Patio Dip, 40
Quick and Easy Clam Dip, 41
Rarebit Dip, 35
Divinity, Sunshine, 183
Donuts, frozen, 192
Down Home Streusel Coffeecake, 164
Dressed Up Gingerbread, 165
Dried Beef Bake, 115
Dried Beef Hash, 111
Drying Flowers, 198
Duckling
A L'Orange, 99
Defrosting, 21
Delectable, 101
Oriental, 100
with Cherries, 100
Dumplings, Dependable, 163

E

Easy-Bake Chicken, 104
Easy Beef Stew Supreme, 110
Easy-Does-It Canapes, 39
Easy Spiced Peaches, 188
Egg Basics, 126
Egg Foo Yung, 128
    Gravy, 128
    Seafood, 128
Eggplant, 149
    Creamy Baked, 140
Eggs, 124
    After Christmas Quiche, 129
    A La Goldenrod, 127
    Benedict, 126
    Cheese & Onion Quiche, 129
    Cheese Souffle, 125
    Cheese Scrambled, 127
    Curried, 127
    Curried Eggs & Shrimp, 128
    Filled Omelets, 127
    Fluffy Hollandaise, 157
    Frozen, 192
    Ham Au Gratin, 130
    Mock Hollandaise Sauce, 126
    Mushroom Quiche, 129
    Omelet Deluxe, 127
    Poached, 126
    Quiche, 128
    Quiche Lorraine, 129
    Sauced Omelets, 127
    Scrambled, 126
    Shrimp & Asparagus Quiche, 129
    Spinach Quiche, 129
    Western Omelet, 127
Elegant Egg Nog, 59
English Beef, 79
English Pork, 87
Escalloped Corn, 139
Escargot, 38
Espresso Royale, 58
Everyday Pot Roast, 76

F

Fabulous baked Fish, 67
Family Breakfast, 26
Family Style Meat Loaf Dinner, 30
Fantastic Chocolate Fondue, 179
Fantastic Fudge, 182
Fast Cheese Frenchies, 165
Fifteen-Second Pizza, 50
Fiji Beef Chunks, 111
Filled Omelets, 127
Fillet of Sole Casserole, 69
Fillets Almondine, 66
Fish and Seafood, 60
    Baked Fish, 67
    Baked Salmon with Mushrooms, 69
    Baked Torsk, 67
    Cantonese Shrimp and Pea Pods, 62
    Chowder, 56
    Coquilles Saint Jacques, 64
    Crab Gumbo, 121
    Crab Mornay, 64
    Cucumber Sauce, 68
    Defrosting, 22
    Fabulous Baked Fish, 67
    Fillets, fried, frozen, 193
    Fillets, Savory, 69

Fillet of Sole Casserole, 69
Fillets Almondine, 66
Fish Surprise, 66
Halibut Hawaiian, 69
Italian Poached Fish, 66
Lobster Tails, 62
Luncheon Shrimp, 63
Newburg Sauce, 157
Oysters and Macaroni Au Gratin, 121
Quick Paella, 65
Salmon Loaf Scandinavian, 68
Salmon Piquante, 68
Salmon Steak Limone, 68
Scallop Curry, 65
Scallops Lorraine, 65
Sea Food Newburg, 63
Shrimp Creole, 63
Spaghetti with Crab Sauce, 63
Spanish Sauce, 65
Sweet-Sour Sauce, 69
White Fish Poached in Wine, 66
Whole Lobster, 62
Fishburger, 48
Fish Chowder, 56
Flank Steak Roll-Up, 76
Florentine Mushrooms, 43
Fluffy Hollandaise, 157
Fondant, 183
Fondue
    Cheese, 131
    Chocolate, 179
    Swiss, frozen, 193
Food for the Gods with Green Beans, 134
Food Shapes, 18
Frankfurters. See Wieners
Frankfurter Special, 45
Freezer to Table Pot Roast, 83
Freezer to Table Rump Roast, 83
Freezer to Table Swiss Steak, 83
French Lamb, 94
French Onion Soup, 54
French Pork, 87
French Rivieras, 46
Fresh Strawberry Refrigerator Jam, 186
Fried Liver and Onion, 97
Frontier Pot Roast, 75
Frostings
    Butterscotch, 171
    Cream Cheese, 184
    Chocolate, 170
    Chocolate Icing, 170
    German Chocolate Cake Topping, 168
    Marshmallow Mist Icing, 170
Frozen
    Brownies, 17
    Cherry Pie, 175
    Fruit, 13
    Peas and Onions Cooked in Serving
        Dish, 17
Fruit
    Brule, 179
    Cocktail Torte, 177
    Curried, 179
    Defrosting, 23
    Holiday Fruit Pudding, 177
    Hot Ambrosia Compote, 178
    Salad Dressing, 158
    Tipsy Fruit Sauce, 158
Fudge
    Fantastic, 182
    Never Fail, 182

G

Garbanzo Casserole, 114
Garlic Studded Leg of Lamb, 93
German Chocolate Cake, 168
German Chocolate Cake Topping, 168
German Pork, 87
German Potato Salad, 142
"Get Together" Buffet, 33
Gingerbread, Dressed Up, 165
Ginger Joys, 185
Ginger Pears, 178
Ginger People, 185
Glazed Carrot Coins, 137
Goulash, 110
Graham Cracker Crust, 174
Grape and Basil Jelly, 189
Grapefruit and Savory Jelly, 189
Grape Glazed Carrots, 137
Gravy, 158
Greek Lamb, 94
Green Beans, 147
    and Bacon Casserole, 134
    Cheesy Tomato, 135
    Food for the Gods With, 134
    Mushroom Creamed, 134
    Cream-Curry, 134
Green Peppers, Stuffed, frozen, 193
Green Peppers, Stuffed, Pots, 82
Grilled Cheese Sandwich, 45
Grits Royale, 155
Ground Beef. Also see Hamburger. 80
    "Add Meat" Dinner, 114
    Browning Dish Hamburgers, 16
    Chili, 113
    Country Pie, 115
    Curried Meat Loaf, 81
    Defrosting, 20
    Gumbos, 47
    Hamburger Creole, 82
    Johnny Marzetti, 114
    Lasagna for 4, 113
    Meat Loaf, 81
    Mom's Tater Tot Hot Dish, 115
    Noodles Bolognese, 113
    One Dish Spaghetti, 113
    Pork and Bean Casserole, 119
    Quick Beef Chip Casserole, 115
    Salisbury Steak, 80
    Sara's Meat Balls, 80
    Saturday Special, 114
    Sauced Loaf, 81
    Saucy Salisbury Steak, 80
    Seasoned Meat Loaf, 81
    Sour Cream Salisbury Steak, 80
    Speedy Shepherd's Pie, 80
    Stuffed Cabbage Rolls, 82
    Swedish Meatballs, 80
    Tasty Herbed Salisbury Steak, 80
    Tomato Sauced Meat Loaf, 81
    Top the 'Taters Dinner, 114
Ground Lamb, Burger Special, 95
Ground Sausage, Italian Mushrooms, 43

H

Halibut, Fish Suprise, 66
Halibut Hawaiian, 69
Ham. Also see Pork. 86
    and Eggs Au Gratin, 130
    and Pineapple Kabobs, 37

Asparagus, Birds, 117
Baked, 91
Brown Sugar, 90
Confetti Casseroles, 117
Creamy Chicken 'N Ham Soup, 57
Glazes, 91
Hawaiian Sweet Sour, 116
Heavenly Loaf, 116
Leftover (cooked) Ham Casserole, 116
Luau Kabobs, 90
'N Oyster Casserole, 117
Patties, Refrigerated - Canned, 196
Roll Ups, 37
Spicy - Slice, 90
Swiss - Sandwiches, 47
Hamburgers. Also see Ground Beef. 46
All American Cheeseburger, 45
Baby Burgers, 37
Barbecues, 47
Browning Dish, 16
Buns, Frozen 23, 192
Burger-Dogs, 46
Creole, 82
Defrosting, 20
Ground Beef Gumbos, 47
Helper, 197
Sandwiches, 44
Instant Cheeseburger, 50
South of the Border Buns, 48
Variations, 46
Hans Christian Anderson, 50
Harvard Beets, 136
Hash, Corned Beef - Canned, 196
Heat Control, 19
Herbed Lamb, 93
Herbed Scallops, 38
Holiday Brunch Buffet, 27
Holiday Fruit Pudding, 177
Hors D'Oeuvre. See Appetizers, 35
Horseradish Sauce, 97
Hot Ambrosia Compote, 178
Hot and Creamy Shrimp Dip, 15
Hot Cheese - Clam Dip, 41
Hot Cheese Dip, 41
Hot Cheese Dip with Fruit, 41
Hot Chocolate 59
Hot Dogs. Also See Wieners. 47
Hot Fudge Sauce, 159
Hot Gingered Pears, 189
Hot Lox and Bagel, 50
Hot Meat and Gravy Sandwiches, 49
Hot Mulled Wine, 58
Hot Toddy, 58
Hot Turkey Salad, 107
How to Cook the Dinner on the Cover, 72
Hungarian Beef, 79
Hungarian Pork, 87

I

"I Forgot to Defrost the Meat" Dinner, 29
Indian Beef, 79
Indian Lamb, 94
Indian Pilaf, 153
Instant Cheeseburger, 50
Instant Chocolate Fondue, 179
Instant Coffee, Tea and Cocoa, 12
Instant Vichyssoise, 57
Irish Lamb, 94

Italian
Dinner for 6 to 8, 32
Lamb, 94
Liver Bake, 115
Mushrooms, 43
Poached Fish, 66
Rice, 153
Shrimp, 37

J

Jams, Preserves and Relishes, 186
Antipasto Relish, 188
Aromatic Apple Jelly, 189
Easy Spiced Peaches, 188
Fresh Strawberry Refrigerator Jam, 186
Grape and Basil Jelly, 189
Grapefruit and Savory Jelly, 189
Hot Gingered Pears, 189
Mild Peach Chutney, 188
Pickled Beets, 188
Jazzy Baked Beans, 135
Johnny Marzetti, 114

K

Kabobs, Ham and Pineapple, 37
Kabobs, Mushroom, 37
Key West (sandwich), 50
Killarney Coffee, 59

L

Ladies' Luncheon, 28
Lamb, 92
Australian, 94
Basic Casserole, 94
Burger Special, 95
Curry, 92
French, 94
Garlic Studded Leg of, 93
Greek, 94
Herbed Leg of, 93
Indian, 94
Irish, 94
Italian, 94
Leftover Lamb Dinner, 30
Lemon Marinated Chops, 93
Marmalade, 95
Pilaf, 95
Riblets in Tomato Honey Sauce, 94
Roast Leg of, 93
Shish Kabob, 92
Stew, 95
Lasagna for Four, 113
Lasagna, frozen, 193
Lazy Beef Casserole, 111
Leftover Ham Casserole, 116
Leftover Lamb Dinner, 30
Leg of Lamb
Garlic Studded, 93
Herbed, 93
Roast, 93
Lemon
Butter Dessert Squares, 184
Dessert Sauce, 159
Marinated Lamb Chops, 93
Meringue Pie, 173
Lima Beans, 147

Colossal Baked, 135
Maple Glazed, 135
Liver, defrosting, 20
Liver, Italian Bake, 115
Liver Pate (in Hans Christian Anderson Sandwich), 50
Liverwurst Pate on Toast, 39
Lobster
Defrosting, 22
Seafood Newburg, 63
Tails, 62
Whole, 62
Lox, (Hot Lox and Bagel Sandwich), 50
Luau Kabobs, 90
Luncheon Meat, Orange-Berry Glazed, 97
Luncheon Shrimp, 63

M

Macaroni and Cheese Dinner, 123, 197
Magic Meltwiches, 50
Manhattan Clam Chowder, 56
Maple Glazed Lima Beans, 135
Marinated Chicken Wings, 38
Marshmallow Mist Icing, 170
Mashed Potatoes, 140
Mashed Potatoes, Orange-Potato Shells, 142
Matterhorn Vegetable Bake, 141
Mauna Loa Sauce, 158
Meatballs, Frozen, 193
Meatballs, Mini, 37
Meatballs, Spiced - Soup, 55
Meat Loaf, Variations, 81
Mexican Style Dinner, Frozen, 193
Microwave Cooking Techniques, 18
Microwave Menus, 24
Beef Bouquetiere Dinner, 25
Busy Day Supper, 31
Children's Luncheon, 28
Company Chicken Dinner, 31
Family Breakfast, 26
Family Style Meatloaf Dinner, 30
"Get Together" Buffet, 33
Holiday Brunch Buffet, 27
"I Forgot to Defrost the Meat" Dinner, 29
Italian Dinner for 6 to 8, 32
Ladies Luncheon, 28
Leftover Lamb Dinner, 30
"No Time To Cook" Company Dinner, 32
"Souper" Lunch, 27
Sunday Brunch, 26
Thanksgiving Dinner, 33
Veal Paprika Dinner, 29
Microwave Stack-ups, 15
Mild Peach Chutney, 188
Minnesota Wild Rice Casserole, 153
Minted Peas, 140
Mocha Filling, 167
Mocha Torte, 167
Mock Hollandaise Sauce, 126
Mom's Tater Tot Hot Dish, 115
Mornay Sauce, 157
Muffins, 14, 165
Muffins, Buttermilk Bran, 164
Mushroom-Barley Casserole, 123
Mushroom-Cheddar Canapes, 41
Mushroom Cheese Fondue Dip, 131
Mushroom Creamed Beans, 134
Mushroom Kabobs, 37

Mushroom Quiche, 129
Mushrooms, Stuffed, 43
  Bacon, 43
  Basic Recipe, 43
  Bleu Cheese, 43
  Chestnut-Celery, 43
  Crab or Lobster, 43
  Florentine, 43
  Italian, 43
  Mexican, 43
  Polynesian, 43
  Shrimp, 43
  Stroganoff, 43
Mustard Loaf, 81

N

Nachoes, Cheese, 39
Nature's Own Candy, 183
Never Fail Fudge, 182
Newburg Sauce, 157
New England Clam Chowder, 56
No Clean-up Instant Lunch, 14
Noodles Almondine, 123
Noodles Bolognese, 113
Noodles Romano, 122
"No Time to Cook" Company Dinner, 32

O

Oatmeal, 154
Okra, 149
Old-Fashioned Cooked Salad Dressing, 158
Olives in Bacon Blankets, 36
Omelet Deluxe, 127
Omelets, Western - Frozen, 194
One Dish Spaghetti, 113
One Man Oatmeal, 154
Onions
  French, Soup, 54
  Fresh, 149
  Herb Bread, 164
  Cheese Sticks, 163
  Sensational - Bake, 140
  Soup Mix, 197
Open Face Beans and Wiener Sandwich, 48
Orange-Berry Glazed Luncheon Meat, 97
Orange Date Bars, Candied, 184
Orange-Glazed Turkey Quarter, 106
Orange-Potato Shells, 142
Orange Sauce, 99
Oriental Beef or Pork Sandwich, 50
Oriental Frankfurters, 119
Oriental Hash, 119
Oriental Ribs, 88
Oriental Tuna, 122
Oven Stew, 110
Oysters and Macaroni Au Gratin, 121
Oyster Stew, 55

P

Pancake Batter, frozen, 192
Pan Drippings, Gravy, 158
Parisian Mocha, 58
Parsnips, 149
Party Appetizer Pie, 38

Pasta, 152
  Egg Noodles, 154
  Lasagna, 154
  Macaroni, 154
  Preparation Instructions, 154
  Spaghetti, 154
Pastry for One-Crust Pie, 172
Pastry Shell From Mix, 172
Patio Dip, 40
Peaches, Easy Spiced, 188
Peaches, Mild Chutney, 188
Peach Spice Pudding Cake, 171
Peanut Brittle, 182
Peanut Butter Kidwiches, 47
Pears in Red Wine, 177
Pears, Ginger, 178
Pears, Hot Gingered, 189
Peas, 150, 196
  and Carrots, 150
  Blackeyed, 150
  Minted, 140
  Split Pea Soup, 54
Pecan Pie, 173
Penuche, 182
Pepper Steak, 77
Perfect Egg Noodles, 154
Pheasant in Wine Cream Sauce, 100
Pickled Beets, 188
Pie Crust Stick or Mix, 172
Pies
  Banana Cream, 173
  Black Bottom, 171
  Butterscotch, 173
  Chocolate Cream, 173
  Chocolate Wafer Crumb Crust, 174
  Coconut Cream, 173
  Coconut Crust, 174
  Cherry, frozen, 175
  Graham Cracker Crust, 174
  Lemon Meringue, 173
  Party Appetizer, 38
  Pecan, 173
  Pumpkin, 174
  Strawberry, 172
  Vanilla Cream, 173
  Vanilla Wafer Crust, 174
  Waikiki Pineapple, 174
Pineapple Upside Down Cake, 170
Pizza, Fifteen-Second, 50
Pizza Roll Appetizers, frozen, 194
Poached Eggs, 126
Polynesian Mushrooms, 43
Pork, 86
  American, 87
  and Apple Pie, 88
  and Bean Casserole, 119
  Barbecued Spareribs, 89
  Basic Casserole, 87
  Belgian, 87
  Chinese, 87
  Chop Bake, 16
  Chops, Barbecue, 88
  Chops Creole, 89
  Defrosting Pork, 21
  English, 87
  French, 87
  German, 87
  Hungarian, 87
  Luau Kabobs, 90
  Oriental Hash, 119
  Oriental Ribs, 88
  Ribs, cooked - frozen, 194
  Roast, 86

  Roast and Sauerkraut, 119
  Scandinavian, 87
  Sliced - Canned, 196
  Smothered Tenderloin, 86
  Stuffed Chops in Wine, 88
Potatoes
  Baked, 150
  Baked, stuffed - frozen, 194
  Boiled, 150
  Buttered, 150
  Cheese Casserole, 121
  Cheese Stuffed, 141
  Fried - Frozen, 195
  German Potato Salad, 142
  Instant Vichyssoise, 57
  Mashed, 140
  Salad, German Style - canned, 196
  Scalloped, 142
  Scalloped - Mix, 197
  Shoestring - frozen, 194
  With Celery in White Sauce, frozen, 194
Poultry, 98
  Chicken A La King, 105
  Chicken Barbeque, 103
  Chicken Braised in Wine, 103
  Chicken Cacciatori, 102
  Chicken Livers Chablis, 105
  Chicken Majorca, 104
  Chicken Marengo, 102
  Chicken Parisienne, 103
  Chicken Saltimbocca, 103
  Coq Au Vin, 102
  Cornish Hens for Two, 107
  Cranberry Sauce, 104
  Delectable Duckling, 101
  Duckling A L'Orange, 99
  Easy-Bake Chicken, 104
  Hot Turkey Salad, 107
  Orange-Glazed Turkey Quarter, 106
  Orange Sauce, 99
  Oriental Duckling, 100
  Pheasant in Wine Cream Sauce, 100
  Roast Chicken, 104
  Roast Cornish Hens, 107
  Roast Duckling with Cherries, 100
  Roasted Half Turkey, 105
  Saucy Turkey and Rice, 120
  Sherried Chicken Breasts, 103
  Single Cornish Hen, 107
  Stuffing Supreme, 104
  Turkey Divan, 106
  Turkey Roast, 105
  Wild Rice Stuffing, 101
Proofing Frozen Bread, 162
Pudding or Custard Mix, 176
Pudding
  Butterscotch, 176
  Chocolate, 175
  Holiday Fruit Pudding, 177
  Rice, 153
  Tapioca Fluff, 176
  Vanilla Fluff, 176
Pumpkin Bars, 184
Pumpkin Pie, 174

Q

Quantities, 18
Quiche, 128
  After Christmas, 129
  Cheese and Onion, 129

Lorraine, 129
Mushroom, 129
Shrimp and Asparagus, 129
Spinach, 129
Quick and Easy Clam Dip, 41
Quick Beef Chip Casserole, 115
Quick Cocoa, 59
Quick Cream of Wheat, 155
Quick Paella, 65
Quick Shrimp Rice, 152
Quickie Corn Chowder, 56

R

Rarebit Dip, 35
Raspberry Swirl Bundt Cake, 169
Ratatouille, 143
Ravioli, canned, 195
Rearranging, 18
Reuben Sandwich, 49
Rhubarb Crisp, 178
Rhubarb Sauce, 179
Rice, 152
   Brown, 155
   Italian, 153
   Long Grain, 153
   Minnesota Wild Rice Casserole, 153
   Pilaf, 153
   Pudding, 153
   Quick, 155
   Quick Shrimp, 152
   Spanish, 152
   Verde, 152
   Wild, 155
   Wild and White Mix, 155
Roasting, 19
Roast Beef, see Beef
Roast Beef Stew, 111
Roast Chicken, 104
Roast Cornish Hens, 107
Roast Duckling with Cherries, 100
Roast Half Turkey, 105
Roast Leg of Lamb, 93
Roast Pork, see Pork
Rock Cornish Game Hens, 22
Rolls, Dinner, 22
Roma Sandwich, 50
Rotating Dish, 18
Rumaki, 36
Rutabegas, 150

S

Salislbury Steak, 80, 194
Salmon Loaf Scandinavian, 68
Salmon Piquante, 68
Salmon Steak Limone, 68
Salmon Baked with Mushrooms, 69
Sandwiches, 44
   All American Cheeseburger, 44
   Barbecued Crab, 49
   Barbecues, 47
   Bolognese, 50
   Burger-Dogs, 46
   Cheese 'N Tuna Buns, 48
   Cheesy B.L.T., 50
   Coney Islands, 48
   Denver, 47

Fifteen-Second Pizza, 50
Fishburger, 48
Frankfurter Special, 45
French Rivieras, 46
Grilled Cheese, 45
Ground Beef Gumbos, 47
Hamburgers, 46
Hans Christian Anderson, 50
Hot Dogs, 47
Hot Lox and Bagel, 50
Hot Meat and Gravy, 49
Instant Cheeseburger, 50
Key West, 50
Lamburger Special, 95
Open Face Beans and Wiener, 48
Oriental Beef and Pork, 50
Peanut Butter Kidwiches, 47
Reuben, 49
Roast Beef Special, 50
Roma, 50
South of the Border, 50
South of the Border Buns, 48
Swiss Ham, 47
Turkey Divan, 49
Wide Open Reuben, 50
Salsa Di Vongole, 158
Sara's Meatballs, 80
Saturday Special, 114
Sauced Loaf, 81
Sauced Omelets, 127
Sauces and Toppings, 156
   Barbecue Sauce, 157
   Bechamel Sauce, 156
   Cheddar Cheese Sauce, 157
   Cheese Toppers, 131
   Chocolate Mint Topping, 159
   Cranberry Sauce, 104
   Cucumber Sauce, 68
   Currant-Raisin Sauce, 156
   Curry Sauce, 157
   Fluffy Hollandaise Sauce, 157
   Fruit Salad Dressing, 158
   Gravy, 158
   Ham Glazes, 91
   Horseradish Sauce, 97
   Hot Fudge Sauce, 159
   Lemon Dessert Sauce, 159
   Mauna Loa Sauce, 158
   Mock Hollandaise Sauce, 126
   Mornay Sauce, 157
   Newburg Sauce, 157
   Old-Fashioned Cooked Salad Dressing, 158
   Orange Sauce, 99
   Salsa Di Vongole, 158
   Spanish Sauce, 65
   Sweet-Sour Sauce, 69
   Teriyaki Sauce, 157
   Tipsy Fruit Sauce, 158
   Velvet Custard Sauce, 159
   White Sauce, 157
Saucy Beef Hash, 111
Saucy Salisbury Steak, 80
Saucy Shrimp Hors D'Oeuvre, 40
Saucy Turkey and Rice, 120
Sauerkraut with Apples, 143
Sausage Noodle Casserole, 116
Savory Fish Fillets, 69
Scalloped Bologna Bake, 118
Scalloped Potatoes, 142
Scalloped Potatoes, Mix, 197
Scallops
   Coquilles Saint Jacques, 64

Curry, 65
Defrosting, 22
Herbed, 38
Lorraine, 65
Scandinavian Pork, 87
Scotch Rocky Road Candy, 185
Scrambled Eggs, 13, 126
Seafood. Also see Fish.
   Egg Foo Yung, 128
   Newburg, 63
   Tantalizers, 39
Sea Salad Canapés, 40
Seasoned Loaf, 81
Sensational Onion Bake, 140
Sherried Chicken Breasts, 103
Shielding, 19
Shish Kabob, 92
Shrimp
   and Asparagus Quiche, 129
   Bisque, 57
   Cantonese Shrimp and Pea Pods, 62
   Creole, 63
   Defrosting, 22
   Hot and Creamy Dip, 15
   in Bacon, 36
   Italian, 37
   Luncheon Shrimp, 63
   Quick Paella, 65
   Saucy Shrimp Hors D'Oeuvres, 40
   Shrimp Stuffed Mushrooms, 43
Sirloin Steak, 75
Smoked Bratwurst, 97
S'Mores, 14
Smothered Pork Tenderloins, 86
Souffle
   Cheese, 125
   Spinach, frozen, 195
"Souper" Lunch, 27
Soups, 53
   Borscht, 53
   Cheese Soup Canadienne, 54
   Chicken Soup with Little Dumplings, 55
   Chili Con Queso, 54
   Chunky Style, canned, 196
   Condensed, canned, 197
   Cream of Turkey, 55
   Creamy Chicken 'N Ham, 57
   Creamy Tomato, 54
   Fish Chowder, 56
   French Onion, 54
   Instant Vichyssoise, 57
   Manhattan Clam Chowder, 56
   New England Clam Chowder, 56
   Oyster Stew, 55
   Quickie Corn Chowder, 56
   Shrimp Bisque, 57
   Spiced Meatball, 55
   Split Pea, 54
   Tomato Soup Exceptional, 57
   Vegetable, 57
   Zippy Madrilene, 56
Sour Cream and Potato Casserole, 143
Sour Cream Salisbury Steak, 80
South of the Border, 50
South of the Border (Sandwich), 50
Spaghetti, canned, 197
Spaghetti, frozen, 197
Spaghetti with Crab Sauce, 63
Spanish Rice, 153
Spanish Sauce, 65
Spareribs, Barbecued, 89
Speedy Baked Potato, 15
Speedy Macaroni and Cheese, 123

Speedy Orange Glazed Yams, 145
Speedy Shepherd's Pie, 80
Spiced Apricots, 177
Spiced Cider, 59
Spiced Meatball Soup, 55
Spicy Carrots, 137
Spicy Ham Slice, 90
Spinach, 151
   Casserole, 144
   Cottage Pie, 143
   Quiche, 129
   Souffle, frozen, 195
   Sweet Sour, 144
Split Pea Soup, 54
Squash
   Acorn or Butternut, 151
   Baked, 144
   Caribbean Baked, 144
   Hubbard, 151
Standing Time, 19
Starting Temperatures, 18
Stew
   Beef, canned, 196
   Lamb, 95
   Oyster, 55
Stirring, 18
Strawberry,
   Cream Filling, 171
   Fresh Strawberry Refrigerator Jam, 186
   Frozen, 192
   Macaroon Torte, 171
   Pie, 172
Streusel Coffeecake, 165
Stroganoff Spectacular, 78
Stroganoff Stuffed Mushrooms, 43
Stuffed Cabbage Rolls, 82
Stuffed Mushrooms, 43
Stuffed Pepper Pots, 82
Stuffed Pork Chops in Wine, 88
Stuffed Tomatoes, 145
Stuffed Zucchini, 145
Stuffing Supreme, 104
Sunday Brunch, 26
Sunshine Divinity, 183
Swedish Meatballs, 80
Sweet Potatoes, 151
   Marsharole, 141
Speedy Orange Glazed Yams, 145
Sweet Sour Sauce, 69
Sweet Sour Spinach, 144
Swiss Ham Sandwiches, 47
Swiss Luncheon Bake, 130
Swiss Steak, 76

T

Tangy Creamed Beets, 136
Tapioca Fluff, 176
Tasty Herbed Salisbury Steak, 80
Tasty Tuna Bake, 122
Tater Tots, frozen, 195
Teriyaki Sauce, 157
Thanksgiving Dinner, 33
Tipsy Fruit Sauce, 158
Toffee Tempters, 183
Tomatoes, 151
   Creamy Tomato Soup, 54
   Sauced Meat Loaf, 81
   Soup Exceptional, 57
   Stuffed, 145
Top The 'Taters Dinner, 114
Torsk, Baked, 67
Triple Fudge Bundt Cake with Glaze, 169

Tuna
   "Add Meat" Dinner, 122
   Cheese 'N Tuna Buns, 48
   Chow Mein, 122
   Noodle Casserole, frozen, 194
   Oriental, 122
   Tasty Tuna Bake, 122
   Tuna Helper, 197
Turkey
   Cream of Turkey Soup, 55
   Defrosting, 22
   Dinner, frozen, 194
   Divan, 106
   Divan Sandwich, 49
   Hot Turkey Salad, 107
   Quarter Orange Glazed, 106.
   Roast Half Turkey, 105
   Saucy Turkey and Rice, 120
   Turkey Special, 120
Turnips, 151

V

Vanilla Cream Pie, 173
Vanilla Fluff Pudding, 176
Vanilla Wafer Crust, 174
Veal, 84
   Chops, Parmigiana, 84
   Creamy Velvet, 85
   Defrosting, 21
   in Sour Cream, 85
   Paprika Dinner, 29
   Scallopine, 84
   Steak in Onion Sauce, 85
   Valencia, 85
Vegetables, 133
   Asparanuts, 134
   Au Gratin Potatoes, 141
   Baked Squash, 144
   Baked Zucchini and Onions, 145
   Beans and Burgundy, 135
   Braised Celery, 138
   Broccoli and Mushrooms in Sour Cream, 136
   Broccoli Italian Style, 136
   Brussel Sprouts Au Gratin, 137
   Brussel Sprouts in Cream Sauce, 137
   Caribbean Baked Squash, 144
   Cheese Stuffed Potatoes, 141
   Cheesy Tomato Beans, 135
   Colossal Baked Limas, 135
   Corn Bubble, 139
   Corn On The Cob, 133, 149
   Corn Off The Cob, 149
   Creamy-Curry Beans, 134
   Creamy Baked Eggplant, 140
   Deviled Cauliflower, 137
   Escalloped Corn, 139
   Food For The Gods With Green Beans, 134
   Frozen Peas and Onions Cooked in Serving Dish, 17
   German Potato Salad, 142
   Glazed Carrot Coins, 137
   Grape Glazed Carrots, 137
   Green Bean and Bacon Casserole, 134
   Harvard Beets, 136
   Jazzy Baked Beans, 135
   Maple Glazed Lima Beans, 135
   Mashed Potatoes, 140
   Matterhorn Vegetable Bake, 141
   Minted Peas, 140
   Mixed-Frozen, 195

   Mushroom-Barley Casserole, 123
   Mushroom Creamed Beans, 134
   Orange-Potato Shells, 142
   Soup, 57
   Ratatouille, 143
   Sauerkraut with Apples, 143
   Scalloped Potatoes, 142
   Scalloped Potatoes from Package Mix, 142
   Sensational Onion Bake, 140
   Speedy Orange Glazed Yams, 145
   Spicy Carrots, 137
   Spinach Casserole, 144
   Spinach Cottage Pie, 143
   Sour Cream and Potato Casserole, 143
   Stuffed Tomatoes, 145
   Stuffed Zucchini, 145
   Sweet Potato Marsharole, 141
   Sweet-Sour Spinach, 144
   Tangy Creamed Beets, 136
   Wine Braised Celery and Mushrooms, 138
   Zucchini Parmesan, 145
Velvet Custard Sauce, 159

W

Waikiki Pineapple Pie, 174
Warm Rolls, 12
Weenie-Mac, 116
Welsh Rarebit, 130
Western Omelet, 127
Wheat, Cream of, 155
Whipped Herb Butter, 111
White Fish
   Poached in Wine, 66
   Fillets Almondine, 66
   Italian Poached, 66
   Savory Fish Fillets, 69
White Sauce, 157
Whole Lobster, 62
Whole Wheat Bread, 162
Wide-Open Reuben, 50
Wieners
   Bourbon, 36
   Butterflied, 35
   Coney Islands, 48
   Frankfurter Special, 45
   Hot Dogs, 47
   Open Face Beans and Wiener Sandwich, 48
   Oriental Frankfurters, 119
   Weenie-Mac, 116
Wild Rice. Also see Rice. 155
Wild Rice Stuffing, 101
Wine Braised Celery and Mushrooms, 138
Wine, Hot Mulled, 58
Wine Sauce Mix, 147

Y

Yellow Cake Mix, 169

Z

Zippy Madrilene, 56
Zucchini, 151
   Baked with Onions, 145
   Parmesan, 145
   Stuffed, 145

Notes